Moral Error Theory

Wouter Floris Kalf

Moral Error Theory

palgrave
macmillan

Wouter Floris Kalf
Department of Philosophy
Utrecht University
Utrecht, The Netherlands

ISBN 978-3-319-77287-5　　　ISBN 978-3-319-77288-2　(eBook)
https://doi.org/10.1007/978-3-319-77288-2

Library of Congress Control Number: 2018941093

© The Editor(s) (if applicable) and The Author(s) 2018
This work is subject to copyright. All rights are solely and exclusively licensed by the Publisher, whether the whole or part of the material is concerned, specifically the rights of translation, reprinting, reuse of illustrations, recitation, broadcasting, reproduction on microfilms or in any other physical way, and transmission or information storage and retrieval, electronic adaptation, computer software, or by similar or dissimilar methodology now known or hereafter developed.
The use of general descriptive names, registered names, trademarks, service marks, etc. in this publication does not imply, even in the absence of a specific statement, that such names are exempt from the relevant protective laws and regulations and therefore free for general use.
The publisher, the authors, and the editors are safe to assume that the advice and information in this book are believed to be true and accurate at the date of publication. Neither the publisher nor the authors or the editors give a warranty, express or implied, with respect to the material contained herein or for any errors or omissions that may have been made. The publisher remains neutral with regard to jurisdictional claims in published maps and institutional affiliations.

Cover credit: gregoryfenile

Printed on acid-free paper

This Palgrave Macmillan imprint is published by the registered company Springer International Publishing AG part of Springer Nature.
The registered company address is: Gewerbestrasse 11, 6330 Cham, Switzerland

Dedicated to Carel, Vera, Laurens, and Sanne

Preface

I have written this book as a contribution to the debate in contemporary metaethics about the plausibility or otherwise of moral error theory, according to which moral judgements are truth-apt but systematically fail to be true. This book is therefore most suitable for professional philosophers and postgraduate students in philosophy. However, and because I explain most philosophical concepts that I introduce, it will also appeal to advanced undergraduates with a solid foundation in metaethics.

This book has two parts. In Part I, I defend moral error theory. Moral error theorists traditionally argue that the truth-makers of moral judgements must be irreducibly normative or objectively prescriptive moral facts and that these facts are too queer to exist. But moral error theorists can also argue that whether some moral judgements are true depends on whether rational minds converge on what is morally right and wrong, which does not support a queerness argument and instead requires moral error theorists to argue that rational minds don't converge on what is morally right and wrong. There are many other choices that moral error theorists must make when they formulate and defend their view, resulting in a large number of possible formulations of moral error theory. I argue that one such formulation renders moral error theory a plausible theory in contemporary metaethics.

In Part II, I switch tack from defending moral error theory to answering the so-called now what question: moral error theory, and now what?

In particular, what should we do with moral discourse after moral error theory? As I will explain, the moral error theorist's commitment to the non-existence of moral facts does not commit her to the non-existence of reasons for belief or prudential reasons. I subsequently appeal to these reasons to argue that after moral error theory we should leave moral discourse largely as it is and only change what the truth-makers of its moral judgements should look like: not moral facts that don't exist but (roughly) prudential facts that do exist. I argue that this 'substitutionist' solution to the now what problem is more plausible than existing solutions to this problem, such as revolutionary fictionalism and revolutionary expressivism. My version of moral error theory conjoined with my answer to the now what question constitutes a new metanormative view which has thus far not been defended in the literature. It also has implications for how we should do normative ethics after moral error theory. In the penultimate chapter, I offer a preliminary discussion of what implications this view might have in political philosophy and normative ethics. Given that I put my metanormative theory to use in an attempt to contribute to our thinking about a practical and political question, this book will also appeal to students and scholars of politics, jurisprudence, and sociology.

How should you read this book? If you are not yet a moral error theorist, or if you are not prepared to accept it for the sake of argument, then you should start with Part I. But if you are already a moral error theorist, or if you are prepared to accept it for the sake of argument, then you can skip most of Part I and go straight to Part II. If you skip Part I, then I advise reading §3.3–3.5 from Part I before reading Part II because you will need to know what I say there in order to be able to assess my arguments in Part II.

I wish to thank a number of people who have helped me tremendously in writing this book. My sincere gratitude to Professor Herman Philipse, who has generously funded my postdoctoral research from his Distinguished University Professorship research budget (Utrecht University, 2015–2019). At Palgrave Macmillan, I thank Brendan George and April James, who have been very helpful in the editorial process. In writing this book I have benefited greatly from conversations with Pekka Väyrynen, Andrew McGonigal, Gerald Lang, John Divers, David Enoch, Ulrike Heuer, Robbie Williams, Ross Cameron, Elizabeth Barnes,

Thomas Brouwer, Michael Bench-Capon, Carl Baker, Richard Caves, Carl Warom, Chris Cowie, Richard Rowland, Pauline Kleingeld, Bruno Verbeek, Joeri Witteveen, Tom Hayes, Fred Muller, Bart Streumer, Jonas Olson, Jeroen Hopster, Michael Klenk, Julia Hermann, and Rosanne Scharff. I have presented part of the material in these pages at various conferences and workshops, and I thank the audiences of: BSET 2012, the postgraduate session (Joint Session of the Aristotelian Society and the Mind Association), and conferences at the Universities of Amsterdam, Utrecht, Groningen, Leeds, Sheffield, Reading, Stirling, Leuven, Bristol, Tilburg, Venice, St Andrews, Oxford, and Delft, and the Central European University of Budapest, the Australian Catholic University, the LUISS Guido Carli University, and Claremont Graduate University in California, USA. Special thanks to an anonymous reviewer for Palgrave, who has provided some excellent suggestions to improve this manuscript before publication.

I thank my parents Carel and Vera and my brother Laurens for their ongoing encouragement, both during and after my studies. My partner Sanne has supported me throughout the process of writing this book. Without her love and encouragement, I could not have written it. Thank you.

Utrecht, The Netherlands   Wouter Floris Kalf

Contents

Part I	**Moral Error Theory**	**1**

1	**Introduction**	**3**
	1.1 The Generic Argument for Moral Error Theory	3
	1.2 Outline of the View	15
	1.3 Three Assumptions	21
	References	23
2	**Conceptual Entailment Error Theory**	**27**
	2.1 Introduction	27
	2.2 Elements of Conceptual Entailment Error Theory	32
	2.3 Mackie's Conceptual Entailment Error Theory	41
	2.4 Joyce's Conceptual Entailment Error Theory: Initial Arguments	44
	2.5 Joyce's Conceptual Entailment Error Theory: The Use Argument	51
	2.6 The Externalism Objection	59
	2.7 Retreat to Content-Internalism with Indeterminate Referential Intentions	67

	2.8	Pervasiveness Objections	69
	2.9	Conclusion	75
		References	75
3	**Presupposition Error Theory**		**81**
	3.1	Introduction	81
	3.2	Semantic Presupposition Error Theory	83
	3.3	Pragmatic Presupposition	91
	3.4	Pragmatic Presupposition Error Theory	94
	3.5	Rationality or Non-Naturalism?	101
	3.6	Externalism, Systematic Falsity, and Cognitivism	106
	3.7	Pervasiveness Objections	108
	3.8	Conclusion	114
		References	115
4	**Rationality**		**119**
	4.1	Introduction	119
	4.2	Queerness	121
	4.3	Joyce's Rationality Argument	124
	4.4	The Reduction of Reasons and Rational Requirements	129
	4.5	The Intrinsic Value of Rationality	138
	4.6	From Categorical Epistemic to Categorical Moral Reasons	142
	4.7	The Companions-in-Guilt Objection	146
	4.8	Other Objections	150
	4.9	Conclusion	153
		References	154

Part II Normative Ethics   157

5	**Some Solutions to the Now What Problem**		**159**
	5.1	Introduction	159
	5.2	Assessment Criteria for Prescriptive Metaethical Theories	162
	5.3	Revolutionary Fictionalism	173

5.4	Revolutionary Expressivism	178
5.5	Conservationism	188
5.6	Abolitionism	190
5.7	Conclusion	194
References		194

6 Substitutionism — 197
- 6.1 Introduction — 197
- 6.2 Mackie's Conceptual Entailment Substitutionism — 198
- 6.3 Pragmatic Presupposition Substitutionism — 205
- 6.4 Intra-Personal Benefits of Schmoralizing — 210
- 6.5 Inter-Personal Benefits of Schmoralizing — 215
- 6.6 Propagandism and Moral Success Theory — 219
- 6.7 Conclusion — 222
- References — 223

7 Application — 227
- 7.1 Introduction — 227
- 7.2 Rawls on Distributive Justice — 228
- 7.3 Nozick on Distributive Justice — 232
- 7.4 Distributive Justice after Error Theory — 235
- 7.5 Conclusion — 239
- References — 240

8 Conclusion — 241
- Reference — 242

Index — 243

Part I

Moral Error Theory

1

Introduction

1.1 The Generic Argument for Moral Error Theory

You are most probably an error theorist about our thought and talk about witches, or our 'witch discourse'. You believe that there can only be witches if there are women with supernatural powers, you believe that no one can have supernatural powers, and so you believe that there are no witches (Smith 1994, p. 64). You also believe that anyone who utters a judgement like 'Annie is a witch' makes the systematic error of uttering a judgement that is truth-apt (i.e., can be true or false) but systematically fails to be true.

In this book, I argue that you should be an error theorist about our thought and talk about morality, or our 'moral discourse', too (Mackie 1977; Joyce 2001; Olson 2014). You may not yet, but you should believe that there can only be morally obligatory (or morally wrong, or morally right, or morally permissible) actions if there are categorical moral reasons to perform these actions, you should believe that there are no such reasons, and so you should believe that there are no morally obligatory (or morally wrong, or morally right, or morally permissible) actions. You should also believe that anyone who utters a judgement like 'giving to the poor is morally obligatory' makes the systematic error of uttering a judgement that is truth-apt but systematically fails to be true.

Categorical moral reasons are reasons for agents to perform a moral action regardless of whether performing that action satisfies one or more of their desires. For instance, Beatrice has a categorical moral reason to give to the poor regardless of whether doing this satisfies her desire to be praised by others (Mackie 1977, p. 35; Joyce 2001, p. 5; Dreier 1997, p. 84; Olson 2010, pp. 64–65). In this book, reasons are always normative reasons in the standard sense of considerations that count in favour of or against performing an action (Scanlon 1998, p. 17). For example, if you are thirsty then "the consideration that drinking would feel good to you" is a normative reason for you to drink (Scanlon 1998, p. 38). The intended contrast is with motivating reasons, which are considerations that motivate agents to perform an action but need not also count in favour of or against the performance of that action (Parfit 1997, p. 99). For instance, and ignoring non-standard cases in which believing false propositions is all-things-considered beneficial for you (for instance, because knowing the truth will drive you insane), you have a merely motivating reason if you accept the consideration that a proposition's *falsity* counts in favour of believing it. Reasons can either be practical, in which case they are typically reasons to perform an action, or theoretical, in which case they are typically reasons to form a belief. I explain how I think about reasons in more detail in §4.4.

The term 'error theory' is sometimes used to denote just a local error theory about morality and sometimes error theory about normativity as such. The latter view has recently been defended by Bart Streumer (2017). Such a global error theory extends to, for example, prudential normativity, which includes reasons to eat healthy and to get enough sleep, and epistemic normativity, which includes the reason to believe all propositions for which you have conclusive evidence that they are true. In this book, error theory always denotes moral error theory unless specified otherwise.

The most generic argument for error theory runs as follows:

Generic Argument for Error Theory
P1   Moral judgements carry a non-negotiable commitment to claim N.
P2   Claim N is false.

P3 If moral judgements carry a false non-negotiable commitment, then they are untrue.
C1 Therefore, moral judgements are untrue (from P1, P2, P3).
P4 If C1, then we should accept error theory of moral discourse as a whole.
C2 Therefore, we should accept error theory of moral discourse as a whole (from C1, P4).

Moral discourse is our practice of uttering moral judgements in moral discussions with our peers about such issues as the permissibility or otherwise of euthanasia and abortion, of uttering moral judgements to teach our children what ought to be done and how to muster the motivation to act on these judgements, of adjusting our moral judgements in light of other people's arguments, of reminding someone of a promise, of praising someone's altruistic behaviour, *et cetera*. I use the terms judgement, claim, sentence, and utterance interchangeably, such that in my vocabulary, all judgements, claims, and sentences are uttered or otherwise communicated, for instance by being inscribed. The relation between moral judgements and fully private moral thoughts will not be at the forefront of my analysis in this book, though it stands to reason that if moral judgements are systematically untrue, then the moral thoughts that these judgements express are also systematically untrue (Väyrynen 2013, p. 44).

P1 is error theory's "non-negotiable commitment" claim (Joyce 2001, p. 3). To understand what this means, consider again error theory about witch discourse. Error theorists about witch discourse have to show that this discourse must be about women with supernatural powers in order to be discourse about *witches* and not something else entirely, such as spinsters. Similarly, moral error theorists have to show that a particular commitment, such as a commitment to categorical moral reasons, is essential to moral discourse for it to be discourse about *morality* and not something else entirely, such as prudential values. For suppose that error theorists do not have a good argument for P1. In that case, some moral success theorists, who think that moral discourse does not commit the systematic error that error theorists attribute to it and who think that moral discourse is successful as it is, can argue that even if there are no categorical moral reasons, moral discourse was never committed to their existence in the first place, and thus that at least some moral judgements are true (Sayre-McCord 1986). Moral success theorists who deny P1 often think that moral discourse is just committed to hypothetical reasons, which are reasons that an agent has because she has a certain desire that will be promoted if she acted on that reason, and which are much easier to defend philosophically (Railton 1986; Brink 1989).

P2 is error theory's "substantive claim" (Joyce 2001, p. 5). Error theorists have to show that there are no categorical moral reasons. This is similar to the task that error theorists about witches have when they must show that there are no supernatural powers. For suppose that error theorists do not have a good argument for P2. In that case, some other moral success theorists can claim that although moral discourse is committed to the existence of categorical moral reasons, such reasons exist, and therefore that some moral judgements are true (Enoch 2011).

P3 is simply an instance of the more general and obviously correct thesis that any claim that carries a false non-negotiable claim is untrue (Streumer 2007, p. 255). For error theory about witch discourse, the judgement 'there exists a witch' is truth-apt and carries a non-negotiable commitment to the claim that there is at least one woman who has supernatural powers. But the last claim is false, and so the judgement 'there exists a witch' must also be untrue. It cannot be the case that the claim 'there exists a witch' is true but that the claim 'there exists a woman with supernatural powers' is not true and that the truth of the first claim requires the truth of the second. The same holds for moral discourse. The judgement 'giving to the poor is morally obligatory' is truth-apt, and it carries a non-negotiable commitment to the claim that there are categorical moral reasons; but that claim is false, and so the judgement 'giving to the poor is morally obligatory' is untrue. It cannot be the case that the claim 'giving to the poor is morally obligatory' is true but that the claim 'there exists at least one categorical moral reason' is not true and that the truth of the first claim requires the truth of the second claim.

P1, P2, and P3 entail C1. Yet from the truth of C1 we cannot deduce the truth of C2 (Evans and Shah 2012, p. 85). That is, we cannot conclude from the fact that moral judgements are untrue that our entire moral discourse is in error. This inference is unwarranted, first, because the

Generic Argument does not specify whether all or only some moral judgements are untrue. Perhaps the deontic part of morality with judgements like 'X is morally obligatory' and 'X is morally right' is systematically untrue, but what to say of judgements about moral goodness or judgements involving thick concepts like COURAGEOUS and VIRTUOUS? If such non-deontic moral judgements are true, then it becomes at least questionable to conclude from the fact that deontic moral judgements are untrue that moral discourse as such is in error. A second reason why this inference is unwarranted is that even if error theory extends from deontic to many other kinds of moral judgements, it remains to be seen whether negated and modal moral judgements such as 'X is *not* morally obligatory' and 'X *might be* morally obligatory' are systematically untrue (Kalf 2013, 2017). For again, if these moral judgements are not systematically untrue, then it seems that we cannot reach the conclusion that our entire moral discourse is in error. P4, if true, bridges this gap.

Generic Argument for Error Theory is the most generic formulation of error theory because it contains the largest number of placeholder terms for which error theorists must find a more precise meaning. For instance, traditionally error theorists have said that moral judgements are untrue because they are "all false" (Mackie 1977, p. 35; Clark 2009, p. 200). Alternatively, we can say that they are untrue because they are "neither true nor false" (Kalf 2013, p. 925). Error theorists must find interpretations of the placeholder term 'untrue', and also for the other placeholder terms in the Generic Argument, because these terms require further unpacking before we have an argument for error theory. Another example of a placeholder term in Generic Argument is 'claim N'. We can't argue that moral error theory is true because we know that it is committed to 'claim N' and that 'claim N' is false. We first need to know what 'claim N' is. This book is an attempt to find specific interpretations of these placeholder terms in Generic Argument that render this argument for error theory maximally plausible.

In addition to defending Generic Argument, error theorists should also tell us what we should do with moral discourse after error theory; that is, after at least some people have become convinced that error theory is the most plausible metaethical theory on offer. As John Burgess has put it, this is the major philosophical puzzle raised by … moral error theory: if an error theory provides the correct descriptive account of moral discourse, how, if at all, ought we to adjust our practices after having discovered the error? (1998, p. 534)

More recently, Matt Lutz has called this the "now what question" (2014, p. 351). Error theory, and now what? Answering the now what question is an exercise in normative thinking: what should we do with moral discourse from the point of view of prudence, and perhaps other normative domains such as epistemology and aesthetics, after error theory? Each of these normative domains (the prudential, the epistemic, the aesthetic) will provide *pro tanto* reasons for treating moral discourse in a certain way, and all these different oughts coalesce into an all-things-considered, overall ought that tells us what to do. The kinds of answers to the now what question that we can expect include, but are not limited to, the conservationist answer that we should continue with moral discourse as though nothing happened (Olson 2014) and the fictionalist answer that we should pretend that moral discourse is not in error (Joyce 2005).

Moral error theorists are not required to answer the now what question. This is because they are not epistemically obligated to abandon their view if they don't have a convincing answer to this question, just like error theorists about aesthetics are not required to answer the now what question for aesthetic discourse, and just like error theorists about religion are not required to answer the now what question for religious discourse. The plausibility of the Generic Argument is not affected by the absence or presence of a working account of what we ought to do with moral discourse after error theory. Unless the objection is that there couldn't be non-moral (prudential and epistemic) oughts if there aren't any moral oughts, and that this is a reason to reject error theory (Cuneo 2007; Rowland 2013). But this so-called *companions-in-guilt objection* will be rejected in §4.7. Nevertheless, if error theorists do answer the now what question, then they broaden their scope from moral to prudential and epistemic normativity, thus offering not just a metaethical but a more complete, *metanormative* theory. And that is a good thing, for being able to tell a convincing metanormative story on the back of one's metaethical theory is a further reason to accept the metaethical theory one favours.

A third question that is relevant to error theory, in addition to the question as to whether the view is plausible and the now what question, is whether the proposed post-error-theoretic metanormative theory consisting of error theory and its answer to the now what question enables us to make some headway in answering some of our questions in political philosophy and normative ethics, such as the question as to what justice in the distribution of resources consists in. So, the third question that is relevant to error theory is: suppose that error theory is true and that our best answer to the now what question is that we should treat moral language in way x; does that leave room for doing political philosophy and normative ethics, and if so, how? I pick this topic in political philosophy and not a topic that falls squarely in the domain of normative ethics for two reasons. First, I believe that the topic of distributive justice should be more central to normative ethics as it is practised today because, like many other topics in normative ethics, it deals with the issue of how we should treat other human beings. Other questions in political philosophy, such as which form of democracy is most desirable, are much further removed from the core business of normative ethicists (Kalf 2014). But distributive justice lies, I think, at least at the intersection of political philosophy and normative ethics. Second, and this will be explained in greater detail in Part II, after moral error theory and thus in the absence of true moral judgements and moral facts, there is no longer a clear sense in which questions about morality differ from the more general question of how we wish to live with each other. This last question clearly also concerns the topic of how we should distribute our resources, and is therefore a topic in normative ethics as we shall have construed it after error theory. In what follows, and when I refer to the penultimate chapter in this book, I will therefore sometimes continue to write that I will apply my metanormative view to a topic in normative ethics even though this should be understood with the qualifications just made.

How can error theorists speak of, or even do, normative ethics? Russ Shafer-Landau writes that if error theory is true, then

> obviously, the prospects for developing a normative ethic are bleak ... If there are no truths within morality—only a truth about morality, namely, that its edicts are uniformly untrue—then the enterprise of normative ethics

is philosophically bankrupt. Normative ethics is meant to identify the conditions under which actions are morally right, and motives morally good or admirable. If nothing is ever morally right or good, then normative ethics loses its point. (2005, p. 107)

However, it matters which formulation of error theory we adopt. Error theorists like Jonas Olson who defend a conservationist answer to the now what question, according to which we should simply go on as before after error theory, can still use moral terms in their moral discussions, and so they can affirm that giving to the poor is morally obligatory (Olson 2014). My own 'substitutionist' answer to the now what question is that we must change what moral judgements' truth-makers should be after error theory. Currently there are no facts that can be moral judgements' truth-makers, but there are different facts that look a lot like moral facts, which Joyce has usefully suggested we should call "schmoral" facts, and which I think we should adopt as schmoral judgements' truth-makers after error theory (Joyce 2007, p. 51; Blackburn 1984; Johnston 1989, 1993). True, in that case we will be doing, if you will, normative *schmetics*, but that just means that we will be identifying the conditions under which actions are schmorally right and schmorally wrong. This is sufficiently different from doing normative ethics to warrant not calling this activity 'normative ethics', but it is still sufficiently like normative ethics to deserve the name 'normative schmetics'.

Given that these are the three main questions for error theory, my aim in this book is threefold:

First, to defend error theory by finding precise formulations of the placeholder terms in Generic Argument, such as 'claim N' and 'untrue', that render error theory more plausible than existing formulations of error theory that use different precisifications for these placeholder terms.

Second, to argue that error theorists should accept substitutionism as their answer to the now what question.

Third, to offer a preliminary discussion of what implications this view might have in political philosophy and normative ethics.

Above I emphasized a number of times that accepting different interpretations of the placeholder terms in the Generic Argument makes a difference to error theory's plausibility. Here is an example of why this is so.

Consider the term 'untrue' as we find it in the Generic Argument. In an important sense, both the view that moral judgements are *false* and the view that moral judgements are *neither true nor false* are acceptable ways of precisifying Generic Argument's claim that moral judgements are *untrue*. This is because what is most important for error theory are the following two theses. The first is that there are no moral considerations that agents ought to take into account in their deliberations about what they should do, such that the only considerations that matter are always non-moral considerations like prudential and perhaps aesthetic considerations. Suppose Celine is enjoying her daily afternoon walk and sees a child drowning in a shallow pond (Singer 1972, p. 231). Should she wade in to save the child and damage her new shoes in the process, or should she continue to enjoy her walk without the interruption of saving the child? The error theorist wants to say that as Celine makes up her mind about what she ought to do, she just has to consider non-moral considerations, such as the prudential consideration that getting her shoes wet would cause her some minor trouble, and she never has to consider moral considerations, such as the consideration that she is morally obliged to save the child. The second of these two most important theses for error theory is that no one can communicate to anyone else a *true* moral judgement that would obligate the addressee to take the moral consideration that this judgement entails into account in their practical decision-making. Because the idea that moral considerations are irrelevant in practical deliberation and because the idea that no moral judgement successfully communicates that there are moral considerations are at the heart of error theory, it does not matter whether the error theorist ends up saying that moral judgements are *false* or that they are *neither true nor false*. What matters is that there are no moral considerations and that every moral judgement that pretends that there is such a consideration is *untrue*. I call this the no moral considerations are relevant argument.

However, in a different sense, the issue of whether to formulate error theory as the view that moral judgements are false or as the view that moral judgements are neither true nor false matters a great deal. For there are important objections to error theory that focus on which of the two specifications of the placeholder term 'untrue' it embraces. This includes the objection that if error theory is formulated as the view that moral judgements are all *false*, then error theory is not coherent because it violates the law of the excluded middle (Pigden 2007). The objection is that the negation of the moral judgement 'giving to the poor is morally obligatory' is also a moral judgement, which must as such, according to the standard error theorist's view that *all* moral judgements are false, be false. But if that is so, then we violate the law of excluded middle, according to which if a positive, atomic judgement like 'giving to the poor is morally obligatory' is false, then its negation 'giving to the poor is not morally obligatory' must be *true*, not false. A formulation of error theory that entails that moral judgements are all neither true nor false, including affirmative moral judgements and their negations, clearly avoids this 'inconsistency objection'. After all, it is not inconsistent to say both that 'giving to the poor is morally obligatory' is neither true nor false and that 'giving to the poor is not morally obligatory' is neither true nor false. In §2.2 and §2.8, I consider some responses to this objection on behalf of the standard error theorist who insists that all moral judgements are false. Here my point is just that the way in which error theorists formulate their theory matters for its plausibility.

My generic formulation of error theory does not have space for a different version of error theory, proposed by Richard Joyce in his book *The Evolution of Morality*, which does not say that moral judgements are systematically *untrue* but instead that they are *epistemically unjustified* because we lack sufficient epistemic warrant for our moral beliefs (2006, p. 233). On this formulation of error theory, we do not commit ourselves, out of epistemic modesty, to the claim that moral judgements are definitely untrue because they are false, or definitely untrue because they are neither true nor false. We just commit ourselves to the claim that they are probably untrue. But Joyce now rejects this label, for knowing that we lack sufficient epistemic warrant for the truth of our moral beliefs is consistent with the existence of moral facts and therefore with the truth of moral realism, and "error theory had better not be compatible with moral realism" (Joyce 2013, p. 354). After all, moral realism entails that there *are* moral considerations that are relevant in our deliberations about what to do, which is precisely what error theorists want to avoid, given their no moral considerations are relevant argument. I therefore keep Generic Argument as formulated.

At this point, you might have started to think that the issue of how to formulate error theory is anything from very to only mildly interesting, but that the fact that error theory implies that all moral judgements are untrue has such obviously implausible consequences that error theory is not worth taking seriously. This objection can take various forms. First, with G.E. Moore we can say:

> It seems ... *more* certain that I *do* know that this is a pencil, [that there are moral facts] and that you are conscious, than that any single one of these sceptical assumptions is true. (Moore 1959, p. 226; italics in original)

And since you too may find it comparatively more certain that there are moral facts than that a sceptical theory like error theory is true, you might conclude that error theory should be rejected. Or, second, with David Lewis we can say that you should

> never put forward a ... theory that you cannot yourself believe in your least philosophical and most commonsensical moments. (1986, p. 135)

And since you too may find that you cannot believe error theory in your most commonsensical moments, you might conclude that error theory should be rejected. Third and finally, you might worry that if we accept error theory, then many people will start to do things that we are currently inclined to call morally wrong, such as engaging in wanton killing and refraining from saving innocent children from drowning in shallow ponds (Cuneo and Christy 2011, p. 96). And since you may think that we mustn't run the risk that people become (even) more evil after error theory, you might think that we should reject error theory.

These kinds of worries fail. The first two versions of the objection are philosophical objections that will be rejected in §4.8. I explain why we should reject the third version of the objection here because in my experience this objection hinders many people from taking error theory seriously.

There are two reasons why we don't have to be afraid that people, after they have become convinced of error theory, will start performing actions that we thought were morally wrong but are not morally wrong, strictly speaking, as "nothing is morally anything", according to error theory

(Kalf 2013, p. 928). The first reason concerns moral motivation. As error theorist Joyce puts it, most people have

> firm and entrenched desires on the side of moral goodness ... Such a person's desires may only be contingent, it is true, but contingency must not be confused with flimsiness. (2006, p. 205)

Moreover, as David Hume writes in his famous essay 'The Sceptic':

> Were I not afraid of appearing too philosophical, I should remind my reader of that famous doctrine, supposed to be fully proved in modern times, "That tastes and colours, and all other sensible qualities, lie not in the bodies, but merely in the senses." The case is the same with beauty and deformity, virtue and vice ... And as it is certain, that the discovery above-mentioned in natural philosophy, makes no alteration on action and conduct; why should a like discovery in moral philosophy make any alteration? (1742/1987, p. 166)

Recent empirical studies also suggest that people are often motivated to perform actions that we are inclined to call morally good, solely on self-regarding grounds (Walker 2013; Frimer et al. 2014). Finally, as the philosopher Derek Parfit says, error theorists' "past beliefs may have continuing effects on what they care about and do" (2012, Vol. 2, p. 462).

In addition to this, and switching from motivation to normativity, I will argue that many of us have prudential reasons to perform actions that we thought were morally obligatory, such as saving drowning children from shallow ponds. These prudential reasons include, but are not limited to, that it will make us feel better to perform these actions, that it will significantly lower the chance that we get ostracized by society if we don't perform these actions, and that it will significantly lower the chance that we will be sent to jail for culpable neglect (§6.4). Joyce writes:

> The popular thought that without morality all hell would break loose in human society is a naïve one. Across a vast range of situations, we all have perfectly good *prudential* reasons to continuing to act in cooperative ways with our fellow humans. In many situations, reciprocal and cooperative relationships bring ongoing rewards to all parties, and do so *a forteriori* when defective behaviours are punished. When, in addition, we factor in the benefits of having a good reputation—a reputation that is based on

past performance—then cooperative dispositions can easily out-compete hurtful dispositions on purely egoistic grounds. (Joyce 2005, p. 300)

And so, given that we are often independently motivated to perform the actions that we were used to describe as morally right and morally obligatory, and given that there are prudential reasons to perform these actions, there will be no moral apocalypse after error theory. Thus, error theory is not so obviously implausible or dangerous that it does not merit our attention.

In the remainder of this chapter, I do two things. First, I explain the outline of my argument for error theory, comparing it with existing arguments offered by Mackie (1977), Joyce (2001), and Olson (2014) (§1.2). Second, I explain three assumptions about metaethics that most error theorists, including myself, accept but don't try to defend because a serious defence of these assumptions would merit at least another book in its own right (§1.3). The project of the book is to see whether we can get a plausible formulation, and defence, of moral error theory on the assumption that these three assumptions are acceptable.

1.2 Outline of the View

In the previous section, I explained that I have three aims in this book, that is, to defend error theory, to defend a particular answer to the now what question, and to explore what implications this view might have in debates in political philosophy and normative ethics. However, because my first aim of defending error theory requires arguing for three premises (P1, P2, and P4), I have a total of five tasks: to argue for P1, to argue for P2, to argue for P4, to argue for my answer to the now what question, and to indicate what I consider to be the implications of my error theory and its answer to the now question for topics in political philosophy and normative ethics. I do not have to argue for P3 because I have already done this above.

The first task is to defend P1, that is, to show that a particular commitment, such as a commitment to categorical moral reasons, is essential to moral discourse for it to be discourse about morality and not something else entirely, such as prudential values. Moral error theorists have traditionally argued for this non-negotiable commitment claim by trying to show that moral judgements like 'giving to the poor is morally obligatory' *conceptually entail* the judgement 'there exist categorical moral reasons'. For instance, Richard Joyce writes:

> An error theory ... involves two steps of argumentation. First, it involves ascertaining what a term *means*. I have tried to explicate this in terms of "non-negotiability" ... in artificially simple terms, the first step gives us something roughly of the form "For any x, Fx if and only if Px and Qx and Rx." We can call this step *conceptual*. The second step is to ascertain whether the following is true: "There exists an x, such that Px and Qx and Rx." If not, then there is nothing that satisfies "... is F." Call this step *ontological* or *substantive*. The concept of *phlogiston* – with its commitment to a stuff that is stored in bodies and released during combustion – and the concept of *tapu* – with its commitment to a kind of contagious pollution – do not pass the test. (2001, p. 5; italics is original)

Just like it follows from conceptual analysis of the concept VIXEN that it refers to 'female fox', and just like it follows from conceptual analysis of TAPU that it refers to 'contagious pollution', it follows from conceptual analysis of MORALLY OBLIGATORY that it refers to a categorical moral reason. And where moral concepts are part of affirmative judgements, the error theorist claims that the judgement 'giving to the poor is morally obligatory' entails that there is a categorical reason to give to the poor, just like the judgement 'Foxy is a vixen' entails that Foxy is a female fox. Accepting this line of argument, and in an attempt to turn Generic Argument into a specific argument for error theory, requires us to rewrite P1 in the Generic Argument as follows:

P1'   Moral judgements conceptually entail claim N.

What should the content of 'claim N' be? Richard Joyce thinks that:

> Conceptually, morality requires ... categorical moral reasons. (MS, p. 2)

Accepting this line of argument requires us to further specify P1' in the Generic Argument, which is as follows:

P1"   Moral judgements conceptually entail the claim that there are categorical moral reasons.

An alternative interpretation of claim N has been provided by error theorist Jonas Olson, who used to accept that categorical moral reasons are the content of claim N but now prefers a different formulation (Olson 2014, p. 117). Olson now thinks that claim N should be about irreducibly normative reasons, where reasons are analysed as facts such that "for a fact to be an irreducibly normative reason is for that fact to count in favour of some course of behaviour, where the favouring relation is irreducibly normative" (2014, p. 118). Olson also accepts the conceptual entailment view:

> we can call the claim that moral facts are or entail irreducibly normative reasons (and correspondingly that moral claims are or entail claims about irreducibly normative reasons) *the conceptual claim*. (2014, p. 124; italics in original)

This means that Olson defends:

P1'''   Moral judgements conceptually entail the claim that there are irreducibly normative reasons.

The difference between categorical and irreducibly normative reasons is that it is built into the definition of the latter that they make an ontological demand on the world, whereas the former leave this open and just require that they "bind" agents regardless of whether they desire to perform the action that a categorical reason tells them to perform (Joyce 2001, p. 37). I call a theory of reasons according to which reasons make an ontological demand on the world an *existence theory of reasons*. There are various theories of reasons that do not fall into this camp, but as I shall explain below, the theory of reasons that provides the best fit with error theory is a theory according to which reasons are considerations that count as reasons because it is rational to count these considerations as reasons. In this case I speak of *reasons of rationality* rather than irreducibly normative reasons, which are postulated by the existence theory of reasons. As I use these terms, 'categorical reason' can refer to 'irreducibly normative reason' and to 'categorical reason of rationality'. This will change in Chap. 4, as at that point, the most plausible interpretation of categorical reason will have been found to be categorical reason of rationality, and I will from that point onwards use the term 'categorical reason' to refer to just categorical reasons of rationality.

My plan is to argue, in Chap. 2, that the traditional argument for P1, which uses conceptual entailment, fails, and to argue, in Chap. 3, that an alternative, highly underexplored argument for P1 does work. This alternative argument for the non-negotiable commitment claim uses *presupposition* instead, and has not yet been formulated in sufficient detail (Kalf 2013). The idea is mentioned in Finlay (2008a, p. 374; 2011, p. 535) and Shafer-Landau (2005, p. 108) and discussed, though all too briefly, and subsequently rejected, in Joyce (2001, pp. 6–9) and Olson (2014, pp. 9–13). To see how presupposition works, first consider the non-moral judgements "the king of France is wise" and "the king of France is not wise" (Strawson 1950, p. 321). These judgements both presuppose that France has a king, but that claim is false, and so both statements about the king of France are neither true nor false (or possibly 'false'; I will comment on this in Chap. 3). Similarly, says the advocate of this alternative formulation of error theory, 'giving to the poor is morally obligatory' and 'giving to the poor is not morally obligatory' both presuppose that there are categorical moral reasons, but that claim is false, and so both statements are neither true nor false.

Since I defend presupposition error theory, I claim that error theorists are best advised not to understand P1 as P1', P1", or P1"', but that they should understand P1 as P1*:

P1* Moral judgements presuppose claim N.

In fact, I think that the content of commitment N is that there are categorical moral reasons, so I will defend P**:

P1** Moral judgements presuppose the claim that there are categorical moral reasons.

To be even more precise, there are two different versions of presupposition error theory—semantic and pragmatic presupposition error theory—and I will defend:

P1*** Moral judgements pragmatically presuppose the claim that there are categorical moral reasons.

A third option for error theorists is to argue not for a conceptual entailment or presupposition but for a 'metaphysical entailment' formulation of their view, which works like conceptual entailment but proposes to drop the requirement that there must be a necessary relation between concepts (Kalf 2013, p. 926). I am thinking of entailment relations that hold in virtue of *a posteriori* identity or constitution claims between moral considerations and categorical reasons, much like the way in which the statement 'this is water' entails 'this is H_2O'. There is no conceptual connection between water and H_2O, yet if there is water, then there is guaranteed to be H_2O. This would not give us an error theory of ordinary moral discourse, but of 'morality', to which, if the advocate of a metaphysical entailment error theory is right, we have epistemic access without prioritizing researching the semantics of moral judgements. Whether, and if so how, a view like this works for the moral case is an interesting project in its own right, and I make some preliminary moves in my article 'Moral Error Theory, Entailment and Presupposition' (Kalf 2013). However, in the present book, I am interested in an error theory of ordinary moral discourse and, moreover, I doubt that we can get to the essence of morality without prioritizing moral semantics (Gampel 1996). I therefore ignore the metaphysical entailment possibility in what follows.

My second task is to argue for P2, that is, to argue that claim N is false. Here my ambition is to show that we are led to error theory on the basis of some widely accepted but controversial assumptions about reasons and rationality. Moral error theorists have used a number of arguments for the claim that categorical reasons don't exist, including the argument that such reasons are "too queer" to exist (Olson 2014, p. 12n17; Mackie 1977, pp. 38–42). They have also argued that although categorical moral reasons are not queer, whether they exist depends on whether they are generated by correct reasoning or rational thinking, but that correct reasoning or rational thinking does not generate such reasons (Joyce 2001, pp. 53–134). In Chap. 4, I explore this kind of rationality and not a queerness moral error theory. An important reason for doing this is that queerness arguments often lack genuine dialectic force and just result in an "incredulous stare", that is, 'you find this queer and think that queerness matters?' versus 'you don't find this queer and that queerness doesn't matter?' (Lewis 1973, p. 86). As Mark Platts writes:

> The world is a queer place. I find neutrinos, aardvarks, infinite sequences of objects, and (most pertinently) impressionist paintings peculiar kinds of entities. (1980, p. 72)

And it looks as though there isn't much one can do by way of arguing to persuade Platts to adopt a different attitude. Nevertheless, for those who think that queerness does matter, I will explain why it stands to reason to think that the non-moral normativity that I appeal to is not too queer to exist (§4.4).

My third task is to argue for P4, that is, to argue that the falsity of C1 is sufficient warrant to become an error theorist about the discourse as a whole. The error in moral discourse must be so pervasive that it is not consistent with a benign revision of moral discourse, which may take the form of ceasing to utter only one kind of moral judgements, such as judgements about deontic morality, and which leaves everything else, such as judgements about virtue, intact. For such a benign revision, because it doesn't enable error theorists to keep their *no moral considerations are relevant argument* and because it renders superfluous the need to make fundamental changes to moral discourse, is inconsistent with error theory's sceptical stance towards morality. Thus, error theorists face the *pervasiveness objection*: though there may be an error in moral discourse, it is not sufficient to render the discourse completely false. I argue that with presupposition rather than conceptual entailment, error theorists have a convincing reply to this objection (§3.7).

This defence of error theory by means of my defence of P1, P2, and P4 constitutes Part 1 of this book. Part II is about what we should do with moral discourse after error theory. There I start with the fourth task for error theorists, which is to solve the now what problem. In Chap. 5, I argue against every existing solution to this problem except the one that I favour, which I argue for in Chap. 6. In that chapter, I argue for a new version of substitutionism, which I call pragmatic presupposition substitutionism. According to it, we should substitute moral judgements that pragmatically presuppose (rather than entail) categorical moral reasons, which don't exist, for schmoral judgements that pragmatically presuppose (rather than entail) hypothetical schmoral reasons, which do exist.

The fifth and final task for error theorists is to explore the implications of their overall picture, including their answer to the now what question, for political philosophy and normative ethics. I discuss some of these implications in Chap. 7. Chapter 8 concludes by summarizing my findings and indicating avenues for further research.

At various points in this Introduction, I have made a number of assumptions about metaethics that I did not defend. I accept these assumptions and I want to see whether error theory or a different metaethical theory provides the best fit with these assumptions. In the remainder of this Introduction, I will explain what the assumptions are, and although I will provide some arguments for them, I will not nearly spend as much time on these assumptions as I will on the five tasks identified above.

1.3 Three Assumptions

The first assumption is that the only plausible metaethical theories are cognitivist theories, according to which ordinary participants in moral language adopt the belief attitude towards moral propositions, and that the meaning of moral judgements is given by the cognitive, truth-apt mental states that they express. This means that non-cognitivist theories, according to which the meaning of moral judgements is given by the non-cognitive, non-truth-apt mental states that they express, will not be considered in this book. An example of a non-cognitivist theory is A.J. Ayer's emotivism, according to which:

> If I say to someone, 'You acted wrongly in stealing that money' [then it] is as if I had said, 'You stole that money', in a peculiar tone of horror ... I produce a sentence which has no factual meaning—that is, expresses no proposition that can be either true or false. (1936, p. 107)

In Ayer's view, "stealing is morally wrong" means "boo! Stealing" (Kalf 2015, p. 1873). The main problem with non-cognitivism, from the point of view of error theory, is that it entails that moral judgements are not truth-apt.

A well-known qualification is that certain sophisticated versions of non-cognitivism, such as various forms of quasi-realism, have been claimed to be able to give us moral truth without cognitivism (Blackburn 1993; Gibbard 1990, 2003). To achieve this, quasi-realists sometimes accept disciplined syntacticism, according to which, so long as a sentence is suitably well behaved—that is, so long as it can be embedded in propositional attitude contexts and plays an appropriate role in conditionals, logical inferences and the like—it is truth-apt (Boghossian 1990, pp. 161–7). And quasi-realists might add to this a version of deflationism or minimalism about truth, according to which truth is not a property of sentences or propositions and according to which there is nothing more to asserting that a sentence is true than simply asserting the sentence (Horwich 1990, p. 15). Alternatively, quasi-realists can say more than, or at least something different from, just what is captured by this sort of *equivalence schema*, and suggest that utterances of the form "S is true" do not predicate "is true" of S and instead merely indicate preparedness on the part of the speaker to assert S (Stoljar and Damnjanovic 2014: §2). My second assumption is that at least a minimally *inflationary* notion of truth is required for moral truth, such that truth is a property of some kind, for instance, though this is not required, truth as consisting in correspondence with facts. This means that quasi-realism cannot be true.

Recently, metaethicists have started to explore the possibility of a hybrid cognitivist-non-cognitivist semantics for moral judgements, according to which part of their meaning is given by the beliefs that they express and part of their meaning is given by the desires that they express (Fletcher and Ridge 2014). One argument for accepting a hybrid semantics for moral judgements is that although we need cognitivism to account for moral truth and the possibility of genuine moral disagreement, we need non-cognitivism to explain moral motivation, given the Humean theory of motivation, according to which our psychologies consist of just desires and beliefs and according to which desires are motivationally efficacious, and beliefs are not. Hume wrote:

Where … objects themselves do not affect us, their connexion [of effect to cause, which reason makes evident to us] can never give them any influence; and 'tis plain, that as reason is nothing but the discovery of this connexion, it cannot be by its means that the objects are able to affect us … reason alone can never produce any action, or give rise to volition … Nothing can oppose or retard the influence of passion, but a contrary impulse … Reason is … only … the slave of the passions, and can never pretend to any other office than to serve and obey them. (1739/1975, pp. 414–15)

However, in Chap. 6 I argue that if error theorists accept my substitutionist answer to the now what problem, they can explain moral motivation with a purely cognitivist semantics and they do not need to become hybrid expressivist-error theorists (Kalf 2017, pp. 118–21).

My third assumption is that philosophers have armchair access to folk intuitions (Johnston 1987; Joyce 2006, p. 102; Finlay 2008b, p. 136; Robinson 2009, p. 321; Marks 2013, p. 9; Dunaway et al. 2013). I believe that, *qua* competent participants in moral discourse, we can judge whether a philosophical interpretation of folk behaviour is or is not in keeping with what the folk would themselves say they are doing if they were competent with the technical, philosophical concepts that philosophers use to describe folk morality. Nevertheless, I do consult the empirical metaethics literature to defend some of the arguments that I make. The project in this book is to see whether we can get a plausible error theory on the assumptions that we must accept cognitivism, a minimally inflationary theory of truth, and that philosophers have armchair access to what the folk would and would not find acceptable philosophical interpretations of their behaviour.

References

Ayer, A.J. 1936. *Language, Truth and Logic*. London: Victor Gollancz.
Blackburn, S. 1984. *Spreading the Word*. Oxford: Clarendon Press.
———. 1993. *Essays in Quasi-Realism*. Oxford: OUP.
Boghossian, P. 1990. The Status of Content. *The Philosophical Review* 99: 157–184.

Brink, D.O. 1989. *Moral Realism and the Foundations of Ethics*. Cambridge: CUP.
Burgess, J.A. 1998. Error Theories and Values. *Australasian Journal of Philosophy* 76: 534–552.
Clark, P. 2009. Mackie's Motivational Argument. In *Reasons for Action*, ed. D. Sobel and S. Wall, 200–218. Cambridge: CUP.
Cuneo, C. 2007. *The Normative Web*. Oxford: OUP.
Cuneo, T., and S. Christy. 2011. The Myth of Moral Fictionalism. In *New Waves in Metaethics*, ed. M. Brady, 85–102. New York: Palgrave Macmillan.
Dreier, J. 1997. Humean Doubts About the Practical Justification of Morality. In *Ethics and Practical Reason*, ed. G. Cullity and B. Gaut, 81–100. Oxford: OUP.
Dunaway, B., A. Edmonds, and D. Manley. 2013. The Folk Probably Think What You Think They Think. *Australasian Journal of Philosophy* 91 (3): 421–441.
Enoch, D. 2011. *Taking Morality Seriously*. Oxford: OUP.
Evans, M., and N. Shah. 2012. Mental Agency and Metaethics. In *Oxford Studies in Metaethics 7*, ed. R. Shafer-Landau, 81–109. Oxford: OUP.
Finlay, S. 2008a. The Error in the Error Theory. *Australasian Journal of Philosophy* 86: 347–369.
———. 2008b. Too Much Morality. In *Morality and Self-Interest*, ed. P. Bloomfield, 136–158. Oxford: OUP.
———. 2011. Errors Upon Errors: A Reply to Joyce. *Australasian Journal of Philosophy* 89: 535–547.
Fletcher, G., and M. Ridge. 2014. *Having it Both Ways*. Oxford: OUP.
Frimer, J.A., N.K. Schaefer, and H. Oakes. 2014. Moral Actor, Selfish Agent. *Journal of Personality and Social Psychology* 106: 790–802.
Gampel, E.H. 1996. A Defense of the Autonomy of Ethics: Why Value Is Not Like Water. *Canadian Journal of Philosophy* 26: 191–209.
Gibbard, A. 1990. *Wise Choices, Apt Feelings*. Cambridge, MA: Harvard University Press.
———. 2003. *Thinking How to Live*. Cambridge, MA: Harvard University Press.
Horwich, P. 1990. *Truth*. Oxford: OUP.
Hume, D. 1739/40. *A Treatise of Human Nature*, ed. L.A. Selby-Bigge. 1978. Oxford: Clarendon Press.
———. 1742. The Sceptic. In *Hume's Essays, Moral, Political, and Literary*, ed. E. Miller, 1987. Indianapolis: Liberty Fund

Johnston, M. 1987. Human Beings. *The Journal of Philosophy* 84: 59–83.
———. 1989. Dispositional Theories of Value. *Proceedings of the Aristotelian Society* 63 (Suppl): 139–174.
———. 1993. Objectivity Refigured: Pragmatism Without Verificationism. In *Reality, Representation, and Projection*, ed. J. Haldane and C. Wright, 85–130. Oxford: Oxford University Press.
Joyce, R. 2001. *The Myth of Morality*. Cambridge: CUP.
———. 2005. Moral Fictionalism. In *Fictionalism in Metaphysics*, ed. M.E. Kalderon, 287–313. Oxford: OUP.
———. 2006. *The Evolution of Morality*. Cambridge, MA: MIT Press.
———. 2007. Morality, Schmorality. In *Morality and Self-Interest*, ed. P. Bloomfield, 51–75. Oxford: OUP.
———. 2013. Irrealism and the Genealogy of Morals. *Ratio* 26: 351–372.
———. MS. *Enough with the Errors! A Final Reply to Finlay*. http://personal.victoria.ac.nz/richard_joyce/acrobat/joyce_2012_enough.with.the.errors.pdf.
Kalf, W.F. 2013. Moral Error Theory, Entailment and Presupposition. *Ethical Theory and Moral Practice* 16: 923–937.
———. 2014. The *Tractatus Theologico-Politicus* and the Received View of Spinoza on Democracy. *Res Publica* 20: 263–279.
———. 2015. Are Moral Properties Impossible? *Philosophical Studies* 172: 1869–1887.
———. 2017. Against Hybrid Expressivist-Error Theory. *Journal of Value Inquiry* 51: 105–122.
Lewis, D.K. 1973. *Counterfactuals*. Oxford: OUP.
———. 1986. *On the Plurality of Worlds*. Oxford: Basil Blackwell.
Lutz, M. 2014. The 'Now What' Problem for Error Theory. *Philosophical Studies* 171: 351–371.
Mackie, J.L. 1977. *Ethics: Inventing Right and Wrong*. Harmondsworth: Penguin Publishers.
Marks, J. 2013. *Ethics Without Morals*. London: Routledge.
Moore, G.E. 1959. *Philosophical Papers*. London: Allen and Unwin.
Olson, J. 2010. In Defence of Moral Error Theory. In *New Waves in Metaethics*, ed. M. Brady, 62–84. London: Palgrave Macmillan.
———. 2014. *Moral Error Theory: History, Critique, Defence*. Oxford: OUP.
Parfit, D. 1997. Reasons and Motivation. *Proceedings of the Aristotelian Society* 71 (Suppl): 99–130.
———. 2012. *On What Matters*. Oxford: OUP (Two Volumes).

Pigden, C. 2007. Nihilism, Nietzsche and the Doppelganger Problem. *Ethical Theory and Moral Practice* 10: 414–456.

Platts, M. 1980. Moral Reality and the End of Desire. In *Reference, Truth and Reality*, ed. Platts, 69–82. London: Routledge & Kegan Paul.

Railton, P. 1986. Moral Realism. *Philosophical Review* 95: 163–207.

Robinson, D. 2009. Moral Functionalism, Quasi-Relativism, and the Plan. In *Conceptual Analysis and Philosophical Naturalism*, ed. D. Braddon-Mitchell and R. Nola, 315–348. Cambridge, MA: MIT Press.

Rowland, R. 2013. Moral Error Theory and the Argument from Epistemic Reasons. *Journal of Ethics and Social Philosophy* 7 (1): 1–24.

Sayre-McCord, G. 1986. The Many Moral Realisms. *The Southern Journal of Philosophy* 24: 1–22.

Scanlon, T.M. 1998. *What We Owe to Each Other*. Harvard, MA: Belknap Press.

Shafer-Landau, R. 2005. Error Theory and the Possibility of Normative Ethics. *Philosophical Issues* 15: 107–120.

Singer, P. 1972. Famine, Affluence and Morality. *Philosophy and Public Affairs* 1: 229–243.

Smith, M. 1994. *The Moral Problem*. Oxford: OUP.

Stoljar, D., and Nic Damnjanovic. 2014. The Deflationary Theory of Truth. In *The Stanford Encyclopedia of Philosophy*, ed. E.N. Zalta. Stanford: Stanford University Press.

Strawson, P.F. 1950. On Referring. *Mind* 59: 320–344.

Streumer, B. 2007. Reasons and Entailment. *Erkenntnis* 66: 353–374.

———. 2017. *Unbelievable Errors*. Oxford: OUP.

Väyrynen, P. 2013. *The Lewd, The Rude, and the Nasty*. Oxford: OUP.

Walker, L.J. 2013. Exemplars' Moral Behaviour Is Self-Regarding. *New Directions for Child and Adolescent Development* 142: 27–40.

2

Conceptual Entailment Error Theory

2.1 Introduction

In this chapter, I argue that the error theorist's standard defence of the first premise in the Generic Argument for Error Theory is inadequate. The first premise was as follows:

P1   Moral judgements carry a non-negotiable commitment to claim N

How should we understand what is meant by the phrase that moral judgements 'carry a non-negotiable commitment'? As I explained in §1.2, given that I want an error theory of moral discourse and not of morality, I cannot appeal to *a posteriori* metaphysical entailment relations. The remaining options for making moral judgements' mode of commitment to categorical reasons more precise are conceptual entailment and presupposition:

P1'   Moral judgements conceptually entail claim N
P1*   Moral judgements presuppose claim N

© The Author(s) 2018
W. F. Kalf, *Moral Error Theory*, https://doi.org/10.1007/978-3-319-77288-2_2

The version of P1 that I will argue against in this chapter is P1', which is part of the traditional formulation of error theory (Mackie 1977, p. 35; Joyce 2001, p. 42; Olson 2014, p. 124). I will only discuss Mackie's and Joyce's arguments for P1'. I don't discuss Olson's arguments because his main contributions to the literature on error theory lie elsewhere, such as an attempt to revive the queerness argument and a defence of conservationism as an answer to the now what question.

In defending the claim that the mode of commitment of moral judgements to claim N must be understood in terms of conceptual entailment, Joyce has consistently taken categorical reasons as the content of commitment N. Contrastingly, Mackie has wavered between at least four accounts of the content of this commitment. At one point, Mackie says that moral judgements conceptually entail objectively prescriptive moral properties, where prescriptivity involves both normativity and motivation:

> Moral ... values ... are a very central structural element in the fabric of the world. But it is held also that knowing them or 'seeing' them will not merely tell men what to do but will ensure that they do it, overruling any contrary inclinations. (1977, pp. 31–2)

Let's call this the central passage for ease of reference. The first sentence is about the objectivity of moral values, and the second sentence is about their prescriptivity. Mackie's conception of the objectivity of moral properties is that they must exist:

> prior to and logically independent of ... such activities as ... valuing, preferring, choosing, recommending, and so on. (1977, p. 30)

The first sentence in the central passage confirms Mackie's view that moral values are objective in this "SuperDuper" and "Platonist" sense of objectivity, according to which morality is objective if, and only if, it is wholly independent of what we may think about it (Tresan 2009, p. 369; Darwall et al. 1992, p. 141n59). This is because it asserts that values are a central structural element in the fabric of the world, and moral agents cannot influence what the central structural elements in the fabric of the world are.

The following is often overlooked, but there are quite some philosophers who share Mackie's idea that morality is objective in this sense, or in a sense very much like it. For instance, in *The Moral Problem*, Michael Smith argues that one of the central features of common-sense morality is the "objectivity of moral judgement":

> we seem to think moral questions have correct answers; that the correct answers are made correct by objective moral facts; that moral facts are wholly determined by circumstances, and that, by engaging in moral conversation and argument, we can discover what these objective moral facts determined by the circumstances are. (1994, p. 6)

Similarly, in his 'Lecture on Ethics', Ludwig Wittgenstein provides a picture of value as

> the absolutely right road ... which everybody on seeing it would, with logical necessity, have to go, or be ashamed for not going. And similarly the absolute good, if it is a describable state of affairs, would be one which everybody, independent of his tastes and inclinations, would necessarily bring about or feel guilty for not bringing about. (1965, p. 7)

Michael Ruse approaches the issue from a biological or evolutionary perspective, and writes that

> morality simply does not work (from a biological perspective) unless we believe that it is objective. (1998, p. 253)

He also writes that

> the ultimate basis of ethics is objective. By this is meant that moral norms exist independently of humans ... we humans intuit or otherwise rationally grasp morality ... In analogy with mathematics [we can] think of such norms as fixed and eternal. (1998, p. 214)

And although he is critical of error theory, Mark Johnston writes that

There is something in the idea that if anything is absolutely and strictly to deserve the name of value it would be a practical demand built into the world in such a way that any merely formally rational being would on pain of inconsistency feel shame if he were not to respect it. This is in effect what John Mackie called the idea of value as 'the objectively prescriptive'. (1989, p. 171)

The second sentence in the central passage asserts that the prescriptivity of moral values amounts to normative force ('telling' someone to do something is a normative relation) and motivational force ('ensuring' that agents do what is right requires that the agent is motivated to do what is right). Thus, on the first interpretation of Mackie on the nature of moral values, which he thinks moral judgements are non-negotiably committed to, moral values are objective, normative, and motivationally efficacious.

Mackie has also been interpreted as saying that moral judgements conceptually entail objectively prescriptive moral properties, but where prescriptivity, though Mackie does mention motivation, only involves normativity (Copp 2010, p. 146; Garner 1990, p. 144). Third, Mackie has been said to hold the view that moral judgements conceptually entail objectively prescriptive moral properties, but that prescriptivity, though Mackie does mention normativity, only involves motivation (Parfit 2012, pp. 448–452). Fourth, Mackie writes that we can make the issue of understanding morality's non-negotiable commitment

> clearer by referring to Kant's distinction between hypothetical and categorical imperatives ... a categorical imperative would express a reason for acting which was unconditional in the sense of not being contingent upon any present desire of the agent whose satisfaction the recommended action would contribute to as a means ... my thesis that there are no objective values is specifically the denial that any categorically imperative element is objectively valid. (1977, p. 27, p. 29)

On this fourth reading of Mackie's account of the content of claim N, it is about categorical reasons. In what follows, and for stylistic reasons, I will follow Mackie in writing about both objectively prescriptive properties and about categorical reasons when I write about his account of the content of commitment N, though I will consistently omit the reference to motivation as Mackie's queerness argument works best without this further commitment (Garner 1990; Olson 2014). Officially though, and because Mackie says that we can make the issue of objective prescriptivity 'clearer' if we talk about categorical reasons, I take it that both Mackie and Joyce accept P1":

P1" Moral judgements conceptually entail the claim that there are categorical moral reasons

There are many commitments that conceptual entailment error theory undertakes if it accepts P1', regardless of what it says about the content of claim N. To be able to assess the pros and cons of this account of the mode of commitment of moral judgements to categorical reasons, I list and explain these commitments in the next section (§2.2). In the two sections that follow, I present Mackie's and Joyce's arguments for P1" and I argue that these arguments fail (§2.3, 2.4, and 2.5). I focus on P1" rather than P1' because the arguments that Mackie and Joyce give for believing that moral judgements carry a non-negotiable commitment and that this mode of commitment should be understood in terms of conceptual entailment cannot be separated from their arguments for using categorical moral reasons as the content of claim N. My discussion of Mackie and Joyce leads to two general objections to P1', which work even if we remain agnostic about the content of claim N (§2.6, 2.7, and 2.8). It is important to have these general arguments as well, because it does not follow from the failure of Mackie's and Joyce's arguments for conceptual entailment error theory that we should reject conceptual entailment error theory as such. The first general objection directly targets the idea in P1' that the mode of commitment of moral discourse to categorical reasons must be understood as conceptual entailment. It does this by working up an alternative account of the content of moral concepts that does not appeal to categorical reasons and by claiming that this alternative theory better accounts for the data about folk morality as we have them (§2.6 and 2.7). The second general objection is that if moral judgements conceptually entail the claim that there are categorical moral reasons, we cannot get P4 in the Generic Argument, because with conceptual entailment, the error in moral discourse is insufficiently pervasive to sink moral discourse as such (§2.8). In the final section, I conclude that error theorists should not say that moral judgements conceptually entail claim N (§2.9).

2.2 Elements of Conceptual Entailment Error Theory

Traditionally, moral error theorists have accepted conceptual entailment, but what are concepts, and what is entailment? In this section I explain these and other commitments of conceptual entailment error theory. I start with concepts, which is the first of a total of six elements of conceptual entailment error theory that I will explain.

Philosophers in the analytic tradition tend to think about concepts as mind-independent entities of some sort, such as constituents of propositions and, more recently, as modes of representation or ways for subjects to think about the objects of their attitudes (Peacocke 1992, p. 3; Williamson 2007, pp. 13–17, pp. 29–30; Väyrynen 2013, pp. 45–48). This recent account of concepts as modes of representation is fruitfully contrasted with an account of concepts that says that concepts are merely devices for reference. Think about the concepts WATER and H_2O. Both concepts refer to the same thing, that is, the watery stuff in our lakes and rivers. But they differ in cognitive significance because you can coherently think 'there is water in my glass and there is no water in my glass' is contradictory and that 'there is water in my glass but there is no H_2O in my glass' is not contradictory. Psychologists and cognitive scientists have a different view of concepts, as they assign to them an explanatory role in mental processing, according to which concepts work as exemplars or prototypes with which thinkers categorize the world. So, for instance, many people's prototype of a tomato includes redness even though redness is not, according to the philosopher, part of the concept TOMATO because tomatoes can be green (Väyrynen 2013, p. 47).

In this book, I work with the philosophers' theory of concepts as modes of representation because I need to be able to distinguish between different concepts as much as possible, which, given the example of green tomatoes given above, is much harder if we use the psychologists' prototype theory of concepts. For the same reason, I will not work with the view that concepts are devises for reference. I will not pronounce on whether abstract entities or propositions are too queer to exist. I am dialectically permitted to do this because I do not use the queerness argument against categorical reasons and because I do not accept conceptual entailment error theory.

The second element of conceptual entailment error theory that I explain concerns the reason why error theorists have focused on conceptual entailment. The reason is that error theorists want the claim that moral properties are objectively prescriptive to be "non-negotiable" in the following sense (Joyce 2001, p. 3). Error theorists want to be able to claim that moral success theorists, such as naturalist realists who deny that moral properties are objectively prescriptive, change the topic from morality to something that simply isn't morality, that they therefore fail to talk about moral discourse, and therefore that they do not pose a challenge to moral error theory, even though the natural properties that they (falsely) think are the referents of moral concepts exist. And entailment relations are non-negotiable in this sense. To see this, consider a standard semantics textbook example of conceptual entailment (Saeed 2003, p. 87). In the example, judgement (1) conceptually entails judgement (2) (if you think that entailments hold between the propositions expressed by these judgements, then feel free to read me as saying this; nothing important hangs on it):

(1) The anarchist assassinated the emperor.
(2) The emperor is dead.

The entailment relation holds because you cannot accept (1) and deny (2) without changing the topic, or changing the meaning of assassination, because it is conceptually necessary that you are dead if you are assassinated.

Similarly, we may be able to get the following:

(3) Giving to the poor is morally obligatory.
(4) There exists at least one categorical moral reason.

In (4), the categorical moral reason is to give to the poor, and I write that there exists 'at least one' categorical moral reason because (3) only considers one moral obligation, not many. But since we know that there are many other actions that we find morally obligatory, such as saving children from drowning in a shallow pond at little cost to ourselves, and since these sentences will also entail (4) if (3) entails (4), we will also get the entailment to (5):

(5) There exist categorical moral reasons.

However, to have a specific entailment relation to work with, I will continue to focus on (4).

The third point of clarification is that moral concepts may have a richer content than is captured by (4). For example, in addition to thinking that a moral concept cannot be a moral concept without a commitment to categorical reasons, you may also think that a concept cannot be a moral concept if it isn't somehow concerned with human interactions (e.g., not killing, not stealing, giving to the poor). A system of morality that features categorical reasons but only categorical reasons "to run round trees left handed, or look at hedgehogs in the light of the moon" is not, you might think, a system of morality (Foot 1978, p. 107). In this book, I will not legislate what, conceptually speaking, ought to be part of the subject matter of morality. I only legislate on its formal characteristics. Thus, I assume that we can recognize the moral when we see it, just like, as Shafer-Landau has put it, we recognize "the pornographic" when we see it (2003, p. 80; see also Brink 1986, p. 29). I do this because I want to make it as easy as possible for my opponent to win. For suppose that I can argue that moral judgements require categorical reasons and that although there are no categorical reasons that speak in favour of adopting a certain policy towards other humans (i.e., no judgement like 'giving to the poor is morally obligatory' is true), there are categorical reasons that favour adopting a certain policy towards animals (i.e., at least some judgements like 'treating animals in a dignified way is morally obligatory' and 'eating meat is morally wrong' are true). If I would also have an argument for the claim that morality is only about our dealings with other humans, then an error theory would still follow, because on such a view judgements about our interactions with animals fail, by definition, to count as moral judgements. Therefore, by leaving the content of morality open, I give my opponent a better chance to emerge victorious from this debate than if I were to restrict its content beforehand.

The fourth point is a general point about the entailment relation between (3) and (4). It gives us only a *restricted* error theory, in the following sense (Kalf 2013). Though (3) entails (4), judgement (6), which embeds (3) under a negation operator, does not carry the entailment:

(6) Giving to the poor is not morally obligatory.

We can see this phenomenon more clearly if we focus not on the contested issue of the content of moral concepts but instead take on a non-moral example (Simons 2006, p. 357):

(7) Ian has stopped drinking coffee in the evening.
(8) Ian has stopped drinking coffee after 8 pm.
(9) Ian hasn't stopped drinking coffee in the evening.

In this example, (7) entails (8): if it is true that Ian has stopped drinking coffee in the evening, then it must also be true that she has stopped drinking coffee after 8 pm. But once we add to (7) a negation operator to get (9), the entailment to (8) disappears. It is not necessary for (it is even inconsistent with) the truth of the proposition that Ian hasn't stopped drinking coffee in the evening that the proposition that Ian has stopped drinking coffee after 8 pm is true.

Additional entailment-cancelling operators include modal operators and conditionals (Simons et al. 2010, p. 310):

(10) Giving to the poor might be morally obligatory.
(11) If giving to the poor is morally obligatory, then giving to the homeless is morally obligatory.

Just like the claim that Ian might have stopped drinking coffee in the evening fails to conceptually entail that she stopped drinking coffee after 8 pm, (10) fails to conceptually entail (4). And similarly, just like the claim that if Ian has stopped drinking coffee in the evening, then she has stopped eating chocolate in the evening does not conceptually entail that Ian has stopped drinking coffee after 8 pm, (11) fails to conceptually entail (4).

In short, conceptual entailment error theory is restricted in the sense that it can only show that judgements like (3) are systematically false, and as a result large swaths of moral discourse that take the shape of judgements like (6), (10), and (11) are not affected by standard, conceptual entailment error theory. It is not the case that you make a systematic error if you utter (6), (10), or (11), for none of these judgements commits you to the existence of a categorical moral reason. Or rather, even though perhaps you don't make a *semantic* mistake, you do perhaps make a kind of *pragmatic* mistake. For it looks as though it does not make sense *in practice* to continue to engage in moral discourse and to utter a judgement embedded under a negation operator ('stealing is not morally wrong') if no affirmative, atomic judgement like (3) is true. Whether this appeal to pragmatics is sufficient to get pervasiveness will be discussed in §2.8. For now, I just want to make clear that strictly speaking, the error theorist's claim that, as Mackie put it, moral judgements "are all false" must be restricted to atomic judgement like (3) that are not embedded under entailment-cancelling operators (1977, p. 35).

Interestingly, traditional conceptual entailment error theorists see the restricted scope of entailment error theory as an *asset* of their theory (Joyce 2007a, §4). For they think that it saves error theory from incoherence. This is because if we say that "X is right" and "X is not right" are both moral judgements, and that they are both false, then we violate the law of the excluded middle (Olson 2014, p. 11; Pigden 2007; see §1.1 above). But the above-mentioned restriction in conceptual entailment error theory saves error theorists from this objection, as with the restriction they can say that because non-negative atomic judgements are embedded under entailment-cancelling operators, they cannot carry a false entailment, and thus that conceptual entailment error theory cannot apply to them. So, 'X is right' is false and 'X is not right' is not false, because it does not carry the poised commitment to categorical reasons.

The fifth element of conceptual entailment error theory takes the form of an objection to it. Take a negated moral judgement, like (6), and accept, with the error theorist who restricts the scope of her theory to atomic moral judgements, that this judgement is not false. Apply the law of the excluded middle, and we must conclude that since (3) is false, (6) is *true*. Now, in assessing this objection, it is easiest to take not a judgement that negates that we have a moral obligation but one that negates that something is morally wrong. So, take:

(12) Refraining from giving to the poor is not morally wrong.

Judgement (12) embeds (13), which error theorists say is false, under an entailment cancelling operator:

(13) Refraining from giving to the poor is morally wrong.

On the restricted formulation of error theory, (12) is *true* and (13) is *false*; no inconsistency there. The objection is that (12) conceptually entails (14), which means that there is now an *atomic* moral judgement that is *true*, which is inconsistent with error theory, which was supposed to be the view that, *at least*, no atomic moral judgement is true:

(14) Refraining from giving to the poor is morally permissible.

The reason that (12) entails (14) is that it is conceptually necessary that what is not morally wrong is morally permissible. Clearly, you can't admit that refraining from giving to the poor is not morally wrong and yet insist that it is not the case that doing this is permissible. And *vice versa*, if something is permissible, then it is conceptually necessary that it is not wrong.

You might think that error theorists can simply say that (14) is false, for that would mean that no affirmative moral judgement is true. This was one of Olson's responses to this problem, as he argued that the objectively "permissive" moral properties that are the truth-makers of judgements like (14) are just as queer as the objectively prescriptive properties that are the truth-makers for any other affirmative moral judgement (Olson 2010, p. 79n4, 2014, p. 118n12). But in fact, error theorists can't make this move, because if (14) is false then (12) will be false as well: recall from §1.1 that any sentence that entails a sentence that is false is itself false. And the problem with (12) being false is that error theory will then be inconsistent again, for then both (12) and (13) are false. This creates a dilemma for error theory. Either we say that (12) is *true* to avoid the inconsistency objection, but if (12) is true then (14) is true, and error theorists cannot say that there is a true affirmative moral judgement. Or else we say that (14) is false, but that means that (12) will have become *false*, in which case we have the inconsistency objection. Either way, error theory is in trouble.

A different response to this problem is also due to Olson, who has recently insisted that a negated moral judgement like (12) does not *entail*, conceptually or otherwise, (14) but instead *conversationally implicates* (14) (2014, pp. 14–15). And conversational implicatures are cancellable: they can be denied consistently with continued acceptance of the utterance that carries the implication (Grice 1975; Strandberg 2012, p. 93). To understand this phenomenon, consider this example from Paul Grice (1975, p. 56):

(15) John walked into a house yesterday and saw a tortoise.

If you utter (15), then, since it mentions 'a' house, your interlocutor is entitled to assume that the house was not John's house. However, you can continue to accept (15) and cancel this implicature by adding 'but mind you, the house belongs to John'. For it is consistent with John walking into *a* house that it is *his* house. Now, if (12) only conversationally implicates but does not conceptually entail (14), then, since this implicature is cancellable, error theory can be consistent ('X is wrong' is false and 'X is not wrong' is true) and yet avoid having to say that some atomic judgements are true, for they can they say that the alleged entailment between 'X is not wrong' and 'X is permissible' does not obtain and that the relation that connects these two judgements is one of a cancellable conversational implicature. Error theorists cancel the implicature, and have a fully consistent, albeit complicated, view on the relations between the various moral judgements that comprise moral discourse.

The problem with this response is that Olson's explanation of the datum that there is some kind of link between (12) and (14) in terms of cancellable conversational implicatures is inferior to the rival explanation of this link in terms of entailment (Streumer 2017, p. 126). After all, although you can seem to say

(16) John walked into a house yesterday and saw a tortoise, but mind you, this was his house,

you cannot seem to say

(17) Refraining from giving to the poor is not morally wrong, but mind you, refraining from giving to the poor is not morally permissible.

This "statement" is one that "fails to get by" (Austin 1971, p. 18).
To this Olson might reply that *error theorists* can accept (17) because what *they* mean is:

(18) refraining from giving to the poor is not morally wrong, but mind you, refraining from giving to the poor is not morally permissible either *because nothing is morally anything.*

However, there are currently very few error theorists out there, and so for the vast majority of us, the link between (12) and (14) is too strong for conversational implicature. Hence, Olson cannot solve this problem for traditional error theory, and this problem constitutes at least a reason to prefer presupposition error theory to conceptual entailment error theory. After all, presupposition error theory, as I explained in §1.1, avoids all of this by saying that the various kinds of judgements discussed (about moral obligatoriness, about moral permissibility, about the negations of these judgements, and all the rest) *are neither true nor false*. And it is clearly consistent to say that 'X is right' is neither true nor false and that 'X is not right' is neither true nor false. However, I won't rest my case on this argument against conceptual entailment error theory and for presupposition error theory. At least one reason for not doing this is that a lot depends on the positive case for presupposition moral error theory, which will be defended in Chap. 3.

The sixth and final point of clarification is that if error theorists use conceptual entailment as their account of the way in which moral judgements carry a non-negotiable commitment N, then error theorists need a theory about our epistemic access to this conceptual entailment. How do we know what is, and what isn't, part of the content of a concept? Joyce has recently claimed that

> There is no agreed upon method or type of evidence for deciding.... conceptual commitments in general. (MS, p. 10)

The absence of agreement on this method is usually explained by reference to a more fundamental controversy about the ontology of concepts and their relation to language (Peacocke 1992; Fodor 1998; Margolis and Laurance 1999). However, Stephen Finlay thinks that error theorists have a "standard answer" that can be employed irrespective of the details of this fundamental discussion (2008, p. 362). For the sake of argument, and in an attempt to help my opponent as much as I can, I will agree with Finlay on this point. Error theorists can say that whether something is or is not part of the content of a concept

> turns on considerations of people's reflective understanding of their moral thought and speech, and of what they may be conscious of when they engage in this thought and speech. This evinces an assumption of the truth of a local form of content-internalism: what we mean morally is fixed by something internal to our mental states, particularly our intentions. (Finlay 2008, p. 362)

In other words, if we wonder what belongs to the content of moral concepts, then we look exclusively at what's "in the head", particularly our referential intentions for moral concepts (Putnam 1975, p. 227). On the content-internalist model of how concepts acquire their content, our referential intentions, which fully determine what it is that we want to refer to using certain concepts, fully determine the content of these concepts. So, if I want to refer to a 'whale' by using the concept WHALE, then this referential intention fully determines the content of this concept. Similarly, if I want to refer to 'categorical moral reason' by using the concept MORALLY OBLIGATORY, then this referential intention fully determines the content of this concept.

These referential intentions can be either collective or individual referential intentions, but if error theory is to be a theory of ordinary moral discourse—including Mary's, Johnnie's, and president Trump's contributions to moral discourse—then it has to tell a story about how people manage to refer to the same things with moral concepts, thereby ensuring "moral univocity" (Schroeter and Schroeter 2013, p. 1, 2014, p. 7). I will be pressing conceptual entailment error theory on whether they can ensure moral univocity in §2.6. For the moment, I will assume for the sake of argument that ordinary users of moral concepts manage to refer to exactly the same thing with moral concepts, and so the collective versus individual distinction will be, at least temporarily, immaterial. The question is whether conceptual entailment error theory based on the content-internalist assumption *and* the assumption that it can secure moral univocity can be made to work.

2.3 Mackie's Conceptual Entailment Error Theory

Is conceptual entailment a plausible interpretation of moral judgement's mode of commitment to the claim that there are categorical moral reasons? In this section, I argue that Mackie's arguments for conceptual entailment error theory fail. I use this discussion as an introduction to my own more general objections, which I present in §2.6, 2.7, and 2.8.

Mackie was a content-internalist, or at least his arguments for P1" assume it. His first argument for the conceptual claim starts by describing the following reaction that the folk display when they learn that they need to abandon their belief in moral values. According to Mackie, this abandonment causes

> at least temporarily, a decay of ... concern and sense of purpose. That it does so is evidence that the people ... have been objectifying their concerns and purposes, *have been giving them a fictitious external authority*. (1977, p. 34; my italics; see also Mackie 1946, pp. 77–8)

External authority means objective prescriptivity. It is clear in the context of this passage that it is intended as a claim about the content of ordinary moral concepts. It is also clear that as Mackie says that the folk '*have been giving* moral values a fictitious external authority', he thinks that what people think about moral values determines what constitutes the content of moral concepts.

Unfortunately, this argument faces an important problem. Is the datum that Mackie presents sufficiently robust? True, there are people who, after losing their faith in a particular religion, experience a decay of sense of purpose. But there are also people who in the same situation feel liberated, start to live life to the fullest, and experience a growing concern for the world around them, because it is the world that matters rather than a deity that they used to hold responsible, in some sense, for what happens in the world. But even if we assume, at least for the sake of argument, that this is a real datum, then we still face the problem that a different explanation, which only attributes belief in intersubjective prescriptivity to the folk, may give us the explanation that we need (Lenman 2013). Intersubjective prescriptivity is a kind of normativity that exists in virtue of people's agreements about what is important. Why do the folk feel terrible when they learn that there are no moral values? Alternative answer: because they have invested heavily in this belief, have made it part of their identity, and have started to care deeply about what they thought was morally right. This seems at least equally plausible as Mackie's explanation of the same datum, but it does not require us to assume that moral values are objectively prescriptive. Mackie's first argument is unsatisfactory.

Mackie's other argument is that the best interpretation of the main works of Western philosophy reveals that philosophers think that using moral concepts entails describing objectively prescriptive properties and that these philosophers analyse ordinary moral concepts. Mackie writes that it

> is the everyday objectivist concept of which talk about non-natural qualities is a philosopher's reconstruction. (1977, p. 34)

Mackie uses the terms 'non-natural property' and 'objectively prescriptive property' interchangeably. Mackie also writes that the traditional moral concepts of the ordinary man as well as of the main line of western philosophy are concepts of objective value. (1977, p. 35)

And he writes:

I think that Kant is struggling to bring out something that is latent in ordinary moral thought [he is] not merely constructing a philosophical fantasy. (1977, p. 60)

Mackie looks at Kant, Aristotle, Hutcheson, Price, Plato, and Sidgwick, but he focuses on Samuel Clarke and writes that, according to him, there are

eternal and necessary differences of things that make it fit and reasonable for creatures ... to act ... antecedent to any respect or regard, expectation or apprehension, of any *particular private and personal advantage or disadvantage, reward or punishment,* either present or future [i.e., to act morally]. (cited in Mackie 1977, p. 31; italics in original)

Moral values are objective because they are 'eternal and necessary', for being eternal and necessary is a way of being prior to and logically independent of all human activities. And moral values are prescriptive because they make it 'fit and reasonable' for agents to act in a certain way, and the relation of making it 'fit and reasonable' for agents to act in a certain way is a normative relation.

What to make of this argument? One issue is that Mackie's remarks about the philosophers he discusses are too quick to count as serious exegesis. Another issue is that we don't get much by way of argument for the claim that the works of those philosophers who have proposed a different understanding of the nature of moral facts and properties can be ignored. What about David Hume, who has been interpreted as an expressivist (Ayer 1980, pp. 84–5; Snare, 1991; Joyce 2009; see Hume 1740)? Or consider Thomas Hobbes, who has been interpreted as defending "a badly subjectivist understanding of 'good'" which holds for 'good' in both its non-moral and moral senses (Hampton 1986, p. 27). Hobbes seems to accept that what is good is simply what we desire, and what we hate is simply what is bad:

But whatsoever is the object of any mans Appetite or Desire; that is it, which he for his part calleth *Good:* And the object of his Hate, and Aversion, *Evill;* And of his Contempt, *Vile* and *Inconsiderable.* For these words of Good, Evill, and Contemptible, are ever used with relation to the person that useth them: There being nothing simply and absolutely so; nor any common Rule of Good and Evill, to be taken from the nature of the objects themselves. (Hobbes 1651, p. 39)

Philosophers clearly disagree about the meaning of 'morally good'. Why trust the Kantian tradition rather than the Hobbesian or the Humean tradition? Consistently with his first argument and his commitment to content-internalism, it seems that Mackie should say that philosophers who got the content of moral concepts right did have access to their referential intentions and that the philosophers who got the content of moral concepts wrong did not have this access. But if this is the claim, then we are simply back with the first argument: in deciding what the referential intentions are, we should consider what kind of authority we give to our "concerns and purposes" (Mackie 1977, p. 77–8). But then we can again ask whether the datum that we, or the philosophers, would have this reaction is sufficiently robust, and we can also ask why the alternative explanation of this datum that just appeals to heartfelt subjective agreements isn't at least roughly equally successful. And as I just argued, this argument did not work. Mackie does not have a satisfactory argument for the conceptual claim.

2.4 Joyce's Conceptual Entailment Error Theory: Initial Arguments

Perhaps Joyce's arguments are better. Joyce writes:

An error theory ... involves two steps of argumentation. First, it involves ascertaining what a term *means*. I have tried to explicate this in terms of "non-negotiability" ... in artificially simple terms, the first step gives us something roughly of the form "For any x, Fx if and only if Px and Qx and Rx." We can call this step *conceptual*. The second step is to ascertain whether the following is true: "There exists an x, such that Px and Qx and Rx." If not, then there is nothing that satisfies "... is F." Call this step *ontological* or *substantive*. The concept of *phlogiston* – with its commitment to a stuff that is stored in bodies and released during combustion – and the concept of *tapu* – with its commitment to a kind of contagious pollution – do not pass the test. (2001, p. 5; italics is original)

It is one of Joyce's main contributions to the literature on error theory that he has tried to improve the argument for P1". Joyce does this by presenting various thought-experiments, including one that solicits a reaction to Plato's Gyges, who has a ring with which he can get away from crime scenes after having killed and robbed at will (Plato, *Republic*, 360b–c). According to Joyce, when we engage in moral discourse, we want to be able to strongly condemn criminals like Gyges:

> we are not content to admit that our claim that there is a reason to refrain from killing is merely a permissible way of speaking from a perspective that endorses the dictates of morality. We are … left with a desire to say something more—*to imbue the moral imperative with a greater authoritative force*. (2001, p. 41; my italics)

Because Joyce talks about 'imbuing' moral imperatives with authoritative force, he should be interpreted as accepting content-internalism: the referential intentions with which we aim to 'imbue' moral imperatives determine what constitutes the content of moral concepts.

In particular, and as I will continue to explain, Joyce thinks that in understanding these imperatives, we do not need an existence theory of reasons, but instead a theory of reasons according to which we have categorical reasons of rationality with moral content. In saying this, Joyce places himself in a tradition of thinkers that goes back at least to Immanuel Kant. David Copp writes: "In the *Groundwork*, Kant aimed to show that morality is 'something real,' … [and] to show that morality is 'something real,' he thought he needed to show that the fundamental principle of morality 'is an imperative, i.e., that the will of every rational being is necessarily bound by it'" (2015, pp. 134–5). Similarly, a few years before Joyce, Bernard Williams, in a collection of papers on Mackie's *Ethics*, wrote:

Consider another picture of what it would be for a demand to be "objectively valid." It is Kant's own picture. According to this, a demand will be inescapable in the required sense if it is one that a rational agent must accept if he is to be a rational agent. It is, to use one of Kant's favourite metaphors, self-addressed by any rational agent. Kant was wrong, in my view, in supposing that the fundamental demands of morality were objective in this sense, but that is not the immediate point, which is that the conception deploys an intelligible and adequate sense of objectivity. It seems to have little to do with those demands being a part of the fabric of the world; or, at any rate, they will be no more or less so than the demands of logic – which was, of course, part of Kant's point. (1985, pp. 174–5)

But why think that the folk are imbuing moral concepts with categorical reasons rather than something else, such as hypothetical reasons, or non-natural qualities, or what have you? Joyce has four arguments for this claim: the argument from Mackie's platitude, the translation test argument, and the use argument, which comes in two versions. I discuss the first two arguments in this section, and I discuss the two versions of the use argument in the next section.

One reason why Joyce thinks that moral oughts are at least about reasons is because he thinks that what he calls Mackie's platitude is true:

it is necessary and a priori that, for any agent x, if x ought to φ, then x has a reason to φ. (2001, p. 38)

A platitude is a truism about a concept, such as the truism about the concept RED that it denotes a colour (Shafer-Landau 2005, p. 111). Similarly, thinks Joyce, it is a truism about the concept OUGHT that it denotes a reason. This looks like an application of the content-internalist methodology: if you wonder what it takes to have an 'ought', think hard about 'oughts' and you will discover that you are trying to refer to reasons when you use the word 'ought'.

The first problem with this is that Mackie's platitude only gives us reasons, not *categorical* reasons. A second problem is that Mackie's platitude doesn't seem to be a platitude (Shafer-Landau 2005, p. 101). No one contests the platitude that red objects are coloured, whereas lots of philosophers (and perhaps other folk) doubt that morality is normative in the sense of entailing reasons; for example, morality may just be normative in what Derek Parfit calls the 'rule-involving' sense:

Rule-Involving Conception of Morality's Normativity

Moral oughts are normative in virtue of being rules, and rules are normative in virtue of distinguishing between what is correct and incorrect or what is allowed and disallowed. (2012, Vol. 1, p. 144)

True, in defence of Joyce, some philosophers have argued that to say that some behaviour is correct or incorrect according to some norm N is not to say something normative (Broome 2007, p. 162; Olson 2014, p. 120). For they think that merely saying this leaves the normative question unanswered, which is the question whether we have *reasons* to comply with the norm in the first place. But the fact that other philosophers who have thought long and hard about these issues have different considered judgements about the relation between normativity and reasons is evidence that Mackie's platitude isn't a platitude. It may still be *true*, of course, that 'for any agent x, if x ought to φ, then x has a reason to φ', but that won't be because it is *platitudinously true*.

Joyce's second argument for the claim that moral concepts describe categorical moral reasons is the translation test argument. According to this argument, if you have a concept x (such as MORALLY OBLIGATORY) and wonder whether it entails concept y (such as CATEGORICAL MORAL REASON), then you ask whether you would accept a discourse that only contains candidate moral concepts *without y* as an eligible replacement of the original discourse of which you wonder whether it requires a concept with a commitment to y (Joyce 2001, p. 3; 2006, p. 200). If the answer is 'no', then a *moral* concept requires a commitment to categorical reasons. Here the important question is: which criteria should we use in assessing this counterfactual? Suppose two generally intelligent people disagree about whether the translation is possible. Who is right?

In this context, consider Peter Railton's defence of moral realism. Railton has argued that a contender moral concept that satisfies many but not all of the platitudes that we associate with morality is good enough to get a moral success theory, permitting us to say that such a candidate moral concept is a moral concept with referents that exist. First, he explains that "claims—and accusations—of moral realism typically extend along some or all of the following dimensions" (1986, p. 164). He then lists a number of these dimensions, including, but not limited to,

> Cognitivism—Are moral judgements capable of truth and falsity? (2) Theories of truth—If moral judgements do have truth values, in what sense? (3) Objectivity—In what ways, if any, does the existence of moral properties depend upon the actual or possible states of mind of intelligent beings? ... (9) Categoricity—Do all rational agents necessarily have some reason to obey moral imperatives? (10) Universality—Are moral imperatives applicable to all rational agents, even (should such exist) those who lack a reason to comply with them? (11) Assessment of existing moralities—Are present moral beliefs approximately true, or do prevailing moral intuitions in some other sense constitute privileged data? (12) Relativism—Does the truth or warrant of moral judgements depend directly upon individually—or socially—adopted norms or practices? (13) Pluralism—Is there a uniquely good form of life or a uniquely right moral code, or could different forms of life or moral codes be appropriate in different circumstances? (1986, pp. 164–5)

There are many contender moral concepts, with each contender concept accepting a different set of answers to the questions listed above. Railton gives the "approximate coordinates" of his "own view in this multidimensional conceptual space", explaining that he will "argue for a form of moral realism which holds that ... a rational agent may fail to have a reason for obeying moral imperatives, although they may nonetheless be applicable to him" (1986, p. 165).

Railton argues that we can accept that the term 'moral value' stands for a certain natural property, if, and only if, the property supplies an *a posteriori* explanation of the features of our moral experience (Railton 1989, pp. 171–2). The availability of this *a posteriori* explanation determines which of the various contender moral concepts should be seen as the true moral concept and determines what we would accept as an adequate translation of a moral discourse that employs a different contender moral concept. Thus, Railton asks Joyce: why accept that the alleged counter-intuitiveness of denying that categorical reasons are part of the content of moral concepts *is more important* than the availability of this vindicatory reduction of moral value to the property that supplies an *a posteriori* explanation of our moral experience?

In a similar vein, David Lewis has argued that we can accept one of a number of roughly equally acceptable "analytic definitions" of VALUE that ensures that it has a referent in the world, reducing it to natural facts about our psychology, and he calls this theory the dispositional theory of value (1989, p. 113). Lewis thinks that we can accept one of a number of acceptable definitions of VALUE because VALUE is equivocally analytic:

> Quine was wrong that analyticity was unintelligible, right to doubt that we have many clearcut cases of it. If differing versions of a concept (or, if you like, different but very similar concepts) are in circulation under the same name, we will get equivocal analyticity. It is analytic under one disambiguation of 'dog' that all dogs are male; under one disambiguation of 'bitch' that all bitches are canine. It is analytic under some precisifications of 'mountain' that no mountain is less than one kilometre high. When analyticity is equivocal, open questions make good conversational sense: they are invitations to proceed under a disambiguation or precisification that makes the answer to the question not be analytic. By asking whether there are mountains less than one kilometre high, you invite your conversational partners to join you in considering the question under a precisification of 'mountain' broad enough to make it interesting; yet it was analytic under another precisification that the answer was 'no'. So even if all is obvious, open questions show at worst that the alleged analyticity is equivocal. I suggest that the dispositional theory of value ... is equivocally and unobviously analytic. (1989, p. 130; see Quine 1951)

The term 'moral value' expresses importantly different and yet in many respects similar concepts, where the various claimant concepts are revisionist with respect to one or a number of platitudes that we associate with moral value, such that:

> Strictly speaking, Mackie is right: genuine values would have to meet an impossible condition, so it is an error to think there are any. Loosely speaking, the name may go to a claimant that deserves it imperfectly ... What to make of the situation is mainly a matter of temperament. (Lewis 1989, pp. 136–7)

If we think that moral concepts have referents if, and only if, they satisfy the platitudes Joyce focuses on, then Joyce is "right to call values 'queer' and [there is an] error of believing them" (Lewis 1989, p. 134). But if we are prepared to admit that an imperfect claimant of MORAL VALUE is good enough, then we get a success theory of moral discourse. Thus, Lewis asks Joyce: why take the alleged counter-intuitiveness of denying that categorical reasons are part of the content of moral concepts to be more important than allowing one's philosophical temperament to decide this issue, which, at least for the good-tempered, supports a moral success theory in the form of a slightly revisionist moral realism?

The main difference between Railton and Lewis is that Lewis accepts a reductionist *analytic* definition of moral value (and that this definition is acceptably equivocal), whereas Railton thinks that the reduction of moral value to items in the world *is a posteriori*, delivering a synthetic property identity through an empirically justifiable *reforming definition* of the (unequivocal) term 'moral value'. Despite this difference, both theories are problematic for the translation test argument. If it is true that there are many claimant referents of MORAL VALUE that are to varying degrees close or not so close to the one that the error theorist wants to focus on, then what decides whether the error theorist is right? The problem with the translation test argument is that it doesn't give us a decision procedure for deciding which translations are acceptable and which ones aren't. True, Joyce presents a number of thought-experiments that invite us to take seriously the intuition that moral demands are categorically valid (e.g., his thought-experiment based on Plato's *Gyges*), but why are these intuitions more important than Railton's criterion that invites us to accept only those contender moral concepts that can contribute to an *a posteriori* explanation of our moral experience, or Lewis's proposal that suggests that the good-tempered accept a moral concept that vindicates morality by not banging "the drum about how philosophy has uncovered a terrible secret: there are not values! (Shock horror ...)" (1989, p. 137)? Can Joyce say something to improve his argument?

2.5 Joyce's Conceptual Entailment Error Theory: The Use Argument

Joyce's third argument, which I call the *use argument*, may give us the decision procedure we need to be able to decide that a "wimpified" moral discourse that does not require categorical reasons and only requires hypothetical reasons is not good enough (Joyce MS, p. 14; see also Joyce 2006, 2007b). On my interpretation, Joyce presents the use argument as the following four-pronged argument: (i) practical oomph is one of many aspects of moral concepts, (ii) 'inescapable authority' is the best philosophical interpretation of practical oomph, (iii) categorical moral reasons, if they existed, are uniquely capable of combining inescapability and authority, and, finally, (iv) inescapable authority is *necessarily* part of moral concepts (so Railton and Lewis are wrong). I discuss steps (i)–(iii) even though the claim that there is some reason to think that morality's demands are categorical is not under dispute in the dialectic between Joyce on the one hand and Railton and Lewis on the other hand (it is just that Joyce and Railton deny that this commitment is essential to moral concepts). I do this because I need to explain Joyce's reasons for accepting (i)–(iii) in order to be able to explain why he thinks that we need to accept (iv) as well.

Let me first clarify the terminology. Practical oomph is a feature of normative judgements that concerns how 'forceful' the normativity of the normative domain is that the judgement is about. Consider morality as one normative domain and etiquette as another normative domain. Moral judgements are somehow more to us, or oomphier, than judgements of etiquette (Joyce 2006, pp. 60–61). According to Joyce:

> That morality has practical oomph is a simple observation; whether that oomph should be cashed out as *clout* is a philosophical problem. (2006, p. 62)

As Joyce uses this term, clout is synonymous with moral judgements' inescapapbility and authority:

> Moral normativity, it might be thought, has both inescapability and authority. Lacking a word for this conjunction, let me decree that a normative system enjoying both of these features has *practical clout*. (2006, p. 62)

The difference between inescapability and authority can be explained by reference to different imperatives expressing reasons for acting (Joyce 2006, p. 61). First, consider inescapability. There are hypothetical imperatives, which are valid if, and only if, the person you address has a relevant desire that will be fulfilled, or has the relevant end that will be promoted, if that person acts on the imperative. So, the imperative 'shut the window!' addressed at a competent adult in the Dutch winter will be valid if, and only if, that person desires to be warm, desires for both of us to be warm if we are in the room together, and so on. There are also categorical imperatives, which are valid regardless of whether the person you address has ends that will be promoted if she acts on that imperative. For example, it is often said in philosophical discussions that 'believe what you have conclusive evidence to believe' is an epistemic categorical imperative and therefore valid regardless of whether you have or lack the end to have true beliefs. This much is familiar at least since Immanuel Kant:

> Now all imperatives command either hypothetically or categorically. The former represents the practical necessity of a possible action as a means to attain something else which one wills (or which it is possible that one might will). The categorical imperative would be that one which represented an action as objectively necessary for itself, without any reference to another end. (1785, AK4, p. 414)

Thus, categorical reasons are *inescapable*: you can't say that you don't have such a reason by citing a desire, such as for instance a desire to be cold. But hypothetical reasons are *escapable*: you can say that you don't have such a reason by citing a desire (such as a desire to be cold).

Now consider the imperatives of etiquette. Philippa Foot calls such imperatives "non-hypothetical imperatives", because, although they are inescapable, they lack *authority* (Foot 1972; Joyce 2006, p. 62). The imperative "don't speak with your mouth full" applies to you regardless of whether desire to comply (it is inescapable), but it "doesn't carry genuine deliberative weight" and is therefore not authoritative for rational agents (Joyce 2006, p. 63, p. 203). This distinction between a categorical and a non-hypothetical imperative reflects Railton's remark, cited above, that "a rational agent may fail to have a reason for obeying moral imperatives, although they may nonetheless be applicable to him" (Railton 1986, p. 165).

On this understanding of inescapable authority, categorical moral reasons are both inescapable (because they are categorical) and have authority (because they are reasons of rationality and as such cannot be legitimately ignored), at least so long as we accept the "practical reasoning theory" according to which a consideration to perform an action is a genuine reason if, and only if, an agent were to reason correctly, she would end up deciding not to do the act (Harman 1986, p. 66). Joyce thinks that all sorts and kinds of considerations that are external to my rational thinking (i.e., considerations that are not 'yielded' by my rational thinking), such as considerations stemming from "a little normative institution according to which everyone ought to pursue autumnal Norwegian products" can be legitimately ignored, because I can always ask 'but what is this to me?' (2001, p. 203). This is why Joyce rejects Olson's idea that moral reasons must be understood as irreducibly normative *facts*, since in that case we can also ask 'what is that fact to me?' But reasons of rationality, thinks Joyce, cannot be legitimately ignored because

> the statement "I acknowledge that were I to reason correctly I would want to φ, but what is that to me?" does not represent a well-formed sceptical position. (2006, p. 195)

In his earlier book Joyce similarly writes:

> Morality is not presented as something that may be legitimately ignored or begged-off. So the question is: what sense can be made of reasons that cannot be evaded, of "real" reasons? The answer ... is that practical rationality yields [such] reasons, for to question practical rationality is self-undermining. (2001, p. 100)

I think that Joyce is right here, as I shall explain in the next chapter. This establishes step (iii) in the use argument, that is, the step that tells us to analyse morality's inescapable authority in terms of categorical moral reasons of rationality. We still need to argue for (i), (ii), and (iv).

Joyce's defence of (i), which was that morality has practical oomph, has already been mentioned above. Joyce uses a number of thought-experiments, including Plato's thought-experiments that involve Gyges, to elicit the intuition that morality's normativity is both inescapable and authoritative (Joyce 2001, p. 41). In morally condemning Gyges's behaviour, we are not happy to admit that moral obligations do not apply to Gyges (they do) or that they are not rationally authoritative for him (they are). Formulated as such, this also establishes step (ii).

This leaves (iv), which was the claim that categorical reasons are necessarily part of moral concepts. Here the use argument does its most important work. If we ask what determines whether something like INESCAPABLE AUTHORITY is part of moral concepts, then, according to Joyce,

> the answer turns on how the concept morality is used. If concept A is used in a certain manner, but turns out to be problematic for various reasons (i.e., it is uninstantiated by the world), and concept B is an instantiated contender for replacing A, then B can be an adequate successor only if it too can be used in the same manner. For example, ... when we discovered that there are no diabolical supernatural forces in the universe, we had no further use for the concept witch. Perhaps we could have carried on applying the word "witch" to women who play a certain kind of local cultural role on the margins of formal society ... but carrying on in this way would not have allowed us to use the word "witch" for the purposes to which we had previously put it: to condemn these women for their evil magical influence and justify their being killed. (Joyce 2007b, p. 65, 2006, p. 201)

Likewise, argues Joyce, for moral concepts. If we take categorical reasons out of moral concepts, then we won't be able to use moral concepts in the same way that we can use them now; therefore, categorical reasons are part of moral concepts.

The dialectical force of the use argument is greater than that of the translation test argument because it is more than merely an appeal to intuition. Armed with the use argument, Joyce can say that the fact that we won't be able to use moral concepts without categorical reasons for the same purposes is more important in our attempt to figure out what should be part of the content of moral concepts than an appeal Railton's *a posteriori* explanation of moral experience or Lewis's equivocal analytic definition of moral value. I think that formulated like this, Joyce's argument deserves more "plausibility points" than Lewis's argument, as the latter is just an appeal to a different intuition than Joyce's, and on the current reading of the use argument, Joyce now has an *argument* for why a certain contender moral concept should be accepted rather than another (Enoch 2011, p. 267). But in contrast to Lewis, Railton does have an argument rather than an appeal to intuition, and I don't think that it is clear that facts about how we use moral concepts are more important than facts about *a posteriori* property identities that provide explanations of our moral experiences.

Yet I am prepared to give Joyce the benefit of the doubt. *If* Joyce's use argument works, then I am prepared to accept that it is more important for a metaethical theory to respect facts about how moral concepts are used than it is for it to be able to provide a vindicatory *a posteriori* explanation of our moral experience, and thus that Joyce's argument is better than Railton's argument. As mentioned above, Joyce has two versions of the use argument. However, I reject each of them in what follows.

Start with the *silencing function argument* (Joyce 2006, p. 111, pp. 204–205). According to this version of the use argument, we must be able to use moral considerations to 'silence' other considerations that might tempt us to steal. But, the argument continues, this only works if moral concepts can be used to describe categorical moral reasons. After all, hypothetical reasons, though they have authority if they are reasons of rationality, lack inescapability (change your desires, and the alleged moral obligation vanishes), and, in that case, moral considerations that describe escapable moral facts cannot silence other considerations. Aspiring moral concepts that cannot be used for this purpose because they don't describe facts about categorical reasons are "schmoral" concepts at best (Joyce 2007b, p. 51).

There are at least two problems with this argument. First, it seems to require that the normativity of moral considerations must be overriding in the sense that once it is recognized it should and does, precisely, silence other considerations, such as for instance the consideration that stealing is exciting. The problem with this is that, although "there is the idea, made somewhat plausible by the seriousness of moral considerations, that moral considerations are overriding", it simply does not seem to be the case that the normativity of moral considerations is always overriding in this way (Johnston 1989, p. 165). Shelly Kagan gives the example of spending money on going to the movies, which ordinary morality considers to be all-things-considered permissible even though ordinary morality also recognizes that we still have a *pro tanto* reason to spend this money on famine relief (Kagan 1989, p. 1; see also Williams 1972, p. 74, 1985, p. 91). In short, the silencing function argument requires that morality's demands are overriding, and the problem is that it seems that, at least sufficiently often, they aren't.

As an alternative, we can try a different formulation of the silencing function argument that does not require that moral considerations are overriding. Joyce writes:

> a moral judgement … is no guarantor that the action will be performed, but so long as it increases the likelihood of the performance then this may be its evolutionary function [because the moral judgement can] … play a dynamic role in deliberation …. Prompting and strengthening certain desires and blocking certain considerations from even arising. (Joyce 2006, p. 114)

We can interpret this passage as stating that moral considerations play a 'dynamic role' in deliberation. Though they 'increase' the likelihood of the agent performing the morally right action (by 'prompting and strengthening desires'), they need not necessarily do this and hence may be overruled by other considerations. Call this the 'dynamic role' interpretation. We can also interpret this passage as stating that moral considerations actually block other considerations from even arising. Call this the 'guaranteeing role' interpretation. The passage is unclear because it supports both interpretations. But the guaranteeing role interpretation requires the overridingness of morality, which I just argued is implausible, and so I accept the dynamic role interpretation in what follows.

The problem with this interpretation is that the weakened account of moral considerations' functional role in an agent's psychology can no longer support the claim that we need categorical reasons if we want to say that moral concepts play this "dynamic but not guaranteeing" role (Cuneo 2012, pp. 123–4; Brink 1989, p. 66). How often must we be able to use moral considerations as "conversation stoppers" in order to be warranted

Conceptual Entailment Error Theory 57

in saying that we need non-overriding categorical reasons (Joyce 2006, p. 111, p. 165)? This seems to require an appeal to intuitions once again, and is as such a setback for Joyce in the dialectic with Railton, who does not rely on intuitions so heavily and who has more of an argument involving claims about *a posteriori* property identities. In sum, either the silencing function argument assumes that moral considerations are necessarily normatively overriding (the guaranteeing role interpretation), but this is implausibly strong. Or else the silencing function argument asserts that moral considerations are overriding only some of the times (the dynamic role interpretation), but then we are not in a position to argue against Railton.

Let us therefore consider the other version of the use argument, which focuses not on the intra-personal level of moral thought but on the interpersonal level of moral conversations. Joyce writes that accepting a concept of obligation without

> clout ... seems to enfeeble our capacity to morally criticize wrongdoers ... we could not *use* ... a value system lacking practical clout ... as we use morality, indicating that clout may be considered a vital aspect of morality (even when we are speaking loosely). (2006, p. 208–209)

The phrase 'even when we are speaking loosely' is a reference to Lewis's 1989 paper 'Dispositional Theories of Value', discussed above, in which Lewis argues that strictly speaking, error theory is true because there is nothing that can function as the referent of our moral concept as some currently use it, but loosely speaking, error theory is not acceptable because there is a claimant moral concept that does not contain all the platitudes that some of us normally associate with it but for which there is a referent. According to this version of the use argument, which is the argument from enfeebled moral criticism, we must be able to use moral judgements to criticize others, but if moral judgements do not describe categorical moral reasons, then we can't use moral judgements for this purpose (Joyce 2006, p. 204; Tresan 2010, p. 232; Finlay 2008, p. 358).

Joyce asks us to consider not only Plato's *Gyges*, but also Jack the Ripper, the famous and as-of-yet-still-unidentified London serial killer from the 1880s, and he asks us to imagine a moral discourse without authority. If we do, then there should be nothing wrong with our moral pronouncements reflecting this ... to the observations that Jack's action was wicked we should be permitted to add "but Jack had every reason to act wickedly on this occasion, and no real reason to refrain". (Joyce 2006, p. 204)

Now it certainly seems that if you are criticizable for not φ-ing, then there must have been *some consideration* that spoke against φ-ing (Nagel 1970, p. 83; Shafer-Landau 2003, p. 193; Finlay 2008, p. 358). But why do we need categorical reasons of rationality to account for this 'speaking against'? Perhaps hypothetical reasons suffice, as Railton and Lewis have emphasized, or perhaps we can use a still weaker conception of morality's normativity that does not involve reasons at all, such as Parfit's rule-involving conception of normativity discussed in §2.4. True, if we cannot appeal to categorical reasons of rationality, then moral criticism does seem to be enfeebled, but is this enough to warrant the claim that such reasons are *required* for morality?

Settling this issue seems to require yet another appeal to intuition. If we face a choice between moral concepts with inescapable authority that allow us to criticize agents and moral concepts that don't allow us to criticize immoral behaviour *at all*, then we might be tempted to say that Joyce has the upper hand over Railton. We still have an appeal to intuition, but Railton's view becomes *so* implausible, that we are permitted to reject it. But this isn't the choice that we face. The choice that we face is between moral concepts with inescapable authority that allow us to categorically criticize agents, on the one hand, and moral concepts that allow us to criticize agents for wrong behaviour relative to the rules of morality (if, for instance, we accept the rule-involving interpretation of morality's normativity), on the other hand. And in this choice situation, it is not clear that *this* enfeebling of our capacity to criticize wrongdoers is sufficient to believe Joyce rather than Railton. Again, at a crucial point in the argument, Joyce requires an appeal to intuition, whereas Railton can continue to appeal to his argument involving *a posteriori* property identities.

In this section, I have argued that Joyce's use argument for P1" does not work. Having argued in §2.4 that his earlier arguments also fail and that we must conclude that Mackie's arguments are in the same predicament (§2.3), I will, in the remainder of this chapter, present two general arguments that are intended to work against the claim that the mode of commitment of moral discourse to the non-negotiable commitment N must be understood in terms of conceptual entailment.

2.6 The Externalism Objection

My first objection to conceptual entailment error theory in general, regardless of whether it accepts or rejects that categorical reasons are the content of the non-negotiable commitment claim, is a more general instance of one of the objections to Joyce's conceptual entailment error theory discussed above. In short, this more general objection is that a context-externalist account of the meaning and reference of moral concepts is a plausible alternative to content-internalism, and that the package-deal 'content-externalism plus moral success theory' is more plausible than the package-deal 'content-internalism plus moral error theory'.

According to context-externalism, the content of moral concepts is not solely determined by our referential intentions, but also at least in part by features of the world that function as reference fixers for these terms (Schiffer 1990). A concept has meaning if, and only if, the property that gives the meaning to the concept can be identified and bears a relevant relation to that property. A famous example of an externalist theory of meaning for moral predicates is Richard Boyd's moral realism that uses a causal theory of reference. For Boyd, the properties that contribute to the satisfaction of "important human needs" function as the referents of moral properties even if they fail to exhibit objective prescriptivity; that is, even if they are normative if, and only if, the relevant agent desires to pursue these properties (1988, p. 203). And Railton, though he is not wedded to a causal theory of reference, is in the same boat with his argument that proceeds by reference to *a posteriori* identity claims. The problem for content-internalist entailment error theory is that with content-externalism, moral concepts are truly applicable to aspects of the world that do not exhibit objective prescriptivity even if the folk think that morality requires objective prescriptivity to be a feature of the world. For with content-externalism, referents of terms, including moral terms, can be opaque to their users, and this is consistent with these users being competent with these terms, though this is not required.

To understand how the meaning of terms can be opaque to their users even though these users are competent with them, consider the non-moral concept MOVES. On an internalist semantics for MOVES, if all (or most) competent speakers of English want MOVES to refer to a monadic property, then MOVES refers to a monadic property. But we know that with this meaning, MOVES fails to refer because it follows from our best theories in physics that moving objects "move" only in relation to other objects, and that MOVES must therefore express the concept of a relational rather than a monadic property (Boghossian 2006, p. 15). This change in the concept MOVES generates a vindication of our discourse about moving objects, and the conceptual change that it requires, from expressing the concept of a monadic to that of a relational property, is acceptable. The claim that ordinary users do not know when something moves is utterly implausible; it is much more plausible to say that they apply the predicate 'moves' correctly. It is just that when they do, they have a false (latent) belief about what it takes for something to move in the physical world that surrounds them.

As I mentioned two paragraphs up, it is also possible that terms have referents that are opaque to some of their users and that these users are not fully competent with these terms. Consider the famous arthritis example from Tyler Burge (1986). Jane says 'I have arthritis in my thigh', hoping to communicate that the ailment in her leg is due to arthritis. The problem is that arthritis is a disease of the joints only, so Jane utters a judgement that contains a concept that has a referent that is opaque to her *and* she is incompetent with the term.

In what follows, I argue that conceptual entailment error theorists face the following trilemma:

Trilemma for Conceptual Entailment Error Theory

First horn: content-internalism (consistent with error theory, but implausible)

Second horn: content-externalism that guarantees that moral terms have referents (inconsistent with error theory)

Third horn: content-externalism that does not guarantee that moral terms have referents (consistent with error theory, but implausible)

Each of its horns is problematic for error theory. The first and the third horn are consistent with error theory, but implausible. The second horn is much more plausible, but it is inconsistent with error theory.

The first step in my argument is to note that there is substantial empirical evidence for the claim that the folk have inchoate ideas about morality, and to such an extent that this rationally underdetermines our choice between a philosophical interpretation of their moral concepts in terms of categorical reasons and a philosophical interpretation of their moral concepts in terms of hypothetical reasons. Wright et al. have written a useful overview article on this extensive body of empirical metaethical research, which has until recently supported the idea that the folk accept that morality is objectively prescriptive (2013, p. 337). They mention, for instance, research by Smetana that suggests that the folk treat moral transgressions as wrong even in the absence of rules and/or the presence of social sanctions (1981). They also mention the famous studies by Kohlberg and Piaget that show that people treat moral considerations as more important than social or personal considerations (Kohlberg 1969, 1986; Piaget 1932).

However, Wright et al. also discuss more recent research that challenges this received view (2013, p. 338). For instance, Shaun Nichols reports that "many college students reject objectivism" but also remarks that some of them are indeed objectivists (Nichols 2004, p. 11). Goodwin and Darley get similar results. They define ethical objectivists as people who "take their ethical beliefs to express true facts about the world" rather than taking their "beliefs to be mind-dependent, and to express nothing more than facts about human psychology" (2008, pp. 1357–1358). Additionally, they distinguish between different "levels of objectivity" (2008, p. 1344). Respondents attain the highest possible level of objectivity if they regard a particular belief as true (or false), and regard someone who disagrees with that belief as surely mistaken. There are also two intermediately objective responses. Respondents reach a lower intermediately objective response if they regard a particular belief as true (or false), but see no need for either party to be mistaken if another person disagrees with that belief. A second and even lower type of intermediate objective response is to regard a particular belief as an opinion, but to regard a disagreeing other as surely mistaken. And "finally", they write, "the least objective response is to regard a particular belief as an opinion, and to see no need for either party to be mistaken if another person disagrees" (2008, p. 1345). With these distinctions on board, their

> first major finding was that individuals were not particularly consistent in their metaethical positions about various ethical beliefs, and were instead highly influenced by the content of the beliefs in question. This finding suggests that unlike the metaethical systems of philosophers, which tend to be uniform in their treatment of a range of ethical beliefs, ordinary individuals' metaethical systems are highly nuanced. (2008, p. 1358)

Goodwin and Darley further report that some people, especially those that ground their ethical beliefs in religion, commit themselves to a higher level of objectivity than those who ground ethics in, for instance, social utility. Again, there is quite a bit of variation in folk metaethics, and it is not at all clear that 'the folk' are 'objectivists'.

We can multiply examples. To give just two further examples, Beebe and Sackris found that folk metaethical commitments vary across different life stages, with decreased objectivism during the college years (2016; see also Beebe 2014). Sarkissian et al. (2011) found that folk intuitions about metaethical objectivity vary as a function of cultural distance, with increased cultural distance between two parties leading to decreased attributions of metaethical objectivity.

This batch of empirical results is evidence for *folk metaethical pluralism*, which is the doctrine that folk moral discourse is not best described by a uniform theory such as cognitivist success theory, a quasi-realist theory, or a cognitivist error theory, but instead by a theory in which divergent and perhaps even seemingly contrary metaethical positions enjoy equal claims to legitimacy (Joyce 2016, p. 90). As Wright et al. put it:

> People do not appear to conceive of morality as a unified (metaethically speaking) domain, but rather as a domain whose normative mandates come

in different shapes and sizes. They view the wrongness of some moral actions as clear and unquestionable, unaltered (and unalterable) by the feelings/beliefs/values of the individual or culture. They view the wrongness of other actions (though still genuinely moral in nature) as more sensitive to, and moulded by, the feelings/beliefs/values of the actor and/or the people whose lives would be (or have been) affected by the action. This possibility is one we've not seen seriously considered in the metaethical literature—and perhaps it is time that it was. (2013, p. 354; see also Cline 2017)

Given this amount of pluralism and in order to get a precisely formulated account of the non-negotiable commitment of moral concepts, the content-internalist conceptual entailment error theorist has to build a number of details into her internalist theory, such as the assumption that on reflection the folk would reject the idea that morality is subjective if they have both the idea that it is objective and the idea that it is subjective, the assumption that on reflection the folk would accept the idea that morality is objective if they believed that it is only subjective, and the assumption that when participants in moral discourse use moral concepts that their referential intentions are univocal. I will refer to these kinds of assumptions as the *content-internalist assumptions*. Without these assumptions, we don't get a clear account of the folk referential intentions that content-internalist conceptual entailment error theorists can use in order to determine the content of moral concepts.

The problem is that with all of the content-internalist assumptions on board, the resulting view looks much less plausible than the externalist alternative. For an important motivation for a content-externalist account of the meaning of moral concepts is that with this account we can avoid error theory and preserve moral discourse as it is. One influential argument for this claim starts from a *principle of charity* according to which we should interpret speakers as holding true beliefs whenever it is minimally plausible to do so (Davidson 1973). Railton's vindicatory reduction enables us to respect precisely this requirement. If the meaning of moral concepts is given in part by aspects of the world, then moral concepts refer, people can be said to have true beliefs, and error theory is false. It is worse, says someone like Railton, to accept the content-internalist assumptions, to accept error theory, and to reject the principle of charity than to reject the content-internalist assumptions, keep the principle of charity, and remain a moral success theorist. 'Worse', that is, in the epistemic sense of 'worse', for the former collection of views, because it undertakes all the internalist assumptions and rejects the principle of charity, is epistemically inferior to the latter collection of views, which does not have to make all these assumptions and which also does not reject the principle of charity.

Advocates of conceptual entailment error theory may respond to this formulation of the externalism objection in a number of ways. One option is to get into the details of the discussion about the principle of charity and to argue that this principle should be rejected in the case of moral discourse. Perhaps an evolutionary explanation of the persistence of systematically false but fitness-enhancing moral beliefs can be used as a counterweight to the principle of charity (Ruse 1998, p. 253; Joyce 2001, pp. 135–174). This argument would go as follows. We agree with Davidson that we want to be able to *understand* what people say. You might have thought that the only way to do this is to say that moral judgements are *true*, at least by and large, but that, the error theorist might insist, puts the cart before the horse. An evolutionary explanation of our ability and inclination to utter moral judgements, where they only have to enable us to live in groups and where it does not matter whether or not these judgements are true, is equally or perhaps even more illuminating when it comes to trying to understand what people say. Unfortunately, it looks as though that, given the complexities that this brings (does reflection on evolution allow us to draw this conclusion, can we overthrow the principle of charity by reference to it, and if evolution is doing all this philosophical work, then whence conceptual entailment error theory to begin with?), conceptual entailment error theorists still have a theory that is epistemically inferior to the much less complicated content-externalist alternative.

At this point in the dialectic, error theorists seem to be committed to either choosing content-internalism with all the content-internalist assumptions, which renders it implausible, or else accepting content-externalism, but this view, given that it guarantees that moral concepts have referents, is inconsistent with error theory. But there is another reply we can try on behalf of conceptual entailment error theory, which is that it can accept content-externalism whilst insisting that we should reformulate the content-externalist theory in such a way that it remains non-committal on the question whether moral terms have referents. One option here is Burge's social externalist theory of the content of concepts, which I already mentioned, and according to which the content of an individual speaker's utterance is determined by facts about other members of the speaker's community, in particular by experts (Burge 1986). These can be experts about diseases, such as arthritis, but they can also be moral experts. This version of externalism is consistent with the non-existence of moral facts: the folk think that moral terms refer to y and the experts think that they refer to x, the true meaning of moral terms is x; however, x does not exist.

The problem with this version of content-externalism as applied to moral terms is that it requires moral expertise, which is implausible (McGrath 2008; McGrath 2009). The issue of moral expertise is contested. But note that, first, I do not deny that some ethicists possess a 'deflationary' kind of moral expertise which does not entail that others should defer to those who have this kind of expertise when it comes to the *content* of moral beliefs. Peter Singer thinks that philosophers have this kind of deflationary moral expertise and mentions such things as the ability to reason logically and knowledge of ethical theories like Utilitarianism and virtue ethics (1988, pp. 153–54). But an *inflationary* kind of moral expertise is implausible, for we cannot determine who the moral experts are, given that there is so much faultless moral disagreement—disagreement that obtains in the absence of false non-moral beliefs and the like—even among professional philosophers (Tersman 2006). Experts about other issues, such as the weather, do have such objective facts reference to which can settle disputes about who was right and who was wrong about a particular issue, and we can separate the true experts from the charlatans because the former learn more and more about these objective facts and gradually gain better access to them (McGrath 2009, p. 322). But in the moral case, we don't seem to have these kinds of facts, unless, of course, we assume that there are objective moral facts that moral experts can have access to; perhaps, though not necessarily, by employing a causal theory of reference. The problem with *this* is that the resulting view is inconsistent with error theory again. Burge's expertise-based content-externalism about the content of concepts is not an option for content-internalist conceptual entailment error theorists.

At this point, the advocate of content-internalist conceptual entailment error theory might insist that there may be externalist theories of reference that neither require a causal theory of reference, nor require moral expertise. I can't prove that all (possible) content-externalist theories of reference face this choice, but I can show that at least one other, and to my mind promising, externalist theory of reference, also faces this choice. This theory is due to Laura and Francois Schroeter (2013, 2014). They develop what they call the connectedness model, which proposes a semantics for moral terms that uses a holistic rationalizing interpretation of a semantic tradition to assign "a univocal semantic value to the tradition as a whole, taking into account the understanding, environment, and history of the entire diachronic and interpersonal tradition" (2014, p. 12). As a consequence, "we no longer [need] to identify some invariant core understanding, shared by all, that suffices to single out a determinate property" as the referent of our moral terms (Schroeter and Schroeter 2014, p. 20). After all, if the entire tradition, after appropriate rationalizing, gives a term its meaning, then some people may be mistaken about the referents of their own terms. This means that the account is appropriately externalist, and for Schroeter and Schroeter the philosophical task is to assign a semantic value to a tradition of using moral concepts, for which we don't need to assume a version of the causal theory of reference. Unfortunately, we do need to assume moral expertise in order to get determinate referents for moral concepts. For part of this rationalization process concerns making sense of the kind of variation in substantive individual understanding of moral concepts that is indicative of the kind of metaethical pluralism that current empirical research into folk metaethical beliefs suggests. Determining whether two token elements of thought—yours and mine, say—express the same concept involves determining whether they "belong to the same disambiguated tradition" (2014, p. 18). 'Disambiguated' because the *philosophers* clear up the tradition by removing from it inconsistencies and the like. But how are experts going to agree on this? What if two self-proclaimed experts meet and disagree? This is the problem of moral expertise all over again.

I started this section with a trilemma for conceptual entailment error theorists. They might accept content-internalism, but then their view is epistemically inferior to content-externalism. Or they might accept content-externalism, but then either they must postulate referents for moral concepts, which is inconsistent with error theory, or they must accept moral expertise, which is implausible. Whichever option the conceptual entailment error theorist wishes to embrace, her view will be inferior to that of her opponent.

2.7 Retreat to Content-Internalism with Indeterminate Referential Intentions

A final reply on behalf of content-internalist conceptual entailment error theory that comes to mind is to not see folk metaethical pluralism as a problem for error theory, but to exploit it in an alternative argument for the conceptual claim. Consider Stephen Schiffer and J.P. Burgess, who argue that the variation in metaethical beliefs that we must attribute to the folk when they use moral terms means that we cannot have *sufficiently determinate* referential intentions with which we can pick out moral properties (Schiffer 1990, pp. 603–4, 606–7, 2003; Burgess 2010, p. 8). As Burgess puts it, although moral judgements take a cognitivist semantics:

> I ... maintain that moral judgements are without truth-value ... My reason is this: It is part of the normal understanding of moral judgements that what truth-value they have is supposed to be independent of the person by whom, and the circumstances in which, they are uttered. Yet though each speaker may have quite definite (albeit unconscious) criteria for applying the term "moral," there is not enough common to all speakers' criteria to provide "Abortion is immoral" with a speaker-independent truth-value. (2010, p. 8)

On this way of thinking about moral concepts, they tell you to look for referents that carry a description like 'Doxylayndowihai'. Where to look? Such things don't exist.

Similarly, Don Loeb has argued that the variation in metaethical beliefs that we must attribute to the folk when they use moral terms means that although we can have *determinate* referential intentions, we cannot have *coherent* referential intentions. Loeb argues that moral language is "semantically incoherent" and derives the "metaphysical implication ... that ... there is nothing in particular to be realist about—no properties ... count as the referents of ... moral terms" (2008, pp. 357–358). The semantic incoherence stems from the persistence of fundamental disagreement between objectivists and subjectivists, supported by the recent empirical metaethics literature, and which is "evidence that inconsistent elements— in particular, commitments both to and against objectivity— may be part of any accurate understanding of the central moral terms" (Loeb 2008, pp. 357–358). On this way of thinking about moral concepts, they tell you to look for referents that carry a description like 'round square'. Where to look? Such things don't exist.

But given the externalist alternative, this only gets the error theorist back to square one. For the content of the referential intentions—be it 'categorical moral reason', 'objectively prescriptive property', 'maximizes utility impartially conceived' as analytic Utilitarians would have it, or indeed something like 'Doxylayndowihai' or 'round square'—does not matter for the comparison between content-internalist conceptual entailment error theory and content-externalist conceptual entailment success theory. We are still faced with the choice between a content-internalist semantics conjoined with error theory and the rejection of Davidson's principle of charity on the one hand and a content-externalist semantics conjoined with success theory and the principle of charity on the other hand. If this is our choice, then error theory is epistemically inferior to success theory with content-externalism, and so we should reject it.

In response, the advocate of this Schiffer/Burgess type or Loeb type of content-internalist conceptual entailment moral error theory might nevertheless insist that the comparison of relative plausibility between these two positions must be reconsidered. This is because there is now an important and relevant difference between content-internalist error theory with and without determinate referential intentions. For earlier, the error theorist had to make the 'content-internalist' assumptions in the face of folk metaethical pluralism and, she continues, this was alleged to have a significant bearing on the comparison between error theory and success theory. But now we don't make these assumptions. We jump straight from the pluralist wide variety of referential intentions to the non-existence of moral properties. True, we do reject Davidson's principle of charity, but at least we don't reject this principle *and* have to make the content-internalist assumptions. My reply to this response is that although it is true that this error theory does not make the content-internalist assumptions, it does make another and important assumption, which is that because *some* folk are objectivists and *some other folk* are subjectivists, there is no determinate or an inconsistent meaning to their concepts. This assumption is, like the set of content-internalist assumptions, epistemically costly in the face of a content-externalist alternative that does not make such an assumption about what the folk might or might not mean at all, and that moreover respects Davidson's principle of charity.

In conclusion, the first general objection to content-internalist conceptual entailment error theory is that the availability of various plausible content-externalist success theories spells too much trouble for it to be viable.

2.8 Pervasiveness Objections

The second general objection to conceptual entailment error theory is the pervasiveness objection. Although there may be an error in moral discourse, it is not sufficiently pervasive to render the discourse completely false. This is not a direct objection to the error theorist's argument for P1'. Instead, it targets the *consequence* of accepting the conceptual entailment argument for P1'. The objection is that if we accept P1', then perhaps we can get C1 in the Generic Argument, but we cannot get C2. Yet towards the end of this section, I will also argue that we can move from one aspect of the lack of pervasiveness of conceptual entailment error theory to a direct objection to P1'.

The pervasiveness objection comes in two versions that I think are damaging for conceptual entailment error theory. There is also a third version of the pervasiveness objection, but this version of the objection has been successfully rebutted by Joyce. I start with this unsuccessful version of the pervasiveness objection and discuss the two damaging versions of the objection in the remainder of this section.

Joyce's arguments for error theory primarily target deontological concepts like MORALLY OBLIGATORY and MORALLY FORBIDDEN, and the problem, as he notes, is that even if these concepts are flawed, his arguments only show that a proper subset of our moral discourse is flawed (2001, p. 175). How about rights, virtues, and judgements about morally good states of affairs? G.E.M. Anscombe's 1958 paper 'Modern Moral Philosophy' provides one formulation of this challenge (1958). Perhaps a conception of morality's subject matter that sees it as wholly deontic, inherited from a religious divine command conception of ethics, cannot be upheld. But as Paul Bloomfield explains, it may "turn out to be the case that error theory is pointing to a part of our modern conception of morality that it would behove us to do without, while doing without does not leave us bereft of morality" (2013, p. 452).

Joyce's response to this version of the pervasiveness objection, which I accept, is that moral concepts are holistically connected, such that a persuasive attack on deontic concepts by means of an attack on the categorical reasons that these concepts describe will count as a persuasive attack on moral discourse as a whole. First, consider claims about inviolable rights. These claims entail categorical reasons because 'I have a right' clearly entails 'you are obligated not to violate it (other things being equal)' and, as we are now accepting for the sake of argument, we have claim P1', according to which moral judgements about obligations entail categorical reasons. The same holds for claims about morally good states of affairs. A morally good state of affairs is one that one is obligated to bring about, and obligations entail, again as we are now assuming, categorical reasons. You might object that it would only be 'good' if you brought about a morally good state of affairs, which is weaker than thinking that we are *obligated* to bring about a morally good state of affairs. But at least if an action is morally good, then you have a right to perform it, and rights entail obligations, which in turn entail, again by hypothesis, categorical reasons. Moreover, argues Joyce, virtues are character traits that one is *obligated* to cultivate, otherwise we find it hard to understand what is *good* about these character traits. And obligations entail categorical reasons. So, an error theory of deontic moral judgements can be transposed to moral judgements that are about rights, moral goodness, and even virtuous character traits. There is no pervasiveness issue here.

A different version of the pervasiveness objection is much more troubling, however. According to it, conceptual entailment error theory can only say that affirmative moral judgements like 'x is obligatory' are false, for negation and modal operators ('not', 'might', 'may', 'could') provide entailment-cancelling embeddings for these judgements. As I explained in §2.2, 'x is not wrong' does not entail that there exists a categorical reason. The problem is that on this conceptual entailment formulation of the error theory, a conversation between two ordinary users of moral language in which one humbly utters (6) and the other responds by uttering (10) is not committed to the systematic mistake, as only (3) does, and (6) and (10) do not, entail (4):

(3)   Giving to the poor is morally obligatory.
(4)   There exists at least one categorical moral reason.
(6)   Giving to the poor is not morally obligatory.
(10) Giving to the poor might be morally obligatory.

As I will argue in the next chapter, presupposition moral error theory much more accurately accommodates this datum, and the fact that it is does is an important reason to prefer it over conceptual entailment error theory. Moral concepts may be holistically connected, such that the failure of judgements about deontic concepts entails a failure of judgements with a non-deontic and merely evaluative or virtue-theoretic subject matter, but conceptual entailment error theory is restricted to atomic moral judgements, and that is insufficiently pervasive.

The conceptual entailment error theorist may insist, in response, that we can explain the mode of commitment of judgements like (6) to (4) via other means than appeal to conceptual entailment. In §2.2, I suggested that conceptual entailment error theorists may be able to do this by reference to cancellable conversational implicatures. The first problem with this suggestion is that it results in an unnecessarily bifurcated view of moral discourse: affirmative moral judgements like (3) conceptual entail (4), but other judgements are committed to (4) via cancellable conversational implicatures. The major alternative, presupposition error theory presents a uniform account of the mode of commitment of moral judgements to categorical moral reasons. The second problem with this suggestion is that the appeal to conversational implicatures is implausible. As I also explained in §2.2, although error theorists can reject the move from (6) to a judgement about moral permissibility—or as in the example I used, from (12) to (14)—on the basis that nothing is morally anything, focusing on ordinary morality requires the postulation of a *non-cancellable* account of the relation between these two sentences in order to explain why in ordinary moral discourse, the folk must move from (6) and (10) to (4):

(12)   Refraining from giving to the poor is not morally wrong.
(14)   Refraining from giving to the poor is morally permissible.

In this case, the problem is that error theory is either incoherent or false. Conceptual entailment error theorists leave large swaths of moral discourse unaffected and cannot give us an error theory of moral discourse as a whole.

The third version of the pervasiveness objection makes use of the empirical data discussed in §2.6, and offers a way into presupposition error theory, which is the topic of the next chapter. According to this objection, error theorists assume that moral concepts have a context-invariant meaning because the referential intentions that they hold responsible for the meaning of moral concepts remain the same across a range of contexts. The problem is that context-invariantism cannot account for the above-mentioned data.

Let us first get clear on the terminology. To understand metaethical contextualism, first consider *epistemic* contextualism, according to which what is expressed by a claim like 'S knows that p' depends partly on the context of utterance. The context may determine, for instance, how much we ask of the agent and her interaction with her environment for us to be warranted in saying that she knows a particular proposition. For example, it will be much harder to know that the world exists in the philosophy classroom than in a different context, such as a casual conversation with relatives at a family gathering. As a result, the *meaning* of 'S knows that p' changes across different contexts of utterance. Epistemic invariantists deny this and hold that the meaning of epistemic judgements like 'S knows that p' does not vary across different contexts of assertion. They may hold, for instance, that the meaning of epistemic judgements is fully determined by the referential intentions that we have whilst uttering these judgements and that these intentions do not themselves vary across different contexts of utterance. Regardless of whether we find ourselves in the context of a philosophical discussion or a casual chat, what it takes to count as knowing something remains the same, since our referential intentions remain the same.

Now consider metaethical contextualism, which has been defended by Björnsson and Finlay, whose view is that

> every meaningful normative utterance of a sentence "A ought to φ" will express a proposition to the effect that A ought-relative-to-information-i- and-standards-s to φ, for some i and s determined by the context of utterance. (2010, p. 8)

Similar to epistemic invariantism, content-internalist conceptual entailment error theory, because it asserts that the meaning of moral judgements is determined solely by our referential intentions that don't vary across contexts, claims that the meaning of moral judgements does not vary across contexts. Content-internalist conceptual entailment error theory claims that what is expressed by a judgement like 'killing is morally wrong' does not depend on the context of utterance. It is a good thing that they don't say this, for otherwise they would have to say that one and the same moral judgement entails that there is a categorical reason against killing in one context of utterance, such as the philosophy classroom, but not in another context, such as ordinary moral conversations. And this would be insufficiently pervasive if there were too many contexts in which a moral conversation does not require the postulation of categorical reasons. Worse, given that traditional error theorists are context-invariantists, it also follows that if we know that the entailment fails to hold in some contexts, we should conclude that it fails to hold in all contexts.

The problem is that there seem to be too many conversational contexts that are just fine (i.e., all the utterances they contain are felicitous) even if we deny the alleged entailment to categorical reasons (Kirchin 2010). What are these conversational contexts? Consider the following case:

Benevolent Doctors

Two doctors disagree about the ethical permissibility or otherwise of ceasing a particular life-saving but painful treatment for a patient. They agree about all the relevant non-moral facts (e.g., how much the patient wants to continue to live, how much support she gets form relatives, how much pain she has), but one doctor utters the judgement 'we morally ought to cease this treatment' whereas the other disagrees and says 'we ought not to cease this treatment'. They both desire the best for their patient and neither wants to set a precedent for other similarly placed patients.

It does not seem as though we need to assume the existence of categorical reasons to understand this conversation. In their respective conversational contexts, thus with a bilateral standing desire to care for their patient and without a desire to set a precedent with their decision, the conclusion that is being reached doesn't have to have objective or categorical applicability. And yet it also does not seem as though their conversation is not a moral conversation. This suggests that even if categorical reasons are required for some moral judgements in some contexts, they are not required for every moral judgement. And it seems that we can multiply examples. Consider an ethical committee assessing the behaviour of these doctors and being asked whether their judgement was a moral judgement and had categorical applicability. Or consider two students of medical ethics who are being given the same task. The problem for conceptual entailment error theory is that since there are contexts that do not require the postulation of categorical reasons and since conceptual entailment is a context-independent, all or nothing affair (if you deny the entailment, then you are "conceptually deficient"; Evers and Streumer 2016, p. 1), this puts pressure on the conceptual entailment error theorist's claim that the entailment holds in *any* context. This argument is what I referred to above as the direct argument against P1' that uses lack of pervasiveness.

In summary, although moral concepts are holistically connected such that an error theory of judgements about moral obligations entails an error theory of other deontic and even non-deontic moral judgements, the error that conceptual entailment error theorists ascribe to moral discourse is limited to atomic moral judgements and specific contexts of utterance. It is therefore insufficiently pervasive to get us an error theory of moral discourse as such; moreover, the last argument we discussed can be turned into an additional direct argument against P1'. These are further reasons to reject conceptual entailment error theory because they come in addition to the externalism objection.

2.9 Conclusion

In this chapter, I have argued that conceptual entailment error theory is implausible. Mackie's and Joyce's arguments for P1" fail, and there are two general objections that target any version of conceptual entailment error theory: the semantic externalism and pervasiveness objection, which admits of a number of different formulations. The pervasiveness objection is not only problematic for conceptual entailment error theory but in fact for any version of this theory, including presupposition error theory, which I will defend in the next chapter. My defence of presupposition error theory will therefore include a response to the pervasiveness objection. I will also explain that presupposition error theory has a good response to a suitable reformulated version of the externalism objection that applies to it, and I argue that other objections fail as well.

References

Anscombe, G.E.M. 1958. Modern Moral Philosophy. *Philosophy* 33: 1–19.
Austin, J.L. 1971. Performative-Constative. In *The Philosophy of Language*, ed. J. Searle. Oxford: OUP.
Ayer, A.J. 1980. *Hume*. New York: Hill and Wang.
Beebe, J.R. 2014. How Different Kinds of Disagreement Impact Folk Metaethical Judgements. In *Advances in Experimental Moral Psychology*, ed. J.C. Wright and H. Sarkissian, 167–187. New York: Bloomsbury.
Beebe, J.R., and D. Sackris. 2016. Moral Objectivism Across the Lifespan. *Philosophical Psychology* 29: 912–929.

Björnsson, G., and S. Finlay. 2010. Metaethical Contextualism Defended. *Ethics* 121: 7–36.
Bloomfield, P. 2013. Error Theory and the Concept of Morality. *Metaphilosophy* 44: 451–469.
Boghossian, P. 2006. What Is Relativism? In *Truth and Realism*, ed. P. Greenough and M.P. Lynch, 13–37. Oxford: OUP.
Boyd, R. 1988. How to Be a Moral Realist. In *Essays on Moral Realism*, ed. G. Sayre-McCord, 181–228. Ithaca: Cornell University Press.
Brink, D.O. 1986. Externalist Moral Realism. *Southern Journal of Philosophy* 24: 23–41.
———. 1989. *Moral Realism and the Foundations of Ethics*. Cambridge: CUP.
Broome, J. 2007. Is Rationality Normative? *Disputatio* 23: 161–178.
Burge, T. 1986. Individualism and Psychology. *Philosophical Review* 95: 3–45.
Burgess, J.A. 2010. Against Ethics. In *A World Without Values*, ed. R. Joyce and S. Kirchin, 1–16. Dordrecht: Springer.
Cline, B. 2017. A Tale of a Moderate Normative Skeptic. *Philosophical Studies*, Online First.
Copp, D. 2010. Normativity, Deliberation, and Queerness. In *A World Without Values*, ed. S. Kirchin and R. Joyce, 141–166. Dordrecht: Springer.
———. 2015. Rationality and Moral Authority. In *Oxford Studies in Metaethics*, ed. R. Shafer-Landau, vol. 10, 134–159. Oxford: OUP.
Cuneo, T. 2012. Moral Naturalism and Categorical Reasons. In *Ethical Naturalism: Current Debates*, ed. S. Nuccetelli and G. Seay, 110–130. Cambridge: CUP.
Darwall, S., A. Gibbard, and P. Railton. 1992. Toward Fin de siècle Ethics: Some Trends. *Philosophical Review* 101: 115–189.
Davidson, D. 1973. Radical Interpretation. *Dialectica* 27: 314–328.
Enoch, D. 2011. *Taking Morality Seriously*. Oxford: OUP.
Evers, D., and B. Streumer. 2016. Are the Moral Fixed Points Conceptual Truths? *Journal of Ethics & Social Philosophy* 10 (1): 1–10.
Finlay, S. 2008. The Error in the Error Theory. *Australasian Journal of Philosophy* 86: 347–369.
Fodor, J. 1998. *Concepts*. Oxford: OUP.
Foot, P. 1972. Morality as a System of Hypothetical Imperatives. *Philosophical Review* 81: 305–316.
———. 1978. *Virtues and Vice*. Los Angeles: University of California Press.
Garner, R. 1990. On the Genuine Queerness of Moral Properties and Facts. *Australasian Journal of Philosophy* 68: 137–146.

Goodwin, G.P., and J.M. Darley. 2008. The Psychology of Metaethics: Exploring Objectivism. *Cognition* 106: 1339–1366.
Grice, H.P. 1975. Logic and Conversation. In *Syntax and Semantics 3: Speech Acts*, ed. P. Cole and J.L. Morgan, 41–58. New York: Academic Publishers.
Hampton, J. 1986. *Hobbes and the Social Contract Tradition*. Cambridge: CUP.
Harman, G. 1986. Moral Explanations of Natural Facts: Can Moral Claims be Tested Against Moral Reality? *Southern Journal of Philosophy* 24: 57–68.
Hobbes, T. 1651. *Leviathan*. Ed. Tuck, R. 1991. Cambridge: CUP.
Hume, D. 1739/1740. *A Treatise of Human Nature*. Ed. L.A. Selby-Bigge. 1978. Oxford: Clarendon Press.
Johnston, M. 1989. Dispositional Theories of Value. *Proceedings of the Aristotelian Society* 63 (Suppl): 139–174.
Joyce, R. 2001. *The Myth of Morality*. Cambridge: CUP.
———. 2006. *The Evolution of Morality*. Cambridge, MA: MIT Press.
———. 2007a. Moral Anti-Realism. In *Stanford Encyclopedia of Philosophy*, ed. E.N. Zalta. Stanford: Stanford University Press
———. 2007b. Morality, Schmorality. In *Morality and Self-Interest*, ed. P. Bloomfield, 51–75. Oxford: OUP.
———. 2009. Expressivism, Motivation Internalism, and Hume. In *Hume on Motivation and Virtue*, ed. C. Pigden, 30–56. London: Palgrave Macmillan.
———. 2016. *Essays in Moral Scepticism*. Oxford: OUP.
———. MS. Enough with the Errors! A Final Reply to Finlay. http://personal.victoria.ac.nz/richard_joyce/acrobat/joyce_2012_enough.with.the.errors.pdf.
Kagan, S. 1989. *The Limits of Morality*. Oxford: OUP.
Kalf, W.F. 2013. Moral Error Theory, Entailment and Presupposition. *Ethical Theory and Moral Practice* 16: 923–937.
Kant, I. 1785. *Groundwork for the Metaphysics of Morals*. Ed. A. Wood. 2002. New Haven: Yale University Press.
Kirchin, S. 2010. A Tension in the Moral Error Theory. In *A World Without Values*, ed. S. Kirchin and R. Joyce, 167–182. Dordrecht: Springer.
Kohlberg, L. 1969. Stage and Sequence: The Cognitive-Developmental Approach to Socialization. In *Handbook of Socialization Theory and Research*, ed. D. Goslin, 347–480. Chicago: Rand McNally.
———. 1986. A Current Statement on Some Theoretical Issues. In *Lawrence Kohlberg: Consensus and Controversy*, ed. S. Modgil and C. Modgil, 485–546. New York: Taylor & Francis.
Lenman, J. 2013. Ethics Without Errors. *Ratio* 26: 391–409.

Lewis, D.K. 1989. Dispositional Theories of Value. *Proceedings of the Aristotelian Society* 63 (Suppl): 113–137.

Loeb, D. 2008. Moral Incoherentism: How to Pull a Metaphysical Rabbit Out of a Semantic Hat. In *Moral Psychology*, ed. W. Sinnott-Armstrong, vol. 2, 355–386. Cambridge, MA: MIT Press.

Mackie, J.L. 1946. A Refutation of Morals. *Australasian Journal of Philosophy* 24: 77–90.

———. 1977. *Ethics: Inventing Right and Wrong*. London: Penguin Publishers.

Margolis, E., and S. Laurance. 1999. *Concepts*. Cambridge, MA: MIT Press.

McGrath, S. 2008. Moral Disagreement and Moral Expertise. In *Oxford Studies in Metaethics 3*, ed. R. Shafer-Landau, 87–108. Oxford: OUP.

———. 2009. The Puzzle of Pure Moral Deference. *Philosophical Perspectives* 23: 321–344.

Nagel, T. 1970. *The Possibility of Altruism*. Princeton: Princeton University Press.

Nichols, S. 2004. After Objectivity: An Empirical Studies of Moral judgement. *Philosophical Psychology* 17: 3–26.

Olson, J. 2010. In Defence of Moral Error Theory. In *New Waves in Metaethics*, ed. M. Brady, 62–84. London: Palgrave Macmillan.

———. 2014. *Moral Error Theory: History, Critique, Defence*. Oxford: OUP.

Parfit, D. 2012. *On What Matters*. Oxford: OUP (Two Volumes).

Peacocke, C. 1992. *A Study of Concepts*. Cambridge, MA: MIT Pres.

Piaget, J. 1932. *The Moral Judgement of the Child*. London: Routledge and Kegan Paul.

Pigden, C. 2007. Nihilism, Nietzsche and the Doppelganger Problem. *Ethical Theory and Moral Practice* 10: 414–456.

Plato, *Republic*.

Putnam, H. 1975. *Mind, Language and Reality*. Cambridge: CUP.

Quine, W.V.O. 1951. Two Dogmas of Empiricism. *The Philosophical Review* 60: 20–43.

Railton, P. 1986. Moral Realism. *The Philosophical Review* 95: 163–207.

———. 1989. Naturalism and Prescriptivity. *Social Philosophy and Policy* 7: 151–174.

Ruse, M. 1998. *Taking Darwin Seriously*. New York: Blackwell.

Saeed, J.I. 2003. *Semantics*. Malden: Blackwell Publishers.

Sarkissian, H., J. Parks, D. Tien, J.C. Wright, and J. Knobe. 2011. Folk Moral Relativism. *Mind & Language* 26: 482–505.

Schiffer, S. 1990. Meaning and Value. *Journal of Philosophy* 84: 602–614.

———. 2003. *The Things We Mean*. Oxford: OUP.
Schroeter, L., and F. Schroeter. 2013. Normative Realism: Co-reference Without Convergence? *Philosophers' Imprint* 13: 1–24.
———. 2014. Normative Concepts: A Connectedness Model. *Philosophers' Imprint* 14: 1–26.
Shafer-Landau, R. 2003. *Moral Realism*. Oxford: Clarendon Press.
———. 2005. Error Theory and the Possibility of Normative Ethics. *Philosophical Issues* 15: 107–120.
Simons, M. 2006. Foundational Issues in Presupposition. *Philosophy Compass* 1: 357–372.
Simons, M., J. Tonhauser, D. Beaver, and C. Roberts. 2010. What Projects and Why. *Proceedings of SALT* 20: 309–327.
Singer, P. 1988. Ethical Experts in a Democracy. In *Applied Ethics and Ethical Theory*, ed. D. Rosenthal and S. Fadlou, 149–161. Salt Lake City: University of Utah Press.
Smetana, J.G. 1981. Preschool Children's Conceptions of Morals and Social Rules. *Child Development* 52: 1333–1336.
Smith, M. 1994. *The Moral Problem*. Oxford: OUP.
Snare, F. 1991. *Morals, Motivation, and Convention*. Cambridge: CUP.
Strandberg, C. 2012. A Dual Aspect Account of Moral Language. *Philosophy and Phenomenological Research* 84: 87–122.
Streumer, B. 2017. *Unbelievable Errors*. Oxford: OUP.
Tersman, F. 2006. *Moral Disagreement*. Cambridge: CUP.
Tresan, J. 2009. Role-Based Interpretations of Moral Judgements: An Objectivist Account. *Social Theory and Practice* 35: 369–391.
———. 2010. Question Authority: In Defense of Moral Naturalism Without Clout. *Philosophical Studies* 150: 221–238.
Väyrynen, P. 2013. *The Lewd, the Rude, and the Nasty*. Oxford: OUP.
Williams, B. 1972. *Morality*. Cambridge: CUP.
———. 1985. Ethics and the Fabric of the World. In *Morality and Objectivity*, ed. T. Honderich, 203–214. London: Routledge.
Williamson, T. 2007. *The Philosophy of Philosophy*. Oxford: Blackwell.
Wittgenstein, L. 1965. A Lecture on Ethics. *The Philosophical Review* 74: 3–12.
Wright, J.C., P. Grandjean, and C. McWhite. 2013. The Metaethical Grounding of Our Moral Beliefs: Evidence for Metaethical Pluralism. *Philosophical Psychology* 26: 336–361.

3

Presupposition Error Theory

3.1 Introduction

In the previous chapter, I argued that error theorists should not argue that moral judgements are non-negotiably committed to claim N because they *conceptual entail* this claim. In this chapter, I argue that there is a much more plausible interpretation of P1 in the Generic Argument for Error Theory. We should not formulate P1 as P1' but as P1*:

P1   Moral judgements carry a non-negotiable commitment to claim N.
P1' Moral judgements conceptually entail claim N.
P1* Moral judgements presuppose claim N.

In fact, I will argue for a more precise version of P1, according to which the non-negotiable commitment of moral judgements is due to categorical moral reasons:

P1** Moral judgements presuppose the claim that there are categorical moral reasons.

© The Author(s) 2018
W. F. Kalf, *Moral Error Theory*, https://doi.org/10.1007/978-3-319-77288-2_3

There are two kinds of theories of presupposition: semantic and pragmatic theories. I discuss them separately because they entail different commitments about how the argument for P1** should be formulated.

The chapter is structured as follows. In the next section, I explain semantic presupposition error theory and I argue that we should reject it (§3.2). In the sections that follow, I explain pragmatic presupposition error theory and I argue that we should accept it (§3.3. 3.4, and 3.5). Thus, I defend the even more specific thesis:

P1*** Moral judgements pragmatically presuppose the claim that there are categorical moral reasons.

After my positive defence of P1***, I will formulate and reject a number of objections to pragmatic presupposition error theory, including the externalism objection that I discussed in the previous chapter (§3.6). This section will also contain my defence of P3 in the Generic Argument:

P3 If moral judgements carry a false non-negotiable commitment, then they are untrue.

However, given the commitments that I shall have undertaken up until that point, I will in fact defend a reformulated version of P3, which is:

P3' If moral judgements pragmatically presuppose a false non-negotiable claim, then they are neither true nor false.

I subsequently argue that pragmatic presupposition error theorists have a plausible answer to the pervasiveness objection and that, as a result, they have a convincing argument for P4 in the Generic Argument, according to which, if moral judgements are systematically untrue, we should accept error theory of moral discourse as a whole (§3.7). Or to be more precise, given the assumptions that I shall have accepted up until that point, I defend:

P4' If C1', then we should accept error theory of moral discourse as a whole.

C1' is the claim that moral judgements are neither true nor false. A conclusion summarizes my argument and introduces the topic of the next chapter, which is my defence of the claim that there are no categorical moral reasons, and which is the only claim I still need to argue for at that point before being able to conclude that we should accept error theory of moral discourse as a whole (§3.8).

3.2 Semantic Presupposition Error Theory

Let us first try to invoke the notion of semantic presupposition in our defence of moral error theory. A first pass on the semantic view of presupposition is offered by Mandy Simons, who writes that lexical items of particular sentences, such as the words "know", "too", and so on, can carry presuppositions, and that "presuppositions are properties of these items" (2013, p. 330). Pekka Väyrynen similarly writes:

> A semantic presupposition is a … property of a sentence that carries the presupposition which is usually traceable to a particular word or construction in a sentence. (2013, p. 109)

Many lexical items often have truth-conditional content, but if they are presupposition triggers, then at least they have presuppositional content. For instance, the word 'know' can have both truth-conditional and presuppositional content. It has truth-conditional content if it contributes to the meaningfulness of a truth-apt sentence like 'S knows that *p*', which will be true if all the conditions for knowledge (in that context) have been satisfied. But the word 'know' can also have presuppositional content. For instance, Kiparsky and Kiparsky argue that the sentence "Berlusconi knows that he is signing the end of Berlusconism" presupposes "Berlusconi is signing the end of Berlusconism" (1970). In Chap. 1, I discussed another example of this kind of presupposition as triggered by the lexical items in a sentence; viz., Strawson's example involving the king of France (1950, p. 321). In that example, it is the possessive construction in the definite descriptions (19) and (20) that suggests that the claim that there is a king of France is a presupposition of both (19) and (20):

(19) The king of France is wise.
(20) The king of France is not wise.
(21) There is a king of France.

We can make the notion of presupposition more precise with the projection test (Simons et al. 2010, p. 309; Simons 2006, p. 359–60; Kalf 2013). This test is used in linguistics and the philosophy of language to determine whether a piece of information (in this case, that there is a king of France) as carried by an utterance belongs to its meaning. It is widely used as a diagnostic for presupposition. The term 'projection' refers to a phenomenon in natural language where an implication survives as an utterance implication if the target statement, in our case judgement (19), is embedded under an entailment-cancelling operator such as the negation operator 'not', which is judgement (20) in our example. The implication, judgement (21) in our example, as carried by (19) 'projects' because it survives as an implication of (19) if we embed (19) under a negation operator to get (20). Regardless of whether we deny or assert that the king of France is wise, that there is a king of France is information that is carried by both sentences. The currently most inclusive and empirically adequate explanation of why (21) survives as an implication of (19) and (20) is that (21) is *not at issue* (Simons et al. 2010, pp. 315–8). In debating whether or not the king of France is wise, the information that he exists is not at issue, projects, and indicates presuppositional information.

On the standard view of semantic presupposition:

If p (the presupposing sentence) is true then q (the presupposed sentence) is true; if p is false, then q is still true, and if q is true, p could either be true or false. (Saeed p. 102; see also Väyrynen 2013, p. 109; Frege 1892)

In our example, (19) is our presupposing sentence 'p' and (21) is our presupposed sentence 'q'. First consider the presupposition relation from left to right, that is, from the presupposing sentence to the presupposed sentence. If (19) 'The king of France is wise' is true, then (21) 'There is a king of France' is true, but if (19) 'The king of France is wise' is false, then

(21) 'There is a king of France' is still true. Now consider the presupposition relation from right to left, that is, from the presupposed sentence to the presupposing sentence. If (21) 'There is a king of France' is true, then (19) 'The king of France is wise' could be either true or false, and the same holds for (20) 'The king of France is not wise'. I find it most plausible to accept that what happens with a sentence that suffers from semantic presupposition failure is that it becomes neither true nor false.

There are alternative accounts of what happens to the truth of sentences that suffer from semantic presupposition failure. One alternative view is that some presupposition failures result in lack of truth-value while others result in falsehood (von Fintel 2004; Beaver and Geurts 2011, §5.2). Yet another view is that sentences that have a false presupposition can nonetheless say something true (Yablo 2006). For instance, and supposing that (19) is false, the judgement 'the king of France is identical to himself' will be true even though it suffers from presupposition failure. Moral error theory clearly requires the truth of the standard view, according to which a judgement that carries a false presupposition is neither true nor false, or else the first alternative view according to which moral judgements that carry false semantic presuppositions are false. However, we don't need to settle this issue here, as we first need to see whether semantic presupposition works in the moral case in the first place, and I will now argue that it doesn't.

Consider a third example of semantic presuppositions, which uses neither a factive verb nor a possessive construction in a definite description. This is an example of a change of state verb presupposition trigger, which is 'stopped' in the example below. I discuss it because it seems the closest analogy to how moral terms might semantically trigger presuppositions:

(22) Sanne has stopped professional sailing.
(23) Sanne has been sailing professionally.
(24) Sanne hasn't stopped professional sailing.

In this example, (22) requires the truth of (23), which is that Sanne has been sailing professionally. After all, this follows from what it means to have stopped sailing professionally. But although we have conceptual analysis of the term 'stopped', we don't have *entailment* because the falsity of (23) does not result in the falsity of (22). Rather, if it is not true that Sanne has been sailing professionally, then (22) ceases to have truth-value or becomes neither true nor false. Judgement (22) is neither true nor false and, in a sense, has become meaningless. It doesn't make sense to say that Sanne has stopped professional sailing if she never used to sail professionally in the first place. And the same is true for (24). It too requires the truth of (23) because of the meaning of 'stopped' and it too becomes meaningless and neither true nor false rather than false if (23) is false.

Change of state verb presupposition triggers are a better model for understanding how moral judgements might semantically presuppose claim N than either factive verb presupposition triggers or possessive constructions in definite descriptions for the following reasons. First, such triggers are better than factive verb presupposition triggers because the latter don't require the sort of analysis that moral judgements require. If A knows that x, then the presupposed information that x is the case is already in the sentence itself, whereas in a moral judgement we don't similarly get the content of the claim that there are categorical reasons or objectively prescriptive properties from simply looking at the moral judgement itself. And, second, the same holds for the king of France example. The information that there is a king of France is already contained within the two presupposing sentences, but the information that there are categorical reasons or objectively prescriptive properties is not similarly contained within the moral judgement. Contrastingly, in the case of change of state presupposition triggers, we need to analyse what it means to have stopped doing something before we can determine what information, if any, is semantically presupposed by the relevant judgements. The analysis was: to have stopped doing something requires that you must have been doing it for at least some time. We seem to require the same sort of analysis of what it means for something to be morally obligatory (or what-have-you) before we can determine what information, if any, is semantically presupposed by the relevant moral judgements.

With this in mind, consider the following three judgements which I used in Chap. 2 to argue against conceptual entailment error theory, and which I will now use to assess the plausibility of semantic and pragmatic presupposition error theory:

(3) Giving to the poor is morally obligatory.
(4) There exists at least one categorical moral reason.
(6) Giving to the poor is not morally obligatory.

If (4) is presupposed by (3) and (6), then semantic presupposition would explain this by reference to the particular words or constructions in these sentences, which in this case must be the phrase 'morally obligatory'. The explanation must be that (3) and (6) require the truth of (4) and this has to follow from what it means to be morally obligated to φ, which is that to be obligated to φ is to have a categorical moral reason to φ. Do (3) and (6) require the truth of (4)?

Perhaps (3) requires the truth of (4) if we assume that what it means to be morally obligated to φ is to have a categorical moral reason to φ. But that we have to assume this is the first and also the most important problem with semantic presupposition error theory. The semantic triggers in moral judgements require, precisely, the kind of conceptual analysis of key terms in the relevant sentences that we are trying to avoid in light of the externalism objection (§2.6). Why not say, perhaps on the basis of an externalist semantics, that it is rather a commitment to hypothetical reasons that is built into the meaning of MORALLY WRONG? Why think that 'morally wrong' isn't semantically polysemous? Can we formulate sufficiently determinate and internally coherent referential intentions for this concept? Should we only consider people's referential intentions in determining the meaning of moral terms? Such heavy reliance on conceptual analysis of MORALLY WRONG renders semantic presupposition error theory as implausible as conceptual entailment error theory.

A second problem for semantic presupposition error theory is that (6) does *not* seem to presuppose (4). The reason that (6) does not seem to presuppose (4) is that although, in the non-moral case we just considered, it does seem to follow from Sanne not having stopped sailing professionally that she has been (and still is) sailing professionally, it does not follow from giving to the poor *not* being morally obligatory that there exists a categorical moral reason. After all, it not being the case that anyone is morally obligated to give to the poor is consistent with no one having any moral obligation at all. Contrastingly, there is no such option to deny the relation between Sanne not having stopped sailing professionally and her past as a professional sailor.

There are two bad consequences for the plausibility of semantic presupposition error theory if (6) fails to semantically presuppose (4). First, in that case, semantic presupposition is not a helpful tool for the error theorist to get a sufficiently pervasive non-negotiable commitment claim. After all, the more different kinds of moral judgements commit their utterers to categorical moral reasons, the greater the portion of moral language that is in error, and the easier it becomes to say that moral discourse as a whole is in error. Second, without projection across negation we don't even seem to have presupposition, at least not given the idea that it is "the standard test for the claim that such-and-such is presupposed in a sentence … to see whether it is preserved under negation" (Langendoen 1971, p. 341).

In response, the friend of presupposition moral error theory might insist that although it *used to be* the standard test for presupposition to see whether projected information preserves under negation, nowadays the fact that (4) is not information that projects across a negation operator is not sufficient reason to deny that (4) is a presupposition of (3). Consider the following situation in which the hearer of (24) is not required to (continue to) accept (25) as presuppositional information of (24). The utterer of (24) felicitously continues her conversation as follows:

(22) Sanne has stopped professional sailing.
(23) Sanne has been sailing professionally.
(24) Sanne hasn't stopped professional sailing.
(25) Sanne hasn't stopped professional sailing; she was a professional surfer.

As Chris Cummins has argued, given that (25) can be felicitously added to (24), this indicates that some semantic presuppositions require at least some contextual information to arise (2016, p. 126). In this case, the context of the conversation is determined by shared information among the speakers about how the conversation has been shaping up until this point and about how it is likely to continue. If we 'prime a context' for the conversation in which one party utters (22) and the other utters (24) by making it shared knowledge that (25) is not, or cannot be, added to the conversation, then (22) and (24) presuppose (23) (Karttunen 1974, pp. 182–183). If on the other hand we "prime a context" for the conversation in which one party utters (22) and the other utters (24) and we make it shared knowledge that (25) is added to the conversation, then (22) and (24) loose this presupposition.

Another description of a case in which the context of utterance determines whether a semantic presupposition arises for the change of state verb *stopped* is due to Mandy Simons (2013, p. 332). Here we don't add sentences to the conversation; we only change something about the background against which the conversation takes place. Imagine a casual conversation between two people who are meeting for the first time. One remarks to the other:

(26) I notice that you keep chewing on your pencil. Have you recently stopped smoking?

Had the conversational context not been primed with the information that we are talking about two strangers, then we would have justifiably concluded that the question presupposes the information that its addressee used to smoke. However, given that we know that it is part of the context in which this conversation occurs that both participants in the conversation know that they are complete strangers to each other, no implication would arise that the speaker believes that the addressee has been a smoker. Instead, she is understood to be merely asking the following question:

(27) Is it the case that you have habitually smoked in the recent past and that you recently ceased to do so?

The normal presupposition of (26) that the speaker has been a smoker has been cancelled by the context in which it has been uttered. Simons says that in situations like this a semantic presupposition is "contextually defeasible" (2013, p. 331).

Perhaps the same holds for (3), (4), and (6). That is, perhaps (3) presupposes (4), but (6) doesn't, and perhaps we can explain why it doesn't by reference to the context in which the conversation takes places (either having linguistic content, as we had in Cummins's example, or non-linguistic content, as we had in Simons's example). The problem is that this does not help the advocate of semantic presupposition error theory because, at least in the two examples I gave above, if context cancels the presupposition of the negated sentence, then it also cancels the presupposition of the original, affirmative sentence, and it doesn't seem as though there are cases in which context allows us to cancel the presupposition of the negated sentence but not the corresponding affirmative sentence, which is what we need in the moral case.

Jonas Olson has formulated a third objection to semantic presupposition error theory. He writes that we could accept a

> non-standard version of moral error theory according to which all first-order moral claims are neither true nor false, due to a failure of presupposition. But this non-standard version of error theory can be questioned. In general, I take claims that predicate non-instantiated properties of some individual or individuals to be false. For instance, a claim to the effect that some person is a witch (where being a witch involves being a woman with magical powers) is false. The same goes for a claim to the effect that acts of torture are morally wrong. (2014, pp. 12–13)

Olson's thought is that perhaps judgements that have a subject-term that fails to refer can be neither true nor false, but because error theorists believe that moral claims predicate non-instantiated properties of individuals (and one might add, states of affairs, character traits, etc.), it would be better if we said that these judgements are *false* rather than neither true nor false. And that is inconsistent with semantic presupposition moral error theory, which says that moral judgements are neither true nor false.

Richard Joyce's response on behalf of semantic presupposition error theory is to claim that

> In a sentence of the form "a is F," which element is the subject and which element the predicate is entirely arbitrary. For any sentence we may nominalize the predicate (provide a name for the property) and make it the subject of the sentence, and thereby express the same proposition. So "Socrates is wise" becomes "Wisdom is had by Socrates". (2001, p. 6)

This means that we can make it the case that in moral judgements the required term fails to refer, and thus we can say that moral judgements are neither true nor false. However, Joyce in fact rejects this response, as he observes that the plausibility of this suggestion depends on "how we choose to theorize about properties, which in turn is dependent on weighing the theoretical costs and benefits of various contending positions" (2001, p. 6). And for Joyce, the costs outweigh the benefits.

My own treatment of the presupposition relation suggests a better response to Olson's objection because it allows us to remain neutral on which theory of properties we accept. Properly understood, as I will argue in the next section, the presupposition of categorical moral reasons in (4) is not carried by individual terms in judgements like (3) and (6), as a semantic theory of presupposition has it. Instead, the presupposition is carried by moral judgements as a whole, prompted by pragmatic features in their context of utterance. This means that it does not matter whether moral terms occupy the subject- or predicate-terms in sentences, so the third objection to semantic presupposition error theory does not apply to pragmatic presupposition error theory. And as I will explain, both the second objection to semantic presupposition error theory (viz., that it has a problem with negated judgements) and the first objection (viz., that it requires conceptual analysis of the kind that sunk the project of using conceptual entailment as the error theorist's account of moral judgements' mode of commitment to claim N) will also be solved if we accept pragmatic presupposition error theory. Ample reason, therefore, to consider pragmatic presupposition error theory.

3.3 Pragmatic Presupposition

Pragmatic presuppositions arise not in virtue of "the content of the propositions expressed" but in virtue of "the situations in which the statement is made" (Stalnaker 1999, p. 48, 1974; Karttunen 1974; cf. Katz and Langendoen 1976). According to the pragmatic theory of presuppositions, a "proposition P is a pragmatic presupposition of a speaker in a given context just in case the speaker assumes or believes that P, assumes or believes that his addressee assumes or believes that P, and assumes or believes that his addressee recognizes that he is making these assumptions, or has these beliefs" (Stalnaker 1999, p. 50). Stalnaker adds that although on the pragmatic theory of presuppositions, it is natural to say that it is persons and not judgements that have or make presuppositions, the theory can be rewritten so that we can assert that judgements carry presuppositions (1999, p. 50).

One example of a pragmatic presupposition comes from Saeed (2003, p. 108):

(28) It was *Harry* who Alice loved.
(29) It was *Alice* who loved Harry.

Here italics indicate stress or intonation, and they prime a context of utterance for these sentences. The first thing to note is that these sentences seem to describe exactly the same situation of Alice having loved Harry; that is, they embody the same proposition:

(30) Alice loved Harry.

Notwithstanding, (28) and (29) are different because they belong to different conversational contexts. In (28), participants have been discussing Alice and they revert their attention to Harry; in (29) they have been discussing Harry and they revert their attention to Alice. Consequently, (28) and (29) give rise to different presuppositions; (28) presupposes (31), and (29) presupposes (32):

(31) Alice loved someone.
(32) Someone loved Harry.

Thus, if I say, 'it was *Harry* who Alice loved', then we get the presupposition that Alice loved someone, but if I say that 'it was *Alice* who loved Harry', then we get the presupposition that someone loved Harry. Without this priming of the context, thus merely with the proposition that Alice loved Harry (30), choosing between either (31) or (32) as presuppositions of (30) would not be possible.

Another example of a non-moral pragmatic presupposition is due to Terence Langendoen (1971, p. 343):

(33) My cousin isn't a boy anymore.

What, if anything, does (33) presuppose? Again, we can only figure this out once we have more information about the context in which (33) is uttered. In everyday contexts in which the focus of the conversation is on the age of the people being talked about, the utterer of (33) asserts that his cousin has grown up and presupposes that he is male. In less common contexts, such as a conversation in an academic seminar about the social construction of gender in which the conversation has been about sex change, the utterer of (33) asserts that his cousin has changed sexes and presupposes that she is young.

In sum, for some judgements, it holds that even if we keep their semantic properties the same in different contexts, what they communicate to hearers is different in these different contexts, and this is best explained by reference to the notion of pragmatic presupposition, according to which pragmatic features of the context determine what information speakers are justified to infer as not at issue, or as common ground, in the discussion as it has been shaping up until a certain point. The information that speakers are justified to infer from the conversation as not being at issue counts as presuppositional information of that conversation.

Can we prime a conversational context that yields a result amenable to pragmatic presupposition error theory? I think we can, though we must ensure not to pack too much information into the conversational context, and for two reasons. First, this would put the cart before the horse as it wouldn't get us the explanation that we want (Väyrynen 2013, p. 61). For example, if we make it shared knowledge that morality has "practical clout", then we are likely to get the result that moral conversations presuppose categorical moral reasons; however, this would be a very artificial way to prime a conversational context and we would not be able to infer from such contrived cases what happens in ordinary moral conversations that are never primed like this (Joyce 2006, p. 57; see also §2.5). The second problem with making the conversational context too rich is that in so doing, we make it much harder to secure non-negotiability. After all, if we change the conversational context, then the presupposition does not arise, or a different presupposition arises, as we had in Langendoen's example. The less information we put into the conversational context, the likelier it becomes that we are in such contexts sufficiently often, and the likelier it becomes that we can secure the result that the commitment to categorical reasons is non-negotiable.

In what follows, I argue that priming a conversational context with the shared information that we are in a serious moral conversation without applicability restrictions (I will explain what these are below) gets us the result that moral judgements like (3) and (6) pragmatically presuppose (4). I explain how this works in the next two sections (§3.4 and 3.5). In the two sections after that, I respond to some objections to pragmatic presupposition error theory (§3.6 and 3.7).

3.4 Pragmatic Presupposition Error Theory

At the heart of my argument for the claim that moral judgements of various kinds, thus including atomic judgements and their negations, pragmatically presuppose (4) is that this picture of moral discourse best accommodates the empirical data as we have them, and which I reviewed in §2.6. Consider a context in which two people, call them Arnold and Bertie, discuss the obligatoriness or otherwise of giving to the poor. Imagine that Arnold utters (3) and that Bertie, tired of the conversation, exclaims (34) rather than (6):

(3) Giving to the poor is morally obligatory.
(6) Giving to the poor is not morally obligatory.
(34) Giving to the poor is not morally obligatory; the poor should simply die in misery.

Perhaps Bertie wants to shock her interlocutor, or perhaps she does not know all the facts, or again perhaps she no longer wishes to consider the issue with full attention. In this conversational context, the pragmatic mechanisms involved (ceasing to discuss the issue seriously and instead merely trying to upset others) do not supply enough information for a determinate presupposition to arise, or for any speaker to justifiably infer that a proposition amenable to error theory has been assumed in the conversation. Towards the end of the previous section, I mentioned the danger of priming a conversation with too much information. But here we have too little information.

Let us therefore try a different strategy. Suppose instead that the two interlocutors are being serious and are trying to get to the bottom of the issue of the moral obligatoriness or otherwise of refraining from killing. Arnold utters (3) and Bertie utters (35):

(3) Giving to the poor is morally obligatory.
(35) Giving to the poor is not morally obligatory because there are no duties of positive assistance, only negative duties of non-interference.

Or perhaps Arnold anticipates that Bertie wants to have a serious conversation and utters (36) rather than (3):

(36) Giving to the poor is morally obligatory because we have a duty of positive assistance to help the poor.

And their conversation can continue, as Arnold might procure arguments involving harms and Bertie might deny that harm-based arguments are relevant for those who are not rich; Arnold might add that it is virtuous to help the poor and Bertie might deny that this is so; Arnold might invoke arguments from the ethics of care and feminist ethics, and Bertie might add that these arguments come to nothing, et cetera. The question is whether priming their conversation with specifically the shared information, available to both Bertie and Arnold, that they are both trying to get to the bottom of this moral issue is sufficient to get a pragmatic presupposition to categorical moral reasons.

To get this result, we must have an argument for the claim that denying (4) is infelicitous in a conversation that has as its aim to decide whether (3) or a spruced-up version of it like (36), or whether instead (6) or a spruced-up version of it like (35), ought to be accepted. To test whether this works, we can imagine Arnold adding (37) to the conversation:

(37) Oh, but mind you, I do not mean to say that once you accept (3) you have to give to the poor regardless of whether you want to or not.

In uttering (37), Arnold doesn't have to be interpreted as making a claim about what Bertie is *all-things-considered* obligated to do. As we saw in §2.5, moral obligations can be outweighed by non-moral, prudential considerations, such as the consideration that spending money on going to the movies rather than on famine relief makes one feel better. Arnold is just committed to the proposition that the force of the moral obligation to give to the poor is independent of the addressee's desires. The obligation is there, so to speak, regardless of whether or not Bertie or anyone else wants it to be there. Thus, error theorists who think that we can formulate pragmatic presupposition error theory with this way of priming the conversational context (i.e., serious vs. non-serious contexts) argue that, thus understood, (37) is not a felicitous contribution to the conversation, and that this indicates that the information that is being denied is not at issue, projects, and indicates presuppositional information. In more general terms, the information that cannot be denied, and which, given that we are only considering folk or ordinary moral discourse, can only be inchoately expressed, is:

(38) You have to perform your moral obligation whether you want to or not.

It does seem to me that in serious conversations like this, (38) is pragmatically presupposed by participants in moral discourse. However, the problem with this way of formulating pragmatic presupposition error theory is that it is insufficiently fine-grained. It cannot capture the felicitousness of the conversation between the two doctors in the Benevolent Doctors case that we discussed in §2.8 and which primes a different context for a moral discussion:

Benevolent Doctors

Two doctors disagree about the ethical permissibility or otherwise of ceasing a particular life-saving but painful treatment for a patient. They agree about all the relevant non-moral facts (e.g., how much the patient wants to continue to live, how much support she gets form relatives, how much pain she has), but one doctor utters the judgement 'we morally ought to cease this treatment' whereas the other disagrees and says 'we ought not to cease this treatment'. They both desire the best for their patient and neither wants to set a precedent for other similarly placed patients.

The relevant question is whether either of the doctors, or perhaps even both, can felicitously add (39) to the conversation:

(39)   Oh, but mind you, I do not mean to say that once you accept my moral judgement you must accept that everyone ought to act in accordance with it in like cases, whether they want to or not.

Given that it had been made explicit in the conversation that the moral judgement is not meant to set a precedent for other similar cases and that both doctors are concerned with beneficence and want the best for their patient, each of our two doctors can felicitously add (39) to the conversation. This result is consistent with the metaethical pluralism that the best current research in empirical metaethics attributes to the folk: depending on certain aspects of the content of the moral conversation, folk commitment to (38) either wavers or disappears without it being the case that the folk think that they have ceased to discuss morality. The problem for this way of formulating pragmatic presupposition moral error theory is that (39) contradicts (38), and given that both doctors are being serious, we find that priming a conversational context with seriousness is not sufficiently fine-grained to ensure that we get the result that (38) is a pragmatic presupposition of moral discourse.

To this line of reasoning you might object as follows. First, you might note that the claim that the doctors in the Benevolent Doctors case *are* discussing morality and yet *are not* committed to the claim that the same moral judgement applies to a patient in identical circumstances denies the supervenience of the moral on the non-moral. The thesis that the moral supervenes on the non-moral is the thesis that there is a relation of modal covariance (not: ontological or causal dependence) between non-moral and moral properties, such that in some (weak supervenience) or all (strong supervenience) possible worlds, there cannot be a moral difference without an underlying non-moral difference (McLaughlin and Bennett 2010, §3.5). But second, you might note that many philosophers think that to deny moral supervenience is to change the subject from morality to something else entirely and that it is therefore a major problem for a metaethical theory if it denies moral supervenience (Blackburn 1985, p. 64; Dreier 2015, p. 283).

In response, I reject the claim that the Benevolent Doctors case denies moral supervenience, for it is consistent with the case as described that the doctors agree that in the *extremely* hypothetical case that another patient will share *every* relevant non-moral property with this patient (same level of parental support, same level of intensity of the desire to continue to live, same relevant medical history, etc.), their decision will set a precedent. What the doctors are after in this case is a rejection of the much more mundane and much more often used idea that their decision will set a precedent for other similarly placed but not non-morally identical patients. This is consistent with moral supervenience.

So far, our most important results have been that conceptual entailment and semantic presupposition error theories don't work, that pragmatic presupposition error theory might work, but that for it to work, we need to prime a conversational context for moral discussions. But these contexts have thus far contained either too much information when we primed them with practical clout or too little information when we primed them with seriousness. To get pragmatic presupposition moral error theory, I propose to distinguish, within the class of serious moral conversation, between, on the one hand, ordinary or common conversational contexts in which both speakers know that they are using moral language without a further song and dance about exceptions and limitations involving, for instance, benevolent agents not wanting to set a precedent for their decision (*core cases*), and, on the other hand, rare or infrequent conversational contexts in which such limitations are explicitly formulated and in which it is common knowledge that these limitations apply (*peripheral cases*). The kinds of exceptions and limitations I have in mind are what I am going to call *applicability restrictions*: whatever the outcome of the moral discussion is going to be, the obligations we are talking about apply to a restricted subset of moral agents, for instance agents who did not agree that their benevolent decisions about what to do in a morally relevant context, such as one in which it is being decided whether to continue medical treatment, should not be taken to set a precedent for other contexts.

With this in mind, reconsider Arnold and Bertie, and distinguish between core cases (common conversational contexts) and peripheral cases (infrequent conversational contexts). In both cases, Arnold and Bertie are discussing whether or not giving to the poor is morally obligatory, are being serious, and are discussing such things as rights, capabilities, harms, benefits, and all the rest of it. So we can imagine that they utter the following moral judgements:

(36) Giving to the poor is morally obligatory because we have a duty of positive assistance to help the poor.
(35) Giving to the poor is not morally obligatory because there are no duties of positive assistance, only negative duties of non-interference.

In *common* conversational contexts, the information that cannot be felicitously denied, that is not at issue, projects, and that indicates presuppositional information, is:

(38) You have to perform your moral obligation whether you want to or not.

In *peripheral* conversational contexts in which applicability restrictions apply, denying (38) is felicitous, so (38) is not presuppositional information of the conversation.

This result is consistent with our intuitions about these cases, with moral supervenience, and, importantly, with folk metaethical pluralism as confirmed by recent empirical metaethics. Recall that empirical metaethicists agree that the folk are sometimes objectivists and sometimes not, depending on what the conversation is about, their cultural background, *et cetera*. Pragmatic presupposition error theory explains this feature of folk moral discourse by reference to the different conversational cues that are present in the various conversations people might have: serious and common conversations, serious and uncommon conversations, nonserious conversations, *et cetera*. It is not as though there is only one right way to think about morality—a way of thinking that commits you to accepting the view that morality is always and by definition about categorical reasons, as the conceptual entailment error theorist has it, and implausibly so. Rather, it is the case that in some conversational contexts morality is about categorical reasons, whereas in others it is not. This explains why some folk sometimes report objective intuitions about morality, and sometimes subjective intuitions; whether or not they believe that morality is objective depends on the context that surrounds the question or the case being described.

How do ordinary speakers recognize that their conversation has been primed with seriousness and no applicability restrictions? The knowledge that no applicability restrictions obtained in the context of a moral discussion is *suppressed* or *latent knowledge* in the sense that it is not something that is in any way announced or that can be inferred from other information available to the participants in the discussion. There are no specific informational cues in the conversation itself, apart from the fact that there is no specific cue that justifies the assumption that one or more applicability restrictions apply. In common conversational contexts, the folk reason as follows. There is not a single piece of information in the conversational context that justifies an inference to the claim that a restriction condition applies; therefore, I am justified to assume that talk about the moral obligations under discussion applies to everyone across the board, whether they want to or not. However, this presupposition is *contextually defeasible*. If there is a cue in the conversation that justifies inference to the claim that a restriction condition applies, such as the decision by the two doctors not to set a precedent with their decision to continue or to stop the treatment of the patient in the example above, then the presupposition vanishes, even if both parties to the dispute are being serious.

Even if this works up to this point, I still have to argue that categorical moral reasons of rationality and not, for instance, objectively prescriptive properties or irreducibly normative reasons are the *best philosophical interpretation* of (38). I will do this in the next section.

3.5 Rationality or Non-Naturalism?

According to pragmatic presupposition error theory, (38) is a presupposition of moral conversations in common conversational contexts. But there is still the issue of whether this means that (38) should be understood along an existence theory of reasons, as in (40), or whether we should rather speak of reasons of rationality, as in (41):

(40) There exists at least one irreducibly normative moral reason.
(41) There exists at least one categorical moral reason of rationality.

I first argue that (41) is a good interpretation of (38). After this, I argue that the other main philosophical interpretation of (38), that is, (40), is inferior to this interpretation.

Rationality To defend my claim that we must analyse (38) in terms of categorical moral reasons of rationality, I invoke Joyce's argument for this claim (see §2.5). Joyce has recently expressed doubt about his own argument, writing that trying to account for (38)

> leaves us groping for categorical ... reasons [of rationality] ... But what on earth would they be like? And the answer is that I really don't know. I can honestly report that to the extent that I am familiar with moral judgement I have a very strong feeling that people want and require something ... objective and non-institutional ... I have come to suspect that my inadequacy in

articulating this idea is not because of any failure of imagination or eloquence. Rather, morality may be imbued with a deeply mysterious kind of force—a kind of primitive feeling of 'being bound by rules and ends' that resists explication. It is as if we have a pre-wired superstition, which—as the intelligent beings that we are—we cannot quite admit as such (and instead spend two thousand years trying desperately to defend). Perhaps Mackie and I fumble to dissect something that by its very nature cannot be brought into the light. (2011, p. 525)

However, I think that Joyce's recent modesty is not necessary. His earlier and more committed argument from his 2001 book *The Myth of Morality*, works. The argument was that appeal to rationality is sufficient and necessary to explain (38). Focus on the sufficiency claim first. Joyce starts by suggesting that we might accept that saying that what it is

> for the agent to have sufficient reason not to [perform a particular action] … is equivalent to saying that, if the agent were to reason correctly, the agent would end up deciding not to do the act. (Harman 1986, p. 66; see also Joyce 2006, p. 194)

This is the theory of reasons according to which reasons are reasons of rationality, that is, they are considerations that count as reasons because it is rational to regard these considerations as reasons.

After this Joyce writes that "a natural question at this point is": why should the fact that, if you were to reason correctly, you would end up doing the act "have any practical authority?" (2006, p. 195). To answer this question, Joyce takes Harman's famous case of hoodlums igniting a cat, names one of the hoodlums Albert, and says:

> Assuming that one of the actions available to Albert instantiates the property *is-such-that-Albert-would-want-to-do-it-if-he-were-to-reason-correctly*, why does this property represent a genuine deliberative consideration for Albert? The answer … is that he cannot intelligibly raise doubt about whether such a property is a practical consideration for him, since the very act of sincerely asking the question evinces certain commitments to standards of correct reasoning. This is just a fact about the act of doubting or questioning in general. The very act of sincerely asking "Why X?" presupposes

that one is in the business of seeking and possibly accepting answers; it presupposes an acknowledgement that the addressee of the question may be in an epistemically superior position to the questioner. But to acknowledge the possible inferiority of one's epistemic position, and to embrace the desirability of improvement, *is* to concede that the opinions that you would have if you were to reason correctly carry deliberative weight. Thus the statement "I acknowledge that were I to reason correctly I would want to φ, but what is that to me?" does not represent a well-formed sceptical position. (2006, p. 195, emphases in original; the case is from Harman 1977, p. 4)

In his earlier book Joyce similarly writes:

> Morality is not presented as something that may be legitimately ignored or begged-off. So the question is: what sense can be made of reasons that cannot be evaded, of "real" reasons? The answer … is that practical rationality yields [such] reasons, for to question practical rationality is self-undermining. (2001, p. 100)

You might object that this gets us into the agency-schmagency discussion and that a moral agent who does not like to perform a moral obligation can weasel himself out of the obligation by denying that he is an agent (Enoch 2006; Tiffany 2012; Smith 2013). But it doesn't get us into that discussion, for that discussion is about whether people like us, who have the capacity for acting for reasons, ought (always) to do this or whether they can at least sometimes avoid having to do this by conceiving of themselves as schmagents, who do not share some or all of the characteristics of agents. This contrasts with the current discussion, which is about people who have declared themselves as agents by asking a question and concerns whether such agents can legitimately question whether they have a reason to φ though they agree that they would want to φ if they were to reason correctly.

Next, consider the necessity claim. You might object that there exist all sorts and kinds of considerations that are external to my rational thinking, that is, considerations that are not 'yielded' by my rational thinking, such as considerations stemming from "a little normative institution according to which everyone ought to pursue autumnal Norwegian products", and you might insist that likewise these cannot be legitimately ignored (Joyce 2006, p. 203). But if you make this objection, then you must explain why this normative institution carries genuine deliberative weight. I agree that these considerations can be normative and have rationality authority if, for example, acting on them satisfies one or more of my desires and if I rationally ought to satisfy my desires (in the next chapter, I will argue that this claim is true). But I insist that in the *absence* of a desire that would be fulfilled by acting on this alleged reason, it makes perfect sense to deny that an action available to you that instantiates the property of *is-such-that-a-normative-institution-tells-you-to-buy-products-produced-in-the-Autumn-in-Norway* is rationally authoritative for you. To insist otherwise would merely amount to "browbeating", that is, trying to convince an agent that she has a reason even though this is not the case (Gibbard 1990, p. 171; also see §6.5).

Non-Naturalist Realism Jonas Olson defends the view that the best articulation of the non-negotiable commitment of folk moral discourse is "that moral facts … are or entail facts that count in favour of or require certain courses of behaviour, where the favouring relation is irreducibly normative" and that these facts make an ontological demand on the world (2014, pp. 117–8; also see Olson 2011). Thus, Olson thinks that (40) is the best philosophical interpretation of (38):

(40)   There exists at least one irreducibly normative reason.

This commits Olson to the view that moral discourse requires *non-naturalist* realism. The problem with such a view is that it cannot explain moral reasons' inescapability: it cannot explain why a moral obligation tells you to perform an action 'whether you want to or not'. This is because Olson has no answer to Korsgaard's "normative question" of how reasons "get a grip" on agents if reasons are facts and not yielded by rationality (Korsgaard 1996, pp. 44–46). Korsgaard, and I agree, thinks that on Olson's existence theory of reasons, agents can always ask whether they should perform the action that their (alleged) reason suggests they should perform, and that reasons thus understood are therefore not inescapable.

In defence of Olson we might conceive of the normative force of irreducibly normative relations as "invisible cords, hooks, and chains" (Mackie 1977, p. 74), or, as Olson proposes, we might liken the normative force of irreducibly normative relations to "magnetic force" (2014, p. 110). With this analogy on board, Olson might insist that if the normative force of irreducibly normative reasons exists and acts like an invisible cord, then one can no longer sensibly ask: but why follow this normativity? For this would be similar to asking something like the following question: 'I am aware that I have sufficient evidence to believe that this cord is literally holding me back as I can feel it tugging on me, but what is that to me?' And that, Olson might conclude, means that this question is as problematic as it is to question practical rationality.

The problem with this attempt to defend Olson is that for Olson and his irreducibly normative facts, the 'but what is that to me?' question remains legitimate and that this is not the case for Joyce and myself when we appeal to the precepts of rationality. What if the world had contained irreducibly normative reasons that tell me to disfigure my body? What if the world had contained irreducibly normative reasons that tell me to refrain from giving to the homeless, or to give to the poor, even if I can barely survive myself? The fact that the world happens to be a certain way (i.e., that it happens to contain some irreducibly normative reasons rather than others) does not seem to be sufficient for the claim that *I have to* act on the reasons that it allegedly happens to contain. I might perceive some kind of magnetic force, but what is that to me? It seems to me that if, after rational thinking, we conclude that we mustn't disfigure other people's bodies but that we also acquire the knowledge that there exists an irreducibly normative fact that tells us to disfigure other people's bodies, we can legitimately ask 'but what is that to me?' and ignore the relevant normative fact. If this is correct, then on Olson's existence theory of reasons, we cannot say that moral reasons are relevantly inescapable—that you 'have to' perform the action for which you allegedly have a reason whether you want to or not. Instead it depends on what rationality obliges you to do. The best philosophical interpretation of (38) is (41), not (40). We have reached the conclusion that moral judgements pragmatically presuppose the proposition that there are categorical moral reasons of rationality.

What happens to moral judgements that pragmatically presuppose the proposition that there are categorical moral reasons of rationality? In §3.2, I argued that there is debate about what happens to the judgements that carry false semantic presuppositions—do these judgements themselves become false or do they become neither true nor false? But in the pragmatic presupposition case and focusing on moral judgements specifically, there is much less room for debate. It is most plausible to say that moral judgements become neither true nor false if they pragmatically presuppose a false proposition. This is because in such a situation *it no longer makes s*ense to continue to debate whether a particular moral judgement is or is not true, and we best capture this pragmatic infelicity of continuing to do so by saying that such a judgement is neither true nor false. Continuing in such a debate is meaningless.

In sum, moral judgements pragmatically presuppose categorical moral reasons of rationality in common conversational contexts, and these judgements are neither true nor false at least if, as I will argue in the next chapter, such reasons don't exist. From now on, whenever I write 'categorical moral reason', I mean a categorical reason of rationality. I will now proceed to argue that this view has the theoretical resources to respond to some objections that can be, or have been, formulated against it.

3.6 Externalism, Systematic Falsity, and Cognitivism

I first argue that the content-externalism objection does not apply to presupposition error theory. The content-externalism objection was that error theorists must argue that the meaning of moral concepts can be fully determined by the folk's referential intentions, but that it is not plausible to accept this. My version of presupposition error theory completely sidesteps this objection. The presupposition concerns moral discourse as such, including atomic judgements like (3), negated judgements like (6), and modal and conditional judgements like (10) and (11), not individual moral concepts that form part of atomic moral judgements. The pragmatic presupposition error theorist simply does not need to accept either moral content-internalism or content-externalism about the meaning of moral concepts because she does not make a claim about the content of moral concepts. We have moral judgements, and regardless of whatever it is that may or may not be part of their semantic content, speakers who utter them commit themselves to categorical reasons via pragmatic mechanisms in common conversational contexts.

The second objection, which I call the systematic falsity objection, is due to Jonas Olson:

> the claim that it is not the case that torture is wrong seems, from the perspective of moral error theorists to be true, since on their view, nothing has the property of being wrong. In contrast, the negation of the claim that the king of France is wise seems to be neither true nor false, since there is no present king of France. This suggests that while claims about the king of France presuppose that there is a present king of France, first-order moral claims, like the claim that torture is wrong, entail that there are moral properties. (2014, p. 13)

But it only seems to the error theorist that 'X is not wrong' is true *if she already accepts* entailment error theory. If the error theorist accepts presupposition error theory instead, then she will have no problem with an analysis of 'X is not wrong' according to which it comes out as neither true nor false. This is because it suffices for error theorists to argue that moral judgements are *not true* (either because they are false or because they are neither true nor false). Recall the no-moral-considerations-are-relevant argument from §1.1. What matters for both entailment and presupposition error theorists is, first, that it is not the case that people have to take moral considerations, such as the moral obligatoriness of refraining from killing, into account in their practical deliberations and, second, that no one can utter a true moral judgement.

The third objection is that if it is true that moral judgements express propositions that are neither true nor false, then we can no longer be cognitivists, since:

> Cognitivism … holds that moral statements … express beliefs and that they are apt for truth and falsity. (van Roojen 2013, §0)

In other words, cognitivists can hold that all, some, or no moral judgements are true and that, if at least one or more moral judgements are not true, then they are false. But cognitivism is not normally understood as the view that at least some moral judgements can be neither true nor false. However, I don't think that cognitivism is most fruitfully formulated like this. For what, indeed, should we say if the truth of these propositions depends on the truth of a presupposition which turns out to be false, and which has the further consequence of rendering the truth-apt propositions neither true nor false, as I think is the case with moral propositions? This possibility does not mean that we must embrace non-cognitivism, as moral judgements remain truth-apt. On my version of error theory, moral judgements express truth-apt beliefs, though in some contexts they carry false pragmatic presuppositions, which has the consequence that it no longer makes sense to continue to discuss the question whether the judgement is true, and thus that it becomes natural in the conversation to say that the judgement has become neither true nor false.

This means that, consistently with their acceptance of the claim that moral judgements express truth-apt beliefs, pragmatic presupposition error theorists can accept:

P3'   If moral judgements pragmatically presuppose a false non-negotiable claim, then they are neither true nor false.

This leaves the pervasiveness objections.

3.7   Pervasiveness Objections

In this section, I argue that the error that pragmatic presupposition moral error theory attributes to moral discourse is more pervasive than the error that conceptual entailment error theory attributes to it. I also argue that the error is sufficiently pervasive to get P4 in the Generic Argument for Error Theory:

Generic Argument
P1 Moral judgements carry a non-negotiable commitment to claim N.
P2 This non-negotiable commitment claim N is false.
P3 If moral judgements carry a false non-negotiable commitment, then they are untrue.
C1 Therefore, moral judgements are untrue (from P1, P2, P3).
P4 If C1, then we should accept error theory of moral discourse as a whole.
C2 Therefore, we should accept error theory of moral discourse as a whole (from C1, P4).

So far, we have defended a number of more specific formulations of various premises in this argument, reaching the following Intermediate Formulation of Moral Error Theory:

Intermediate Formulation of Moral Error Theory
P1*** Moral judgements pragmatically presuppose the claim that there are categorical moral reasons.
P2 This non-negotiable commitment claim N is false.
P3' If moral judgements pragmatically presuppose a false non-negotiable claim, then they are neither true nor false.
C1' Therefore, moral judgements are neither true nor false (from P1***, P2, P3').
P4' If C1', then we should accept error theory of moral discourse as a whole.
C2 Therefore, we should accept error theory of moral discourse as a whole (from C1', P4).

I have argued for every premise in this argument except P2, which I will defend in the next chapter, and P4', which differs from P4 in that it mentions C1' and not C1. The question here is: is P4' plausible?

In both the Generic Argument and the Intermediate Argument, the first three premises and the first conclusion are ambiguous because I did not fully specify what is meant by 'moral judgement'. I have done this on purpose because moral error theorists do not agree among themselves which types of contributions to moral discourse count as a moral judgement. Richard Joyce thinks that only atomic moral judgements like (3) count as moral judgements (2007, §4). Contrastingly, Charles R. Pigden writes: "(in many cases at least) the negation of a moral judgement … is itself a moral judgement" (2007, p. 450). And I have argued that imperatives like "don't steal!" or "give to the poor!" are also contributions to moral discourse that ought to be debunked, both by standard conceptual entailment error theorists who believe that moral judgements express false beliefs and by pragmatic presupposition error theorists (Kalf 2017, p. 113).

As I explained in §1.1, the issue of which kinds of moral judgements should be debunked matters a lot for error theory. First, if there are true moral judgements then error theory is false. This was the reason why Joyce restricted his error theory to just atomic judgements, as the negations of atomic judgements must, by the principle of the excluded middle, be true, in which case, if negated moral judgements are themselves moral judgements, we must reject error theory. Second, there is the pervasiveness issue: if only atomic moral judgements are to be debunked, then many contributions to moral discourse are error free, which besets the question whether this result is sufficient for the truth of C2, which is that we must be error theorists of moral discourse as a whole.

Pragmatic presupposition error theory does well on both of these issues. For according to it, affirmative moral judgements as well as all kinds of other moral judgements, including negated and modal judgements that contain entailment-cancelling operators, carry the poised commitment, whereas on the traditional error theory only atomic or perhaps also negated moral judgements carry this commitment. For instance, the presupposition (41) projects across ways of embedding (3) that involve various sentential operators, as in (10) and (11):

(10) Giving to the poor might be morally obligatory
(11) If giving to the poor is morally obligatory, then giving to the homeless is morally obligatory

So, though (10) will not *entail* (41) because the modal operator it uses provides an entailment-cancelling embedding for (3), it does *presuppose* (41) on account of the fact that if Arnold utters (10) and Bertie utters, say, (6), (41) is not at issue, projects, and indicates presuppositional information, at least in common conversational contexts without applicability restrictions. Something similar holds for (11), which cannot entail (41) but which does pragmatically presuppose (41) because (41) is not at issue in a conversation that features (11), or at least this holds in common conversational contexts that do not feature applicability restrictions. This means that, first, the principle of the excluded middle does not apply to judgements that are neither true nor false: though a moral judgement and its negation are both moral judgements, you do not violate the law of the middle if you discredit both, for discrediting these judgements means insisting that they are both neither true nor false, rather than both false. And, second, every contribution to the conversation, in the right context, carries the commitment, so we also get pervasiveness.

Does this error theory of ordinary moral discourse, which we here understand as consisting in various kinds of moral judgements that contain moral concepts, extend to other parts of our discourse that we might think are 'ethically inflected' even though the relevant contributions to it do not contain any moral concepts or words, thick or thin? Cora Diamond has argued that whether a string of words expresses a moral judgement depends not on whether it contains moral terms, but on its function or use (1996, p. 237). Diamond's specific Wittgensteinian take on this may or may not be defensible, but the phenomenon seems to be real. I can communicate to you that I think that you are morally obligated to refrain from performing a certain action merely by sniffing at you in a particular way, or if I just ask 'really?' in a particular tone of voice. The traditional conceptual entailment error theorist has a hard time explaining how this works. After all, these sentences or gestures do not contain moral concepts, and so they cannot semantically commit those who utter or display them to the existence of categorical moral reasons. I take it that presupposition error theory earns a plausibility point here because it can explain, and rather easily, how sentences that do not contain moral concepts, and how gestures that aren't even sentences, but that do express moral appraisal, can commit their users to moral reasons. Presupposition error theory can explain this because it takes the nature of moral discourse's mode of commitment to moral reasons to be explained by reference to the pragmatics of moral conversations, and the explanation of how sentences without moral concepts and gestures communicate moral appraisals also uses pragmatics. If you utter 'stealing is not morally wrong' and I reply '*really?!*', then, without applicability restrictions, our conversation as a whole, thus including the '*really?!*', pragmatically presupposes the existence of categorical moral reasons.

A quick remark on terminology. If I am right that contributions to moral discourse that do not take the form of *judgements*, such as imperatives and questions, are systematically untrue, then it may seem a good idea to change the formulation of the argument for error theory to reflect this change. For instance, rather than having P1***, we should perhaps accept P1****:

P1****   All contributions to moral discourse pragmatically presuppose the claim that there are categorical moral reasons of rationality.

However, for purely stylistic reasons I will continue to use the locution 'moral judgements', though it should be understood that my pragmatic presupposition error theory extends to every contribution to moral discourse, even those contributions that do not take the shape of a judgement, such as gestures.

Pragmatic presupposition error theory is clearly more pervasive than conceptual entailment error theory, but is it sufficiently pervasive for P4? The following consideration justifies thinking that this is so: every single contribution to a moral dicussion is untrue if that conversation pragmatically presupposes categorical moral reasons. The question, though, is whether the fact that there are also conversational contexts in which this presupposition does not arise epistemically obligates us to abandon the conclusion that the error we get from pragmatic presupposition error theory is sufficiently pervasive for P4. So at this point in the dialectic, the relevant question is: is the fact that the erroneous commitment only occurs in some contexts sufficient warrant for the claim that moral discourse as such is in error?

I don't think that we should answer that the right kinds of contexts must occur sufficiently often. For instance, perhaps we can say that if in 95% of cases moral conversations are primed with seriousness and the absence of applicability restrictions, the error in moral discourse is sufficiently pervasive to justify P4. But I don't think that this kind of numerical value gives us the answer that we want. After all, it is not clear that 94% makes a difference. We need a more principled reason. A better option is to say that serious conversational contexts that are not characterized by applicability restrictions are the *most important contexts*. By this I mean that participants in moral conversations primed with seriousness but also with the presence of some applicability restrictions *cannot continue to use moral language effectively* after it has become common knowledge that moral conversations primed with seriousness and the absence of applicability restrictions carry a false non-negotiable pragmatic presupposition. The effectiveness of the former kind of moral language depends on that of the latter. If we know that moral discussions in core cases don't work, then peripheral moral discussions will become obsolete as the need to use moral language will be completely removed after the error theory for core moral discussions. No need to announce an applicability restriction for moral obligations if there are no categorical moral obligations at all. The ineffectiveness of core moral discussions permeates that of peripheral moral discussions.

In sum, *every* contribution to moral discussions is in error in the right context (including negated judgements, imperatives, ethically inflected and affirmative judgements that do not use moral concepts, etc.) and the fact that moral judgements are in error in these contexts means that uttering moral judgements in 'error-free' contexts loses its point. The error that pragmatic presupposition error theory attributes to moral discourse is sufficiently pervasive to get P4':

P4'   If C1', then we should accept error theory of moral discourse as a whole.

This concludes my response on behalf of pragmatic presupposition error theory against the pervasiveness objections, and my defence of P4'.

3.8 Conclusion

Some philosophers find it preposterous to think that categorical moral reasons of rationality are the non-negotiable commitment of moral discourse, as it is preposterous to think that a

> belief so recherché could be part of common sense moral thinking. (Brink 1984, p. 120)

These philosophers think that

> ordinary people when they use moral words are not intending to ascribe objective prescriptive properties to actions. (Hare 1981, p. 86; 1999, p. 2)

In this chapter, I have argued that pragmatic presupposition error theory, according to which moral judgements pragmatically presuppose rather than entail categorical moral reasons, is in fact plausible. This establishes error theory's non-negotiable commitment claim:

P1*** Moral judgements pragmatically presuppose the claim that there are categorical moral reasons of rationality.

I have also argued that the following version of P3 from the Generic Argument for Error Theory is true:

P3' If moral judgements pragmatically presuppose a false non-negotiable claim, then they are neither true nor false.

Finally, I have argued that the following version of P4 from the Generic Argument for Error Theory is true:

P4' If C1', then we should accept error theory of moral discourse as a whole

This means that every premise in the argument for error theory has been defended now, except P2, which I will defend in the next chapter.

References

Beaver, D.I., and B. Geurts. 2011. Presupposition. In *Stanford Encyclopedia of Philosophy*, ed. E.N. Zalta. Stanford: Stanford University Press.
Blackburn, S. 1985. Supervenience Revisited. In *Exercises in Analysis*, ed. I. Hacking, 47–68. Cambridge: CUP.
Brink, D.O. 1984. Moral Realism and the Skeptical Arguments from Disagreement and Queerness. *Australian Journal of Philosophy* 62: 111–125.
Cummins, C. 2016. Using Triggers Without Projecting Presuppositions. *Topoi* 35: 123–131.
Diamond, C. 1996. Wittgenstein, Mathematics, and Ethics. In *The Cambridge Companion to Wittgenstein*, ed. H.D. Sluga and D.G. Stern, 209–244. Cambridge: CUP.
Dreier, J. 2015. Explaining the Quasi-Real. In *Oxford Studies in Metaethics*, ed. R. Shafer-Landau, vol. 10, 273–297. Oxford: OUP.
Enoch, D. 2006. Agency, Shmagency: Why Normativity Won't Come from What Is Constitutive of Action. *The Philosophical Review* 115: 169–198.
Frege, G. 1892. *On Sense and Reference*, eds. M. Black and P. Geach. 1952. Translations from the Philosophical Writings of Gottlob Frege. Oxford: Blackwell.
Gibbard, A. 1990. *Wise Choices, Apt Feelings*. Cambridge, MA: Harvard University Press.
Hare, R.M. 1981. *Moral Thinking: Its Levels, Point and Method*. Oxford: OUP.
———. 1999. *Objective Prescriptions and Other Essays*. Oxford: Clarendon Press.
Harman, G. 1977. *The Nature of Morality*. Oxford: OUP.
———. 1986. Moral Explanations of Natural Facts: Can Moral Claims Be Tested Against Moral Reality? *Southern Journal of Philosophy* 24: 57–68.
Joyce, R. 2001. *The Myth of Morality*. Cambridge: CUP.
———. 2006. *The Evolution of Morality*. Cambridge, MA: MIT Press.
———. 2007. Moral Anti-Realism, In *Stanford Encyclopedia of Philosophy*, ed. E.N. Zalta. Stanford: Stanford University Press.
———. 2011. The Error in 'The Error in the Error Theory. *Australasian Journal of Philosophy* 89: 519–534.
Kalf, W.F. 2013. Moral Error Theory, Entailment and Presupposition. *Ethical Theory and Moral Practice* 16: 923–937.
———. 2017. Against Hybrid Expressivist-Error Theory. *Journal of Value Inquiry* 51: 105–122.

Karttunen, L. 1974. Presupposition and Linguistic Context. *Theoretical Linguistics* 1: 181–194.
Katz, J.J., and D.T. Langendoen. 1976. Pragmatics and Presupposition. *Language* 52: 1–17.
Kiparsky, P., and C. Kiparsky. 1970. Fact. In *Progress in Linguistics*, ed. M. Bierwisch and K. Heidolph, 143–173. The Hague: Mouton.
Korsgaard, D. 1996. *The Sources of Normativity*. Oxford: OUP.
Langendoen, D.T. 1971. Presupposition and Assertion in the Semantic Analysis of Nouns and Verbs in English. In *Semantics*, ed. D.D. Steinberg and L.A. Jakobovits, 341–344. Cambridge: CUP.
Mackie, J.L. 1977. *Ethics: Inventing Right and Wrong*. Harmondsworth: Penguin Publishers.
McLaughlin, B., and K. Bennett. 2010. Supervenience. In *Stanford Encyclopedia of Philosophy*, ed. E.N. Zalta. Stanford: Stanford University Press.
Olson, J. 2011. Getting Real About Moral Fictionalism. In *Oxford Studies in Metaethics*, ed. R. Shafer-Landau, vol. 6, 181–204. Oxford: OUP.
———. 2014. *Moral Error Theory: History, Critique, Defence*. Oxford: OUP.
Pigden, C. 2007. Nihilism, Nietzsche and the Doppelganger Problem. *Ethical Theory and Moral Practice* 10: 414–456.
Saeed, J.I. 2003. *Semantics*. Malden: Blackwell Publishers.
Simons, M. 2006. Foundational Issues in Presupposition. *Philosophy Compass* 1: 357–372.
———. 2013. On the Conversational Basis of Some Presuppositions. In *Perspectives on Linguistic Pragmatics*, ed. A. Capone, F. Lo Piparo, and M. Carapezza, 329–348. Heidelberg: Springer.
Simons, M., J. Tonhauser, D. Beaver, and C. Roberts. 2010. What Projects and Why. *Proceedings of SALT* 20: 309–327.
Smith, M. 2013. A Constitutivist Theory of Reasons: Its Promise and Parts. *Law, Ethics, and Philosophy* 1: 9–30.
Stalnaker, R. 1974. Pragmatic Presuppositions. In *Semantics and Philosophy*, ed. M.K. Munitz and P.K. Unger, 197–213. New York: NYU Press.
Stalnaker, R.C. 1999. *Context and Content*. Oxford: OUP.
Strawson, P.F. 1950. On Referring. *Mind* 59: 320–344.
Tiffany, E. 2012. Why Be an Agent? *Australasian Journal of Philosophy* 90: 223–233.
van Roojen, M. 2013. Moral Cognitivism Vs. Moral Non-Cognitivism. In *Stanford Encyclopedia of Philosophy*, ed. E.N. Zalta. Stanford: Stanford University Press.

Väyrynen, P. 2013. *The Lewd, the Rude, and the Nasty*. Oxford: OUP.
von Fintel, K. 2004. Would You Believe It? The King of France Is Back! In *Descriptions and Beyond*, ed. A. Bezuidenhout and M. Reimer, 269–296. Oxford: OUP.
Yablo, S. 2006. Non-Catastrophic Presupposition Failure. In *Content and Modality*, ed. J.J. Thomson and A. Byrne, 164. Oxford: OUP.

4

Rationality

4.1 Introduction

In the previous chapter, I argued that moral judgements presuppose categorical moral reasons of rationality, which, for brevity's sake, I will sometimes also call categorical moral reasons. In the present chapter, I argue that there are no categorical moral reasons. Thus, I argue for P2':

P2' The claim that there are categorical moral reasons is false.

P2' is a more specific version of P2, which features in the error theorist's Generic Argument:

P2 The non-negotiable commitment claim N is false.

But at this point in the dialectic, there is no alternative specification of P2, such as a specification that mentions not categorical moral reasons of rationality but irreducibly normative reasons, that is as plausible as P2'. Therefore, an argument for P2' suffices for the error theorist in the current dialectical context.

This chapter is structured as follows. In the next section, I reject the common but flawed queerness defence of P2' (§4.2). After this, I explain Richard Joyce's rationality argument for P2', which does not use queerness and instead asks whether categorical moral reasons are yielded by rationality, and I argue that this defence of P2' is also not convincing (§4.3). In the sections that follow, I present my own, positive defence of P2'. I first explain in more detail what it means to say that the fate of categorical moral reasons rests wholly on whether they are yielded by rationality (§4.4). I then argue that although rationality yields both categorical and hypothetical epistemic and prudential reasons, it does not yield categorical moral reasons (§4.5 and 4.6). I subsequently argue that this entails that the companions-in-guilt objection fails, and I explain why my response to this objection is better than existing responses (§4.7). I close by arguing that other objections to the error theorist's substantive claim, such as the objection from epistemic conservatism, also fail (§4.8). A conclusion sums up my main findings and introduces the topic of part II (§4.9).

I make two preliminary points before I proceed. First, what follows in these pages is a defence of the claim that P2' is true on the basis of some widely accepted but controversial assumptions about rationality and normativity. I explain how we are led to error theory if we accept these assumptions, and a more detailed defence of error theory would have to contain a more detailed defence of these assumptions. The status of these assumptions is different from the status of the assumptions I made in Chap. 1. Those assumptions did not receive any defence, whereas the assumptions I make in this chapter receive some, albeit limited defence. Second, I do not discuss the argument from disagreement, or the argument from "relativity" as J.L. Mackie calls it (1977, p. 36). I have two reasons for omitting this argument. First, I don't need it to defend P2' and, second, it is not a good argument. This is because persistent, even intractable, disagreement is consistent with the existence of moral properties, since both parties to a disagreement may be incapable of gaining epistemic access to the moral facts (Kahane 2013; Joyce 2013, p. 354).

4.2 Queerness

An often-discussed, and almost equally often-rejected, argument for P2' uses the (alleged) queerness of moral facts (Mackie 1977; Olson 2014). In assessing queerness arguments, we must distinguish between three ways in which properties can be queer. They can be ontologically proliferating, sui generis, or mysterious (Shepski 2008; Huemer 2005, p. 200). However, none of these interpretations of queerness gives us a good argument from queerness.

First, you might think that postulating an entity or property that expands our ontology renders it too queer to exist. However, this is clearly false, and Lee Shepski gives the example of postulating the existence of Pegasus (2008, p. 357). There is nothing queer about a horse with wings even though postulating its existence expands our ontology; after all, evolution might well have created such an animal. The same holds for expansions of our ontology with mysterious properties. On this way of thinking about queerness, what would allegedly make a property queer is our failure to comprehend it. Unfortunately, it does not follow from our failure to comprehend 'round squares' or 'Doxylayndowihai' that these things are too queer to exist. If anything, we have an argument from the meaninglessness of moral language to the non-existence of round squares (Shepski 2008, p. 357; also see §2.7 above). The final option that Shepski presents is to interpret the property of being queer as the property of being sui generis. Can being sui generis or being different from everything else in the universe make a property too queer to exist? Right off the bat, it doesn't seem like it can. Take the property of being alive, which is different from everything else in the universe. Is it therefore queer and, because of that, non-existent? It seems that the answers would have to be 'no' and 'no'. Mark Platts generalizes this point when he writes:

> The world is a queer place. I find neutrinos, aardvarks, infinite sequences of objects, and (most pertinently) impressionist paintings peculiar kinds of entities. (1980, p. 72)

In response, Richard Garner writes:

> Moral facts are not just unusual … they are unusual in an unusual way. (1990, p. 143)

However, the question remains whether, if we know that a property is unusual in an unusual way, we are entitled to think that it does not exist. Again, this doesn't seem to follow. The property of being alive is unusual in an unusual way, but this property certainly exists.

Mackie has two additional interpretations of the queerness argument, but neither of these arguments is better. The first argument focuses on the queerness of our epistemic access to moral facts. Mackie thought that if objectively prescriptive moral values existed, then our epistemic access to them would require "a special sort of intuition" (1977, p. 39). His reasoning was that we need this special faculty because moral properties are ontologically special (Brink 1984, p. 123). Mackie reasoned that whatever it is that makes moral properties too queer to exist would also render our faculty for detecting moral properties too queer to exist, and thus that it would be "lame" to postulate the existence of this faculty (Mackie 1977, p. 39). However, this version of the queerness argument does not help because it does not tell us *why* this faculty, or indeed moral properties themselves, are too queer to exist. The options seem to be being ontologically proliferating, being sui generis, and being mysterious, but these options do not yield a plausible queerness argument. Mackie's third and final version of the queerness objection fails for the same reason. It too has a different target, namely, the supervenience relation between moral and non-moral properties (Mackie 1977, p. 41). But it too does not tell us why this relation is too queer to exist. This argument also fails.

Jonas Olson has recently tried to revive the queerness argument for error theory. However, his argument boils down to an appeal to intuition:

> irreducibly normative favouring relations appear metaphysically mysterious. How could there be such relations? Non-naturalists could retort that it is not clear what kind of explanation we ask for here. They could maintain that it is a fundamental fact about reality that there are irreducibly normative reason relations, and they could refuse head-on to admit that there is anything *queer* about such relations. This illustrates that the issue here is at a bedrock metaphysical level. It is difficult for error theorists to convince those who find nothing queer about irreducible normativity. And

vice versa, of course. So the stubborn response from the non-naturalist seems to leave her and the error theorist in a stalemate, starring incredulously at each other. (2014, p. 136)

Olson offers a good discussion of arguments for and against queerness, but when push comes to shove, this is all there is to his argument, that is, a report of the intuition that moral properties seem to be queer. Olson does suggest that a way out of this stalemate would be to assess whether *other arguments* tip the balance in favour of realism over nihilism, holding fixed the fact that *some* philosophers find irreducible normativity queer. Examples of the kinds of arguments he discusses are companions-in-guilt arguments, Enoch-style deliberative indispensability arguments, and Moorean anti-sceptical arguments (Olson 2014, p. 138). Olson's project is to make a case for the intuition that moral facts are queer and then to ask whether a metaethical view without irreducible normative reasons is acceptable or whether, and quoting Russ Shafer-Landau, "we have no choice but to embrace the mysteries" (2003, p. 205).

I think that Olson's arguments against such objections as the Moorean objection and indispensability arguments are excellent and convincing, but I don't think that his defence of the queerness argument works. After all, someone who doesn't *at all* share Olson's intuition that irreducibly normative reasons are at least somewhat queer can, even after accepting all the other arguments that Olson gives, legitimately accept the existence of irreducibly normative reasons as normative bedrock. This is because that person can accept that *on the assumption that there is a reason* to think that moral properties are at least a bit queer, we should be nihilists rather than realists, but she can insist that on the assumption that moral properties aren't at all queer, which they are entitled to, given the symmetry of the incredulous stare in either direction, we should accept realism rather than nihilism.

I think there is a better argument for P2'. It does not use queerness but rationality instead. I explain it in what follows.

4.3 Joyce's Rationality Argument

Joyce's argument for P2' is not based on the alleged queerness of moral facts but on the idea that moral facts consist in reasons that are yielded by rationality but that rationality does not yield such reasons (2001, pp. 53–134; Olson 2014, p. 123n23). In this section, I explain Joyce's argument and I explain why I think that it must be improved. I suggest the improvements in the remainder of this chapter.

Recall from Chap. 2 that Joyce thinks that moral discourse commits us to reasons-talk (2001, p. 100). In particular, it commits us to reasons of rationality, for such reasons are the only reasons that are inescapable and authoritative in the required sense, given that questioning practical rationality is self-undermining. Joyce writes:

> the question is: What sense can be made of reasons that cannot be evaded ... of "real" reasons? The answer ... is that *practical rationality* yields [such] reasons, for to question practical rationality is self-undermining. "I acknowledge that practical rationality says I should Φ, but why should I have any interest in that fact?" fails to express a well-formed sceptical position, and this cannot be upheld if we replace "practical rationality" with ... any other normative system. (2001, p. 100)

So for Joyce, reasons are not facts with normative efficacy that are part of the furniture of the world and that rational agents mush somehow be attuned to picking up as reasons (I called this the existence theory of reasons in §1.2 above). Instead, reasons are considerations that rational agents *accept as reasons*. Practically, says Joyce, this means that actual agents must be justified in believing that their *idealized selves* would *advise* them to accept these considerations as reasons. Joyce thinks that these idealized agents must be identical to actuals agents like you and I, except for the fact that they have full information and ideal powers of reflection. This means that, for example, they don't affirm the consequent and invariably apply *modus ponens* when required (Joyce 2001, p. 100). We shouldn't accept an account of the idealized agent on which she is not otherwise identical to the actual agent, argues Joyce, because then agents may be *alienated* from their normative reasons. And the problem with allowing for alienation is that this threatens the result that questioning practical rationality is self-undermining. Agents who are alienated from their reasons can ask 'I acknowledge that practical rationality says I should Φ, but why should I have any interest in that fact?' in a way that *does* express a well-formed sceptical position. Thus, just giving an agent advice from the point of view of someone not sufficiently closely tied to who they are is just giving them advice from a normative system that does not have a *grip* on them as rational agents.

Joyce thinks that this means that there are no categorical moral reasons because by steering clear of alienation, we make all reasons "agent-relative", which entails that although one fully rational agent is justified in believing that *her* idealized self would alter *her* desires in way *x*, a different agent, who may or may not be in the same situation, may not get the same piece of advice from *his* idealized self (2001, p. 80). And that goes against the categoricity of moral reasons. The starting point—the actual agent—makes all the difference. The reason why different agents get different advice is that we must accept as our theory of practical rationality a version of *"non-Humean instrumentalism"* and because this theory does not oblige all agents to perform morally obligatory actions (Joyce 2001, p. 78, my italics).

Instrumentalism means: the only business that practical rationality is in is telling agents to perform those actions that satisfy one, some, or all of their desires, or else to drop at least one relevant desire. Non-Humean means: some desires are rationally assessable. Joyce thinks that David Hume believed that desires are not rationally assessable in any way. As Joyce writes in his book *The Evolution of Morality*, "correct practical reasoning is … a desire-sensitive affair" (2006, p. 198). The problem for morality is that although rationality can oblige agents to alter their desires because we should be non-Humeans, it can only ask us to do this if our overall set of desires 'S' will become "more coherent and unified", which is only a *procedural* account of non-Humean rationality and is as such sensitive to input from the set of desires that an agent happens to have (Joyce 2001, p. 72; see also Smith 1994, p. 159; the practice of referring to an agent's set of desires with the capital 'S' derives from Williams 1981). My desires, given that I desire to care for others, will be more unified if I also gave to famine relief, which I currently have no preference for either way. John's desires, however, will be more unified if he desired to refrain from giving to famine relief, given that he desires to ignore people's plights. A *substantial* account of non-Humean rationality would be able to force John to muster a desire to give to famine relief. Think of Immanuel Kant and his requirement that rational agents test the maxim that underlies the action that they are contemplating of performing for consistency with the Categorical Imperative. But this substantial account, thinks Joyce, is not consistent with the procedural bit of non-Humean instrumentalism. So we will never get the result that *all* agents ought to muster a desire to give to the poor. If you don't have sufficiently many prosocial desires to begin with, then the procedural requirements for unity and coherence that the non-Humean instrumentalist posits, and although these requirements force you to alter some of your desires because questioning rationality is self-undermining, will never be able to oblige you to muster a desire to give to famine relief.

For Joyce, the reason that we should adopt a non-Humean instrumentalist theory of practical rationality, and not a different theory altogether, is "the theory's capacity to do better than Humean instrumentalism regarding the accommodation of prudence" (2001, p. 100n16, pp. 68–73). Joyce alludes to Thomas Nagel's argument in the *Possibility of Altruism*, according to which it is unconvincing to accept, as the Humean instrumentalist does, that if A knows that he will have a desire for X next Tuesday, then this only gives him a reason to act so as to bring about X if he now has a desire that his future self will have his desires satisfied, but not otherwise (1970). By contrast, the non-Humean instrumentalist does not require that the present agent A has the desire that his future selves will have their desires satisfied, only that if A were to be fully informed, and were to reflect carefully, then he would want his actual self to act in a way that contributes to the satisfaction of the desires of his future selves. This is a huge improvement over those desire-based theories of reasons that take any old *actual* desire to give me a reason to act and that deny that I have a reason to act if I don't have a *present* desire to perform that action.

Here is my first objection to Joyce's argument: this is a pretty weak reason to accept non-Humean instrumentalism in the present dialectical context. First, why start with prudence? True, it does seem to be important to secure the result that our theory of reasons can explain why I do have a reason now to make sure that I can perform an action later if that action furthers my well-being at that later point in time even if I do not presently desire to do what I need to do in order to be able to perform that action in the future. But by parity of reasoning, the advocate of moral success theory may insist that a similar argument obliges us to accept that a theory of practical rationality must be able to vindicate categorical moral reasons. She might argue that it would likewise be very implausible to accept a theory of reasons that cannot give us the result that I have a reason to care for you if you are in need. We need a more principled reason to accept a certain account of practical rationality over another.

Joyce offers an additional argument for non-Humean instrumentalism, which seems to be more principled. According to this argument, "the non-instrumentalist necessarily commits an error" (2001, p. 101). The error is supposed to be that it is a necessary condition on normative reasons that they must be able to motivate agents; in Bernard Williams's phrase, that all reasons must be internal (1981). But non-instrumentalism commits us to the view that there can be normative reasons that are not able to motivate us; in Williams's phrase, that there can be external reasons. And the problem is that, as Williams famously argued, we cannot make sense of reasons that we are supposed to have but that are not at least in principle able to motivate us. Now Williams does think that there is a "sound deliberative route" from desires to reasons (1981, p. 120):

> A clear example of practical reasoning is that leading to the conclusion that one has reason to φ because φ-ing would be the most convenient, economical, pleasant etc. way of satisfying some element in S ... As a result of [sound deliberation] an agent can come to see that he has reason to do something which he did not see he had reason to do at all. In this way, the deliberative process can add new actions for which there are internal reasons, just as it can also add new internal reasons for given actions. The deliberative process can also subtract elements from S. Reflections may lead the agent to see that some belief is false, and hence to realise that he has in fact no reason to do something he thought he had reason to do. More subtly, he may think he has reason to promote some development because he has not exercised his imagination enough about what it would be like if it came about. In his unaided deliberative reason, or encouraged by the persuasions of others, he may come to have some more concrete sense of

what would be involved, and lose his desire for it, just as, positively, the imagination can create new possibilities and new desires.... We should not, then, think of S as statically given. The process of deliberation can have all sorts of effect on S, and this is a fact which a theory of internal reason should be very happy to accommodate. (Williams 1981, pp. 104–5)

But what counts as sound deliberation is determined by procedural requirements, and as such Williams cannot give us categorical moral reasons. For what we need for categorical moral reasons of rationality is that every agent will have these reasons after rational reflection or 'sound deliberation', and the problem is that it is not built into the notion of sound deliberation that one must end up admitting that one has a reason to give to the poor, or to refrain from stealing.

In response to this argument, we might admit that if it is true that reasons must be able to motivate us, then reasoning must be a desire-sensitive affair and thus that we can't get categorical moral reasons. But the question is: why think that it is a necessary condition on normative reasons that they must be able to motivate us? Joyce' strategy is to discuss and reject famous objections to this aspect of Williams' view including those by Millgram (1996), Hampton (1998), and Korsgaard (1996). Moral success theorists may wish to employ one or more of these objections in order to save their theory from Joyce's error-theoretic arguments, but I will not pronounce on whether Joyce's replies to Milgram, Hampton, and Korsgaard work. For me the main problem with Joyce's argument is that his strategy is piecemeal. Perhaps it turns out that Milgram, Hampton, and Korsgaard can be defeated, but another Hampton or Korsgaard might join the ranks tomorrow and defeat Joyce's arguments.

What I would like to have is a more principled argument for the claim that there are only procedural rational requirements. And I think that we can have this argument if we *ground* the norms that ideally rational agents may and may not appeal to in determining what we should do. We mustn't rest content with *postulating* that coherence and unity matter (procedural requirements) and that the universalizability of our desires (a substantive requirement) does not matter, even if this postulation, as Joyce may well have shown, survives after sustained attacks by the likes of Hampton and Korsgaard. My own view is that we can improve Joyce's argument by giving this principled argument, which appeals to the function of our capacity to use rationality in our decision-making processes.

4.4 The Reduction of Reasons and Rational Requirements

In this section, I start my own positive defence of P2'. I argue that the *content* or *subject matter* of categorical moral reasons precludes them from existing whilst the content of epistemic and prudential reasons secures their existence. My first task is to argue that hypothetical or categorical prudential and epistemic reasons exist because they are yielded by rationality.

In §1.1, I defined reasons as considerations that speak in favour of or against performing a certain action (Parfit 1997; Scanlon 1998). John Broome writes that on "the common opinion ... rationality consists in responding correctly to reasons" (2013, p. 5). On the common opinion, in order to be rational, I ought to figure out what my reasons are, for instance by looking in the world for irreducibly normative facts, and then, importantly, I must act on my reasons, which is what responding correctly to reasons amounts to. I can do this either by forming a belief (theoretical rationality) or by forming at least an intention to act (practical rationality). But Broome "rejects" the common opinion and instead develops an account of rationality that "depends on the notion of a requirement of rationality" (2013, p. 5).

Unlike reasons, rational requirements are not considerations that speak in favour of or against performing a certain action. Instead, they govern the holding of various combinations of mental states, such as desires and beliefs, irrespective of whether one has a reason to be in these states in the first place (Broome 1999, 2013; Kolodny 2005). The most famous and most widely accepted example of a rational requirement is the instrumental principle: regardless of the content of your ends or intrinsic desires—to own a Ferrari, to travel to Paris, or to scoff at your neighbour—you are required by rationality either to take the means to your ends or else to give up your ends. Formally, and reading 'RR' as 'rationality requires that':

Instrumental Principle (IP)

> RR (if you have an intrinsic desire that p and a belief that you can bring about p by bringing about q, then either you have an instrumental desire that you bring about q or else you drop the intrinsic desire that p).

But like some reasons, rational requirements are *categorically normative*. You ought to perform the action (i.e., the mental action of either dropping your end or taking the means to attain or realize your end) that the requirement tells you to perform, and you have to do this whether you want to or not. Qua structural or metaphysical features, rational requirements are as categorically normative as categorical reasons and are therefore potential candidates for being the truth-makers of moral judgements. If, that is, we can make sense of the idea of *a rational requirement with moral content*, which the Instrumental Principle does not have, as it is a procedural and not a substantive rational requirement.

Now consider the following rational requirement, the existence of which, just like the existence of the Instrumental Principle, I have not yet argued for and which I only mention in order to explain that rational requirements, if they exist, can have categorical normative force and that they can have moral content:

Universal

> RR (if a subject has an intrinsic desire that p, then either p itself is suitably universal, or satisfying the desire that p is consistent with the satisfaction of desires whose contents are themselves suitably universal). (Smith 2010, p. 127)

Universal is a rational requirement 'with moral content' because what it requires you to do is recognizable as a moral action. Suppose that Fiona has three intrinsic desires: to provide all rational agents with adequate nutrition, to provide all rational agents with decent education, and to kick all rational agents who wear grey shoes. Universal, though it is not a *reason* because it does not consist of a consideration that speaks in favour or against doing something (such as that kicking rational agents *harms* them or that providing rational agents with adequate nutrition *benefits* them), does require Fiona to eradicate the third intrinsic desire from her set of desires 'S' in her psychology. Just as it is part of what it is to be rational is that you either take the means to your ends or abandon your ends, it is also part of what it is to be rational, says the advocate of the existence of this rational requirement, that you only keep those desires whose satisfaction is consistent with the satisfaction of other agents' desires whose content is similarly universal.

On this way of thinking about rationality, sitting down and checking one's set of intrinsic desires for compatibility with Universal is a moral action—or, if you will, a *preparatory moral action*. A preparatory moral action cleanses your set of desires in light of the rational requirements with moral content and just happens in your head, 'preparing' you for action in the world. And yet, this preparatory action is bound to have consequences in the world at some point or other. For if you no longer have the intrinsic desire to kick all rational agents who wear grey shoes, then you will no longer be able to use its motivational power to get yourself to start kicking agents with grey shoes if you encounter them. Similarly, there could be rational requirements that oblige agents to form desires to perform (rather than to refrain from performing) certain actions, where the action of forming this desire is a preparatory moral action and where acting on this desire to make a difference in the world is, if you will, a *full-blown moral action*.

So far, I have only discussed requirements of prudence and morality. But similarly, we can have rational requirements with epistemic content that require us to perform preparatory epistemic actions, such as getting rid of a desire to believe propositions solely on the basis of wishful thinking, or forming a desire to believe propositions for which we have conclusive evidence. After this, and when the moment comes that I find some conclusive evidence, I will be in a position, because I have the required motivationally efficacious desire, to believe the propositions whose truth is secured by this evidence.

Is there a reason to think that one, some, or all of these rational requirements can be grounded, such that we improve Joyce's piecemeal defence of the existence of some of them? I think there is. To see why, start with Michael Smith, who thinks that the Instrumental Principle

> is best understood in much the same way as we understand claims like 'It ought to be the case that knives cut well' ... this "ought"-claim derives from the metaphysically mundane fact that *knife* is a functional kind. (2010, p. 124; emphasis in original)

A knife is something whose function it is to cut. Given this, knives can be ordered according to how well they serve that function. Knives that cut serve that function better than knives that don't, knives that cut more efficiently serve that function better than knives that cut less efficiently, and so on. Furthermore, we can say that it ought to be the case that knives cut well "because this is nothing more than an efficient way of saying that all these evaluative claims are true" (Smith 2010, p. 125; see also Chrisman 2016, p. 214).

So, ought-claims about knives can be explained by reference to their function, which is to cut. Similarly, the Instrumental Principle can be explained by reference to the function of your psychology, which is to produce action by attaining true or at least reliable beliefs and by satisfying desires (Smith 2010, p. 125; see also Sullivan-Bissett 2017). So, psychologies can also be ordered according to how well they serve their function:

> Psychologies in which intrinsic desires combine with means-end beliefs in the way required to produce action ... better serve the function of the psychology of an agent than do those in which intrinsic desires and means-end beliefs do not combine in this way; psychologies in which intrinsic desires and means-end beliefs reliably combine in this way serve that function better than those in which they combine in this way albeit unreliably; and so on. [The Instrumental Principle], which is just an "ought"-claim about the relationship between desires and means-end beliefs, is simply an efficient way of saying that this raft of evaluative claims is true. (Smith 2010, pp. 124–5)

And—for those still worried about queerness—just as with knives and their associated ought-claims, "no Moorean non-natural qualities are required" to vindicate true ought-claims involving rational requirements (Smith 2010, p. 124). As David Copp puts it, "realism about rational requirements ... is compatible with metaphysical naturalism" (2007, p. 314). Call this theory of normativity that can explain how rationality can categorically demand the performance of actions such as preparatory moral and preparatory epistemic actions *the function theory of normativity*.

I have just grounded the Instrumental Principle as a prudential requirement in the functional profile of our psychologies. This is a reason to believe that the Instrumental Principle exists. A second example of a requirement with prudential content is:

Practical Consistency

RR (your set of desires is consistent).

Practical Consistency also enables us to satisfy our desires because a set of desires that contains mutually inconsistent desires (such as a desire to give to the poor and a desire to keep all one's money to oneself) cannot be satisfied. And so, this requirement can also be grounded in the function of our psychologies. This is a reason to believe that this rational requirement exists.

An example of an epistemic requirement is:

Conclusive Evidence

RR (you believe what you have conclusive evidence to believe).

Like the Instrumental Principle, this rational requirement enables agents to produce action through the attaining of true or at least reliable beliefs and the satisfaction of desires, in this case because it enables agents to acquire true beliefs. There may also be epistemic requirements that speak against attaining true beliefs, such as the requirement not to believe what you know will drive you insane, but that does not mean that agents are not categorically rationally obliged to act in accordance with Conclusive Evidence. It just means that the overall rational ought must weigh up the contributions of Conclusive Evidence and the other requirements before it can tell us what we should do, in an epistemic sense of should, all things considered. Rational requirements like Conclusive Evidence and Practical Consistency specify pro tanto oughts.

In sum, according to the function theory of normativity for rationality, there exist, in an ontologically innocent sense of 'exist', requirements the abiding by which enables us to form true beliefs (theoretical rationality) and to satisfy our desires (practical rationality). This is categorical rational normativity with epistemic content (Conclusive Evidence) and prudential content (Practical Consistency). Two questions are important at this point in the dialectic. First, are there categorically normative rational requirements with moral content that can be grounded in the functional profile of our psychologies? And before that, given that the truth of moral judgements depends on the truth of their presupposition to categorical moral reasons, how do we get from categorically normative rational requirements with moral content to categorical moral reasons of rationality?

I start with the second question. I agree with Mackie that if an

> agent has a reason for doing something ... his desires along with ... causal relations constitute the reason. (1977, p. 66)

For example,

> If smoking has the effects it is alleged to have, then if a heavy smoker wants to live long and be healthy, and doesn't get much enjoyment from smoking, and, if he gave it up, would not feel it much of a loss and would not switch to other indulgences, such as overeating, which were likely to be even worse for his prospects of long life and health, then he ought to give up smoking. When we put in enough factual conditions about the agent's desires and about causal, including psychologically causal, relations, the 'ought' conclusion follows. But no new relation is involved. 'Ought' ... says that the agent has a reason for doing something, but his desires along with these causal relations constitute the reason. (Mackie 1977, pp. 65–66)

The hypothetical imperative "may evaporate" if the agent changes her desires or if it turns out that what we thought was a causal means to satisfying the agent's desires is not in fact such a means (Olson 2014, p. 153). But if we do not change our desires and if we are not mistaken about what is a causal means to satisfying our desires, then this imperative has genuine normative force. I am dialectically permitted to adopt this view because I have already explained where the normativity of reasons, understood as consisting in desires and causal relations, comes from: it comes from the rational requirements that tell us which desires we can and cannot have. Another reason to adopt this theory of reasons is that it enables us to make sense of the idea, central to the practical reasoning theory of reasons, that rationality 'yields' reasons: this just means that rationality tells me which desires I should adopt, and that these desires along with the right causal relations constitute the reasons.

I could also have adopted a different theory of reasons, such as Donald Davidson's theory, according to which:

> Whenever someone does something for a reason ... he can be characterized as (a) having some sort of pro attitude toward actions of a certain kind, and (b) believing (or knowing, perceiving, noticing, remembering) that this action is of that kind. (1963, p. 685)

On this theory of reasons, reasons don't consist in desires and causal relations but in desires and other mental states. For my purposes, it does not matter much which of these two theories reasons we pick, or whether we accept a third option. What matters for my purposes is whether there exist categorically applicable rational requirements with moral content that oblige me to adopt a certain desire, and that this desire subsequently teams up with another property to constitute a categorical moral reason. Whether that further property ends up being a belief or a causal relation does not matter for me. It would matter if we could not make sense at all of the idea that desires partly constitute reasons, but it seems to me that we can and that Mackie's view is plausible.

On my view, then, *categorical* reasons are constituted by causal relations and desires that we are *rationally required* to have and regardless of any other desires that we may have. *Hypothetical* reasons are constituted by causal relations and desires that we are *rationally permitted but not required or forbidden* to have. For example, if I am rationally required to adopt the desire to give to the poor regardless of whatever else I desire, then I should have a desire to give to the poor, which, when joined with the right causal relations, means that I have a categorical moral reason to give to the poor. An example of a hypothetical reason would be you having a desire to doodle for a minute, which you are rationally permitted to have and which, if the right sort of causal relation also obtains, constitutes a reason for you to doodle, though not for me because I do not have the rationally permissible desire to doodle.

Before I continue to argue that this picture of reasons and the genesis of their categorical or hypothetical normative force leaves no room for categorical moral reasons even though it does vindicate the existence of categorical epistemic reasons, I respond to two objections. First, you might think that I am not dialectically permitted to assume this minimalist description of the function of our psychology, limited to the satisfaction of desires and the acquisition of true beliefs (Schafer 2015). For you might think that this makes it too easy to argue that there are epistemic rational requirements, since there is clearly something in the description of the function of our psychology that has something to do with epistemology, that is, getting true beliefs. And equally, you might think that this makes it too easy to argue that there are no moral rational requirements, since there is nothing in this description of the function of our psychologies that has anything to do with morality. So, you might think that to even things out, we have to say that it is also part of the description of the function of our psychologies to enable us to get along. And once we have done this, we can derive the existence of moral requirements just as easily as we can derive the existence of epistemic requirements.

In response, note that independently of your view on the plausibility of the function theory of normativity, and indeed also independently of your view on the plausibility of error theory, it is obviously plausible to assume that we have our psychologies in order to produce action through the attaining of true or at least reliable beliefs and the satisfaction of desires, and that our psychologies are malfunctioning when they fail to enable us to do this. However, it is not obviously plausible to assume that we have our psychologies in order to get along, and that our psychologies are malfunctioning when they fail to enable us to do this. For getting along is just *one way* of using your beliefs and desires to act: frustrating other people's lives as much as possible is *another way* of doing this. Action as such is more fundamental than 'moral' action. Since putting the proposed additional information into the description of what is essential to our psychologies is not as obviously plausible as saying that it is essential to our psychologies that we have them to produce action through the attaining of true or at least reliable beliefs and the satisfaction of desires, we will be begging the question against the error theorist if we do this nonetheless. Better to stick to my minimalist psychology, in which case both error theorists and success theorists have some philosophical work to do, and in which case both might still win. Success theorists need to argue that morality is entailed by this minimalist account of the purpose of our psychologies. Error theorists need to argue that such a relation of entailment does not obtain. I will argue in the next two sections that this entailment relation does not obtain, but the proposal to accept a short-cut route to moral rational requirements by broadening the description of the functional profile of our psychologies should not be accepted.

The second objection is that grounding the existence of rational requirements in the functional profile of our psychologies invites the alienation objection. The alienation objection was that even if we manage to invent all kinds of arguments for the claim that a certain normative institution exists that tells us to do something, rational agents can ask "so what?", legitimately ignore these norms, and disregard the alleged requirements as pseudo-requirements (Joyce 2001, p. 83). Joyce's solution was to postulate an ideally rational version of the agent's *actual* self that does the advising, in which case it no longer makes sense to ask 'why should I listen to this normative institution?' For you are listening to yourself. The problem is, you might think, that I accept an impersonal story about what matters: regardless of what you care about, or who you are, you must accept that you must muster a desire to believe propositions for which you have complete evidence. Why can't agents ask 'so what?' and ignore this advice?

In response, it matters what the ground of normativity is said to be. If a metaethical position entails that agents ought to take the consideration that a fact that has *nothing to do with them* constitutes a reason for them to behave in a certain way (e.g., the fact that this is an objectively prescriptive property) then, I agree, the so what question can be asked. But if you engage in an activity, such as reasoning, and if that activity gives you requirements, then you cannot ignore these requirements. Or of course, you physically can ignore these requirements, but once you ask for reasons, then you are in the activity, and bound by the rational requirements that it specifies.

The question we should now ask is whether, given that the function theory of normativity is plausible and that it allows us to vindicate the existence of categorical epistemic and prudential reasons, it also vindicates the existence of categorical moral reasons.

4.5 The Intrinsic Value of Rationality

So far, I have been quite liberal with my understanding of the content of epistemic and moral requirements. I have assumed without argument that believing propositions on the basis of conclusive evidence has to do with epistemology and that providing adequate nutrition for other rational agents has to do with morality. Should we be more precise? I don't think we should. As I explained in §2.2, relying on our ability to "know the moral when we see it" helps my opponent as much as possible (Shafer-Landau 2003, p. 80). After all, by not limiting what can count as moral content from the start, I cannot be accused of complaining that, when confronted with a good argument that rationality issues a requirement to refrain from killing animals, this does not count as a rational requirement *with moral content*. I accept that a lot of content, including this content, counts as moral content.

I have argued that rational requirements like the Instrumental Principle and various epistemic requirements like Conclusive Evidence exist, but I did not vindicate the existence of moral rational requirements, such as

Universal. I have also argued that given the description of the function of our psychologies as producing action through the attaining of true beliefs and the satisfaction of our desires, it will be difficult to ground the existence of rational requirements with moral content directly into our psychologies. After all, there is nothing in what our psychologies are there for that requires us to postulate a rational requirement with moral content. However, a number of authors have tried to argue that the existence of rational requirements without moral content *entails* the existence of rational requirements with moral content (Smith 2007, p. 285, 2009, p. 103, 2011, pp. 354–60, 2012, pp. 311–12, 2013; Sterba 2013; Parfit 1984, §55; Nagel 1970, p. 3). I discuss and reject two versions of this entailment argument for moral success theory: one in this section and one in the next. This will not establish P2' beyond all doubt. But I will present an argument for the claim that the two arguments I will dismantle are the *only two possible kinds of arguments*, and this gives us reason to think that what I say against my opponents here generalizes to other opponents who aim to revive one of these two kinds of arguments. When Joyce argued against his (and Williams's) opponents, he did not have this kind of claim about how to generalize his claims.

Here is the first version of the entailment argument for moral success theory. Consider the belief formation processes that regularly occur in agents like you and I who possess the capacity to believe propositions on the basis of conclusive evidence (facilitating this, recall, is part of the function of our psychologies). Suppose that you are in the process of inferring that q from two premises: the premise that p and the premise that p implies q. You have arrived at the following point: you have settled that p, you are in the process of settling that p implies q, and you are anticipating performing the required inference and forming the belief that q. What qualities do you have to have, *qua* believer with the capacity for rational deliberation, to believe that q on the basis of sufficient evidence? The answer is that you need to be able to *rely* on your past self who settled that p, to be *vigilant* in the moment in which you are settling that p implies q, and again to be able to *rely* on your future self to draw the inference that q (Smith 2009).

For brevity's sake, I will just focus on reliability and ignore vigilance, though everything I say applies, mutatis mutandis, to vigilance. In order to be reliable in the required sense, you require a standing desire not to irrationally interfere with your future self's rational deliberation. After all, *not* having such a desire may get you in a situation in which you find yourself believing propositions on the basis of the distorting influence of, say, wishful thinking. This gets us the following rational requirement with epistemic content:

Reliance

>RR (if you have and exercise the capacity to believe for reasons, then you desire not to irrationally interfere with your future self's deliberation).

Here is an argument for an entailment relation between Reliance and a further rational requirement with moral content:

>**First Entailment Argument**
>P5   The rational requirement Reliance exists, and protects rational deliberation as such.
>P6   If Reliance protects rational deliberation as such, then it would be *rationally arbitrary* to just protect rational deliberation *in oneself* but to refuse to protect it *in other agents*.
>P7   Rational agents don't make rationally arbitrary decisions.
>
>**No-Rational-Arbitrariness**
>RR (you don't make rationally arbitrary decisions)
>
>C3   Therefore, rational agents should protect rational deliberation in other agents
>P8   Part of what it is to respect C3 is to accept:
>
>**Reliance-Others**
>RR (if you have and exercise the capacity to believe for reasons, then you desire not to irrationally interfere with your future self's or anyone else's deliberation).
>
>C4   Therefore, Reliance-Others exists.

In other words, if we accept the existence of the non-moral rational requirement Reliance, then we are *automatically committed* to the rational requirement Reliance-Others in virtue of No-Rational-Arbitrariness and the truth of P5, according to which rationality is intrinsically valuable. I capture this with the term 'entailment' in my 'entailment argument'. And Reliance-Others has moral content because it concerns treating other agents with respect, which we can clearly recognize as moral content. So, if this argument works, moral error theory is false, as there is at least one categorical moral reason in virtue of the rational requirement Reliance-Others that categorically forces us to adopt a desire not to harm others.

But First Entailment Argument does not work. There may be a number of problems with this argument, but at least P5 should be rejected. P5 is required for the argument to go through because without it, there would be nothing rationally arbitrary about accepting Reliance but refusing to accept Reliance-Others. Rational agents could in the absence of P5 insist that by accepting Reliance but not Reliance-Others, they are simply accepting the only principle of rationality in the vicinity that can be given a naturalistically respectable grounding in the functional profile of *their own* psychology. For *their own* psychology to work, it is not necessary to see to it that *other agents'* psychologies work. The question is whether P5 is plausible. Those who wish to defend this premise may turn to Kantian moral philosophy, in which we find the idea that

> what is most important ... is not the normative significance of my *individual* rationality but rather the normative significance of rationality as such—however it is realized. (Schafer 2015, p. 698)

But whence the required support for the claim that 'what is important is the normative significance of rationality as such'? The problem with P5 is that this part is *not supported* by the function theory of normativity. True, we did say that rational requirements ought to be grounded in the function of our psychologies. We also said that *Reliance* is so grounded. But from this it does not follow that rational requirements are there to respect 'rationality as such' and thus that we can extend the defence of Reliance to Reliance-Others. Rather, it is the case that rational requirements exist if, and only if, they help us to satisfy our desire and get true beliefs. We had good reason to accept the function theory of normativity, and this theory does not lend support to P5. And without P5, First Entailment Argument fails.

4.6 From Categorical Epistemic to Categorical Moral Reasons

I turn to a different kind of entailment argument, which drops the assumption that rationality is intrinsically valuable and instead seeks to show that it is rational *for each individual rational agent* to be moral. The suggestion is that it follows directly from the epistemic requirement to believe only what we have good evidence to believe that we ought to listen to, and therefore keep alive, other agents with the capacity for rational deliberation. Recall that it is part of the function of our psychologies to produce true beliefs. But we know that agents who have the capacity for rational reflection make mistakes. Just one of many examples is that we sometimes affirm the consequent and thus fail to get a logically valid argument, for instance due to the distorting influence of the specific content of the argument, and we also know that if agents with the capacity for rational reflection work together, they are less likely to make these mistakes (Cheng and Holyoak 1989). So, you might think: it is rational for agents with the capacity for rational deliberation to work together. And this is so not because there is something intrinsically good about rationality *as such* but because respecting other agents' capacity for rationality improves our *individual* psychologies' ability to perform their function of collecting true beliefs. No need for P5. We just work with whatever the error theorist who accepts the function theory of normativity is happy to work with (viz., categorical epistemic reasons), and still we get a moral success theory. After all, an individual agent can achieve the kind of cooperation that decreases the chance that she herself erroneously affirms the consequent by following:

Respect

> RR (if you have and exercise the capacity to believe for reasons, then you desire to respect other agents' capacity for rational deliberation).

For by respecting other rational agents I can use their rationality and let them teach me how to avoid affirming the consequent. And Respect has content that we can recognize as moral content because it requires us to eradicate intrinsic desires for, say, killing other rational agents.

However, it is possible that individual agents all by themselves abide by all the non-moral rational requirements that can be grounded in their psychologies. This will also enable them to perform their function, as in that case they will also not affirm the consequent, at least if they follow:

Not-Affirm-Consequent

RR (if you have and exercise the capacity to believe for reasons, then you refrain from affirming the consequent).

But in that case, these agents will no longer *need* to respect rationality that is instantiated in other agents in order to maximize the number of true beliefs they obtain. They can just follow all the individual non-moral rational requirements like Not-Affirm-Consequent. From the point of view of their own psychologies, they can let others perish or indeed actively contribute to their demise, for even without other agents any single individual agent can attain all true beliefs by following Not-Affirm Consequent. No need to affirm Respect and therefore no need to abandon error theory.

Note that this does not mean that most agents will as a matter of fact, or even ought to, actively contribute to the demise of other agents, for most agents have a standing desire to care for others and to refrain from hurting others. And everyone is required by the Instrumental Principle either to take the means to satisfy this desire or else to drop the desire, and it is very unlikely that this desire will be dropped. The point here is that for the vindication of morality we need categorical normativity, but this argument does not give us such normativity.

In light of my objection to this second entailment argument, the advocate of a moral success theory can retreat but insist that it is true that we have more than one way to enable our psychology to perform its function. The options are (a) just follow Respect, (b) just follow Not-Affirm-Consequent, or (c) follow both. And perhaps we should decide to follow, say, (a) just Respect, in which case moral success theory seems to follow.

Unfortunately for the success theorists, it is not clear that we should pick (a). First compare (a) to (b). Which requirement best allows our psychologies to perform their function? Suppose you decide to follow (a). What happens if all the other rational agents you now need for your own psychology to perform its function lose their ability to recognize instances of affirming the consequent? The answer is that your own psychology will no longer be able to perform its function, as you counted on other agents to help you spot situations in which you affirm the consequent. Better not take chances and pick (b) or (c). So, compare accepting (b) to accepting (c). As it is difficult to internalize all the rational requirements such as Not-Affirm-Consequent that govern belief-formation processes (logic is difficult and time is limited, after all), and given that there is a *chance* that you find another agent who can help you to avoid affirming the consequent, it seems that you are better off keeping other agents alive, just so that you can benefit from their insights when you need them. This line of reasoning justifies accepting (c).

But how do you know whether the agents whose advice you trust give you *good* advice? Suppose one agent you meet, and whom you diligently kept alive, says: 'believe *x*, not *y*, because in going for *x* you affirm the consequent and in going for *y* you apply modus ponens'. Why follow her and not another agent who says: 'believe *y*, not *x*, because in going for *y* you affirm the consequent and in going for *x* you apply modus ponens'? The answer is: you can only know this if you yourself *already* appreciate the non-moral rational requirements that matter for belief-formation, such as Not-Affirm-Consequent, and when you yourself already know when to apply this requirement. But then it makes much more sense to focus on internalizing those non-moral requirements, and again in order to enable yourself to do this you do not have to rely on others.

The friend of this kind of moral success theory may retreat once more and admit that there is no rational requirement like Respect, which just requires agents to not disrespect others. But she might insist that a rational requirement in which we find both non-moral and moral content within the scope of the 'rationality requires that' operator can be defended. For instance, reconsider:

Reliance-Others

RR (if you have and exercise the capacity to believe for reasons, then you desire not to irrationally interfere with your future self's or anyone else's deliberation).

The argument will be that we should go for Reliance-Others rather than Reliance because with the former we take on board the chance that others help us to correct our reasoning when they give us *good* advice. But if that is the argument that is supposed to vindicate the existence of Reliance-Others from the perspective of helping individual psychologies to perform their function of getting true beliefs as well as possible, then we still need an external criterion for deciding whether the advice that other agents offers is in fact helpful. And for this we need to abide by all the non-moral rational requirements, including Not-Affirm-Consequent, in which case we are already doing everything right—we are already allowing our psychologies to perform their function—and we don't need others. In sum, we don't need to accept a rational requirement like Reliance-Others. The second entailment argument also fails.

These two entailment arguments are the only kinds of entailment arguments that we can have. Either moral rational requirements are entailed by other requirements and the value of rationality itself or they are just entailed by other requirements. My objection against the first entailment argument was that postulating the value of rationality for all was not justified by the function theory of normativity, and so it seems that there cannot be other versions of this kind of argument against my view. This objection can be generalized. My objection against the second entailment argument can also be generalized, for it seems that every argument that appeals to a need to keep other agents alive because they can help us to become better reasoners (such as an argument from the epistemic value of reliance or an argument from that of vigilance) will require this agent to first separate the good reasoners from the imposters. And that just requires the agent to become a better reasoner herself, by accepting the rational requirements there are, and simply does not require her to accept prosocial requirements like Respect that demand the performance of preparatory moral actions.

We have good reason to deny that moral requirements can be grounded in the functional profile of agents itself, to deny that we can vindicate their existence by postulating the intrinsic value of rationality as such, and to deny that these requirements are entailed by non-moral requirements. We also have good reason to accept the function theory of normativity and that my objections to entailment arguments from epistemic to moral requirements generalize. I conclude that we have good reason to deny that there are rational requirements with moral content. At this point in the dialectic, the moral error theorist's antagonist often switches tack to a companions-in-guilt objection. But, I will now argue, such an objection is not plausible.

4.7 The Companions-in-Guilt Objection

Consider the companions-in-guilt objection to moral error theory (Stratton-Lake 2002; Cuneo 2007; Lillehammer 2007; Rowland 2013, 2016; Das 2016, 2017):

Companions-in-Guilt Objection (CGO)

> If the arguments for the moral error theory are sufficient to establish that the moral error theory is true, then those arguments are sufficient to establish that the epistemic error theory is true (the parity premise). The epistemic error theory is false (the epistemic existence premise). So, the arguments for the moral error theory are not sufficient to establish that the moral error theory is true. (Cowie 2014, p. 408)

Both the parity premise and the epistemic existence premise are widely accepted. For instance, about the first premise, Philip Stratton-Lake writes:

> The difference between [moral] and epistemic reasons is not that they stand in different warranting relations to certain things (one relation queer and

the other innocuous), but that they warrant different things. [Moral] reasons warrant pro-attitudes and sanctions whereas epistemic reasons warrant beliefs. If, therefore, one has doubts about the normative (warranting) relation itself, these doubts could not be localized in such a way as to avoid scepticism about epistemic as well as [moral] reasons. (2002, p. xxvi; see also Bedke 2010, p. 56)

And in defence of the second premise, Terence Cuneo has presented a number of arguments, including the argument that without epistemic reasons, moral error theory becomes dialectically toothless (2007, pp. 117–18). More recently, Richard Rowland has argued that if we deny the epistemic existence premise, then we must accept the implausible consequence that no one knows anything (2013, p. 13).

My own reply to this objection is that we must deny the parity premise. This is because although I agree with the likes of Stratton-Lake that there is no *metaphysical* difference between moral and epistemic reasons, their difference *in content* means that the former reasons don't exist, whereas the latter do. It is not true that if there are no categorical moral reasons, then there are no categorical epistemic reasons. For after all, what we use to deny the existence of reasons is not their metaphysical structure or ontological commitment, but just whether they are 'yielded' by rationality. There is nothing queer about categorical reasons as such, it is just that epistemic reasons are yielded by rationality but that moral reasons are not.

This reply is better than the existing replies currently on offer. For instance, Bart Streumer denies the parity premise on the basis that we should accept an error theory of normativity as such, including epistemic and moral normativity (2013, 2017). There are many things we could say about this metanormative position but because it entails abandoning the kind of local moral error theory that I defend in favour of a different error theory, and because I have my own reply the CGO that does not require me to abandon my local moral error theory, I ignore Streumer's theory in what follows.

Christopher Cowie has two responses to the CGO, both of which are in keeping with a local moral error theory. But his responses are different from mine, and less plausible. First, Cowie argues that the CGO could not possibly work because it faces the following dilemma. Either the advocate of the CGO shows that there is a disparity between moral and epistemic reasons such that the latter "have some special property" that moral reasons don't have and that gives us a reason to accept that epistemic reasons exist (Cowie 2014, p. 412). The problem with this response, says Cowie, is that it denies the parity, which so obviously holds between moral and epistemic discourse. Or else we accept the parity, but then the CGO becomes dialectically redundant (Cowie 2014, p. 415). This is, Cowie thinks, because we will then need a direct argument against epistemic reasons, such as a Moorean argument according to which the obviousness of the existence of epistemic properties defeats any philosophical argument to the contrary. But if this argument works, then appealing to the CGO has become superfluous.

There are many aspects to Cowie's discussion that should be commended, but I don't think that this is a good response to the CGO (also see Rowland 2016; Das 2016, 2017). There are problems with each of the horns of his dilemma. The problem with the first horn is that it requires us to take a stance on the thorny issue of whether epistemic reasons are somehow more naturalistically respectable than moral reasons. We might think that there is an ontologically unproblematic property—true belief—which plays a central role in epistemic discourse, such that something cannot qualify as epistemic discourse without being connected to that property. And we might think that, by contrast, there seems to be no such uncontentious candidate in the case of moral discourse. There does not seem to be an ontologically innocent property, or set of properties, such that something does not count as moral discourse unless this property plays a central role in it (Fletcher 2017). My error theory and the response to the CGO that it invites is better than the error theory that Cowie has in mind and that uses an existence theory of reasons because my error theory avoids this entire metaphysical conundrum. It agrees that there is nothing metaphysically problematic about categorical reasons, be they moral or epistemic, and just asks: which reasons are yielded by rationality?

The main problem with the second horn of Cowie's dilemma is that it is not true that the CGO is redundant in a discussion about the existence of moral and epistemic reasons once we accept the parity thesis. This depends on the details of the dialectic. For example, in the absence of a working Moorean argument (or any direct argument against the existence of moral and/or epistemic properties for that matter) we might decide to employ David Enoch's method of tallying plausibility points and use the CGO as a tiebreaker (Enoch 2011, p. 267). We can imagine a dialectical situation in which the arguments for and against a moral success theory and for and against an epistemic success theory entail that we ought to be epistemic success theorists, but that they don't swing us either way on whether we should be moral error theorists. The CGO, if it works, can help us decide in that case, compelling us to become moral success theorists. Therefore, it remains important to show, as I think I can, that the CGO doesn't work at all, in which case it also cannot be used just as a tiebreaker.

Cowie also has a second and different "Master Argument" against the CGO, which takes the form of a different dilemma (Cowie 2016, p. 126). Cowie asks: what are categorical epistemic reasons? There are two options, he says. On the first horn, epistemic reasons are merely evidential support relations, that is, relations which are not normative (and whose relata are also not normative) such that they merely indicate a probability-raising relation that holds between some evidence and a hypothesis. In this case, the parity premise is false, for although epistemic reasons might be (merely) evidential support relations, moral reasons need to be normative, and indeed categorically normative. On the second horn, epistemic reasons are not simply non-normative evidential support relations and are, like moral reasons, categorically normative. But then we cannot get the existence of epistemic reasons in the CGO due to the queerness of such relations.

It is especially the previous sentence that spells trouble for Cowie's argument. Cowie repeats a number of times that wielding a successful CGO "requires ... establishing the epistemic existence premise (in the dialectical context)" (2016, p. 117). And the dialectical context legislates, he thinks, that we cannot beg the question against the error theorist. Cowie reasons as follows: the error theorist has arguments against the existence of irreducible normativity, thus anyone who claims without adequate defence that there is such normativity makes an impermissible, unfair move in the discussion. But I think that it is precisely unfair to demand that the critic of error theory must have in hand an argument that establishes the existence of epistemic reasons before this discussion starts. The whole point of the CGO is that it enables us to look at the *consequence* of claiming that the error theorist is right that there are no categorical moral reasons. This argument of Cowie's is therefore also not convincing. Better, I think, to accept my response to the CGO, which is to insist that there is nothing metaphysically troubling about either moral or epistemic reasons but that there fails to be a relevant parity between them because what matters is whether these reasons are yielded by rationality and, unfortunately, moral reasons are not yielded by rationality.

The availability of a reply to the CGO consistent with my argument in the previous sections gives us further reason to accept:

P2'   The claim that there are categorical moral reasons is false.

Before concluding with a formulation of the specific argument for error theory that I have now been able to defend on the basis of the Generic Argument for Error Theory that I presented in §1.1, I will first, in the next section, discuss and reject some additional objections to my moral error theory. These objections do not target a specific premise in the argument. They also apply to other versions of moral error theory, but at this point in the dialectic, these versions of error theory are not as plausible as my error theory, and so my defence of moral error theory against these objections will use the resources of my formulation of error theory.

4.8   Other Objections

First, consider the principle of epistemic conservatism:

> a person is to some degree justified in retaining a given belief just because that person has that belief. (Daly and Liggins 2010, p. 223)

This is an argument against error theory if (a) the principle is true and if (b) the degree of justification we have for the belief that morality exists before we started doing metaethics is greater than the degree of justification we have in the error theory after we have done metaethics. In response, error theorists can either claim that the principle of epistemic conservatism carries no weight at all or that it carries some weight (Huemer 2005, p. 99; Daly and Liggins 2010, p. 223). The former, hard-line response is possible, but it is difficult to defend, and error theorists don't need to defend it. Instead, they can accept that the principle carries some weight but insist that the balance of evidence favours error theory nonetheless. The book as such is an argument for the view that the balance of reasons favours my view.

The second objection starts from the observation that if we do philosophy, we are trying to reach a reflective equilibrium between our pre-theoretical beliefs about various things on the one hand and the theories we construct to explain these things on the other hand. The objection is that error theory can never feature in such a reflective equilibrium because it denies that some pre-theoretical beliefs, such as the belief that stealing is wrong, are true (Daly and Liggins 2010, p. 216). This objection fails as well. It asserts on unwarranted a priori grounds that no reflective equilibrium that contains error theory is forthcoming.

Third, consider the following maxim of honesty:

> never put forward a ... theory ... you cannot yourself believe in your least philosophical and most commonsensical moments. (Lewis 1986, p. 135)

On the basis of this maxim we can formulate what I call the objection from honesty. On the assumption that we cannot believe error theory in our least philosophical and most commonsensical moments, it supports the view that we shouldn't believe error theory at all. We should not underestimate what we can bring ourselves to believe. Indeed, unless there is countervailing evidence, we should take those philosophers who claim that they believe moral error theory and other "unbelievable" claims, such as the compositional nihilist's claim that there are no chairs, at their word (Merricks 2001). Charles Pigden writes, "Absent brain injury or massive self-deception, I am the best authority on what I believe, and I can assure you that I believe something that can reasonably be described as ... the error theory" (2007, p. 441). I concur, and take this to be sufficient reason to reject the third objection.

The final objection is that error theorists must adopt a view on the modal status of their theory, but that whichever view they take, their theory is implausible. The question is: is error theory a necessary truth (i.e., are categorical moral reasons absent from all possible worlds) or is it a contingent truth (i.e., are categorical moral reasons only absent from this and perhaps some other but not all possible worlds)? The problem with the view that it is a necessary truth is that it cries out for an explanation why the folk nevertheless believe in morality. The problem with the other view is that it seems to make it possible for us to introduce moral properties into the actual world by improving our capacity for rational deliberation (Kalf 2015, pp. 1871–1872). And that would mean that our error theory is insufficiently stable: after learning the truth of error theory, we simply make the required changes in the actual world so that it becomes sufficiently like a nearby world in which there are moral properties, and moral properties will be instantiated in our world.

However, I think that neither horn is plausible. As has often been noted, especially by error theorists, evolution can explain why so many of us have the strong belief that some actions are morally right or wrong even though there is nothing that can be the truth-maker of the judgements we use to formulate the thought that these actions have moral properties (Joyce 2001, Ch. 6, 2006; Ruse 1998; Street 2006). The first horn of the dilemma is not a problem for error theorist. I however believe that moral properties are only contingently non-existent. Had we evolved differently—with a psychology the proper function of which is to enable us to get along with others and that grounds categorical moral reasons—then we would have had categorical moral reasons in this world. I am happy to admit that the world in which we did evolve differently exists (see, e.g., Lewis 1986). But this world it is not our world. Moreover, given my function theory of normativity, the world in which there are moral facts cannot be reached easily. Things would have been different if, as I suggested in an earlier paper, the existence of moral facts depends on whether rational agents *converge on* what the moral facts are but in which people are too tired or lethargic to do the reasoning, as Michael Smith and Hallvard Lillehammer have argued (Smith 1994, p. 84; Lillehammer 2004, p. 84; Kalf 2015, p. 1871). For in that case, all we'd need to do to introduce moral properties in the actual world is improve the conditions for rational convergence on moral issues, for example better education, better nutrition, and so on. But my claim is that the existence of moral facts depends on whether they can be grounded in the functional profile of our psychologies. And a world in which we change the functional profile of our psychologies is much harder to reach, for how should we alter the course of evolution after this has already taken shape? I conclude that the modal objection is not a strong objection to moral error theory either.

4.9 Conclusion

In this chapter I have argued that there are no categorical moral reasons. This means that my Generic Argument for Error Theory has now been made fully specific, as follows.

Specific Argument for Error Theory

P1***   Moral judgements pragmatically presuppose the claim that there are categorical moral reasons.
P2'   The claim that there are categorical moral reasons is false.
P3'   If moral judgements pragmatically presuppose a false claim, then they are neither true nor false.
C1'   Therefore, moral judgements are neither true nor false (from P***1, P2', P3').
P4'   If C1', then we should accept error theory of moral discourse as a whole.
C2   Therefore, we should accept error theory of moral discourse as a whole (from C1', P4').

This concludes the first part of this book, which aimed to defend moral error theory.

The question I will address in part II is: what should we do with moral discourse after moral error theory (Lutz 2014)? In Chap. 5, I will argue against every answer to this question that I am aware of, except one. The exception will be discussed, and defended, in Chap. 6. In Chap. 7, I apply my overall moral theory (viz., presupposition and rationality error theory combined with my preferred answer to the now what question) to a pressing problem in contemporary political philosophy and normative ethics, offering a preliminary discussion of what implications the view might have in this area of practical philosophy.

References

Bedke, M.S. 2010. Might All Normativity Be Queer? *Australasian Journal of Philosophy* 88: 41–58.

Brink, D.O. 1984. Moral Realism and the Skeptical Arguments from Disagreement and Queerness. *Australian Journal of Philosophy* 62: 111–125.

Broome, J. 1999. Normative Requirements. *Ratio* 12: 398–419.

———. 2013. *Rationality Through Reasoning*. Oxford: OUP.

Cheng, P.W., and K.J. Holyoak. 1989. Pragmatic Reasoning Schemas. *Cognitive Psychology* 17: 397–416.

Chrisman, M. 2016. *The Meaning of Ought*. Oxford: OUP.

Copp, D. 2007. *Morality in a Natural World*. Cambridge: CUP.

Cowie, C. 2014. Why Companions in Guilt Arguments Won't Work. *The Philosophical Quarterly* 64: 407–422.

———. 2016. Good News for Moral Error Theorists; A Master Argument Against Companions in Guilt Strategies. *Australasian Journal of Philosophy* 94: 115–130.

Cuneo, C. 2007. *The Normative Web*. Oxford: OUP.

Daly, C., and D. Liggins. 2010. In Defence of Error Theory. *Philosophical Studies* 149: 209–230.

Das, R. 2016. Why Companions in Guilt Arguments Still Work: Reply to Cowie. *The Philosophical Quarterly* 66: 417–435.

———. 2017. Bad News for Moral Error Theorists: There Is No Master Argument Against Companions in Guilt Strategies. *Australasian Journal of Philosophy* 95: 58–69.

Davidson, D. 1963. Actions, Reasons, and Causes. *Journal of Philosophy* 60: 685–699.

Enoch, D. 2011. *Taking Morality Seriously*. Oxford: OUP.

Fletcher, G. 2017. Pain for the Moral Error Theorist? A New Companions-in-Guilt Argument. *Australasian Journal of Philosophy* Online First.

Garner, R. 1990. On the Genuine Queerness of Moral Properties and Facts. *Australasian Journal of Philosophy* 68: 137–146.
Hampton, J. 1998. *The Authority of Reason*. Cambridge: CUP.
Huemer, M. 2005. *Ethical Intuitionism*. London: Palgrave Macmillan.
Joyce, R. 2001. *The Myth of Morality*. Cambridge: CUP.
———. 2006. *The Evolution of Morality*. Cambridge, MA: MIT Press.
———. 2013. Irrealism and the Genealogy of Morals. *Ratio* 26: 351–372.
Kahane, G. 2013. Must Metaethical Realism Make a Semantic Claim? *Journal of Moral Philosophy* 10: 148–178.
Kalf, W.F. 2015. Are Moral Properties Impossible? *Philosophical Studies* 172: 1869–1887.
Kolodny, N. 2005. Why Be Rational? *Mind* 114: 509–564.
Korsgaard, D. 1996. *The Sources of Normativity*. Cambridge: CUP.
Lewis, D.K. 1986. *On the Plurality of Worlds*. Oxford: Basil Blackwell.
Lillehammer, H. 2004. Moral Error Theory. *Proceedings of the Aristotelian Society* 104: 95–111.
———. 2007. *Companions in Guilt*. London: Palgrave Macmillan.
Lutz, M. 2014. The 'Now What' Problem for Error Theory. *Philosophical Studies* 171: 351–371.
Mackie, J.L. 1977. *Ethics: Inventing Right and Wrong*. Harmondsworth: Penguin Publishers.
Merricks, T. 2001. *Objects and Persons*. Oxford: OUP.
Millgram, E. 1996. Williams' Argument Against External Reasons. *Nous* 30: 197–220.
Nagel, T. 1970. *The Possibility of Altruism*. Princeton: Princeton University Press.
Olson, J. 2014. *Moral Error Theory: History, Critique, Defence*. Oxford: OUP.
Parfit, D. 1984. *Reasons and Persons*. Oxford: OUP.
———. 1997. Reasons and Motivation. *Proceedings of the Aristotelian Society* 71 (Suppl): 99–130.
Pigden, C. 2007. Nihilism, Nietzsche and the Doppelganger Problem. *Ethical Theory and Moral Practice* 10: 414–456.
Platts, M. 1980. Moral Reality and the End of Desire. In *Reference, Truth and Reality*, ed. Platts, 69–82. London: Routledge & Kegan Paul.
Rowland, R. 2013. Moral Error Theory and the Argument from Epistemic Reasons. *Journal of Ethics and Social Philosophy* 7: 1–24.
———. 2016. Rescuing Companions in Guilt Arguments. *The Philosophical Quarterly* 66: 161–171.
Ruse, M. 1998. *Taking Darwin Seriously*. New York: Blackwell.

Scanlon, T.M. 1998. *What We Owe to Each Other*. Harvard: Belknap Press.
Schafer, K. 2015. Realism and Constructivism in Kantian Metaethics (1): The Kantian Conception of Rationality and Rationalist Constructivism. *Philosophy Compass* 10: 690–701.
Shafer-Landau, R. 2003. *Moral Realism*. Oxford: Clarendon Press.
Shepski, L. 2008. The Vanishing Argument from Queerness. *Australasian Journal of Philosophy* 86: 371–387.
Smith, M. 1994. *The Moral Problem*. Oxford: OUP.
———. 2007. Is There a Nexus Between Reasons and Rationality? In *Moral Psychology*, ed. S. Tenenbaum, 279–298. Amsterdam: Rodopi.
———. 2009. Desires, Values, Reasons, and the Dualism of Practical Reason. *Ratio* 22: 98–125.
———. 2010. Beyond the Error Theory. In *A World Without Values*, ed. R. Joyce and S. Kirchin, 119–140. Dordrecht: Springer.
———. 2011. Deontological Moral Obligations and Non-Welfarist Agent-Relative Values. *Ratio* 24: 351–363.
———. 2012. Naturalism, Absolutism, Relativism. In *Ethical Naturalism: Current Debates*, ed. S. In Nuccetelli and G. Seay, 226–244. Cambridge: CUP.
———. 2013. A Constitutivist Theory of Reasons: Its Promise and Parts. *Law, Ethics, and Philosophy* 1: 9–30.
Sterba, J.P. 2013. *From Rationality to Equality*. Oxford: OUP.
Stratton-Lake, P. 2002. Introduction. In *The Right and the Good*, ed. P. Stratton-Lake and W.D. Ross, ix–lviii. Oxford: OUP.
Street, S. 2006. A Darwinian Dilemma for Realist Theories of Value. *Philosophical Studies* 127: 109–166.
Streumer, B. 2013. Can We Believe the Error Theory? *Journal of Philosophy* 110: 194–212.
———. 2017. *Unbelievable Errors*. Oxford: OUP.
Sullivan-Bissett, E. 2017. Biological Function and Epistemic Normativity. *Philosophical Explorations* 20, Online First.
Williams, B. 1981. *Moral Luck*. Cambridge: CUP.

Part II

Normative Ethics

5

Some Solutions to the Now What Problem

5.1 Introduction

In part I of this book, I argued that moral error theory is plausible. In part II of this book, I switch tack from arguing for moral error theory to solving the now what problem (Chaps. 5 and 6) and applying the resulting set of views (error theory and my answer to the now what question) to one problem in political philosophy in order to further corroborate my claim that we can continue to use moral language fruitfully after moral error theory, even when we focus on a topic that does not belong to normative ethics proper (Chap. 7). A final chapter summarizes my argument in the entire book and considers some of the work that lies ahead for moral error theorists (Chap. 8).

The now what problem is the practical problem of what to do with moral discourse after error theory. As I explained in §1.1, although Matt Lutz invented the term the "now what problem", this problem has been with us at least since Mackie (Lutz 2014, p. 351; Mackie 1977, pp. 105–239). Jussi Suikkanen formulates the now what problem as a question, that is, the 'now what question':

in the case that one accepts ... moral error theory, what ... should happen to one's first-order moral thought? (2013, p. 172)

Stephen Ingram provides a different formulation of this question:

If error theory is true, an obvious question arises ... What should we do with moral discourse and moral judgement once we realise that they fail to refer to anything real? (2015, p. 28)

The difference between these two formulations of the now what question is that Suikkanen is only concerned with what should happen with our moral thought after error theory, whereas Ingram asks what should happen with both moral language (which he refers to as moral discourse) and moral thought (which he refers to as moral judgement). As I will explain, it is adamant for a successful answer to the now what question that we know both what we should do with our moral thought after error theory and what we should do with our moral language after error theory. Therefore, in what follows, I use Ingram's formulation of the now what question. For purely stylistic reasons, I switch between referring to the now what problem and the now what question, bearing in mind that although the one is formulated as a problem and the other as a question, what matters is the issue of what to do with moral language and thought after error theory.

In this chapter, I consider every solution to the now what problem except one, which I discuss in the next chapter. None of the answers that I discuss in this chapter is plausible, but the only answer that's left, and which I discuss in the next chapter, is plausible. The answers that I discuss in this and the next chapter all take the form of a *prescriptive* metaethical theory (which I will also sometimes call a *revolutionary* or *revisionary* metaethical theory) rather than a *descriptive* metaethical theory.

Descriptive metaethical theories, among which we find the error theory, should be assessed according to how well they accommodate the various properties of our actual moral thought and talk, such as its truth-aptness and motivational efficacy (the internal accommodation project), and according to whether the philosophical commitments they invoke about metaphysics, semantics, and the like are defensible (the external accommodation project) (Timmons 1999, p. 12; Southwood 2010, pp. 8–9). As I explained in Part I, error theorists argue that a well-executed internal accommodation project shows that categorical moral reasons of rationality are required for morality and that a well-executed external accommodation project shows that there are no such reasons.

Prescriptive metaethical theories set a norm for how we ought to use moral thought and moral language after error theory, and should be assessed according to how well they secure practical advantages and avoid theoretical disadvantages (Svoboda 2017, p. 50). For prescriptive metaethical theories, the internal project is not to give an account of moral discourse as it actually is, but to account for moral discourse as it should be. A prescriptive theory's external accommodation project is identical to the external accommodation project that descriptive metaethical theories have, that is, to ensure that its semantic, metaphysical, and epistemological commitments are defensible. Prescriptive metaethical theories have with one exception always taken the form of answers to the now what question, and therefore assume the truth of moral error theory. The exception is Stephen Ingram's argument that robust realists should be abolitionists because that puts them in a better position to ensure that people act in accordance with their moral obligations (Ingram 2015). However, in this chapter, I am only concerned with prescriptive metaethical theories as answers to the now what question.

What are the practical advantages that a prescriptive metaethical theory should be able to secure if we accepted it as our norm for how to approach our first-order moral discourse after error theory? More generally, what are the assessment criteria with which we should judge the various prescriptive metaethical theories on offer? I answer this question in the next section (§5.2). In the remainder of this chapter, I argue that every existing answer to the now what question except one is implausible. I first discuss revolutionary fictionalism, according to which we should pretend that morality exists, either by make-believing moral propositions or by believing moral propositions that have been prefixed with a fictionalist operator to get a proposition like 'in the moral fiction, giving to the poor is morally obligatory' (§5.3). Second, I assess revolutionary expressivism, which says that we should use moral language to express non-truth-apt conative states like desires rather than, as we currently do, truth-apt beliefs (§5.5). Third, I consider conservationism, which says that we should conserve moral discourse as it is even though it contains the error (§5.5). Finally, I discuss abolitionism, according to which we should abolish moral discourse (§5.6). There is also the propagandist option, according to which we should hide the truth about error theory from the folk and according to which the *cognoscenti* should adopt any of the prescriptive metaethical theories just mentioned or else the theory I discuss in the next chapter. However, I will discuss the propagandist view only in relation to the successful prescriptive metaethical theory that I will discuss in the next chapter. This is because propagandism is a disjunctive view (the *cognoscenti* should accept a particular prescriptive theory and the folk should not know about error theory or the now that question at all), and for this view to be acceptable, both disjuncts have to be acceptable. But since I will argue in this chapter that none of the views mentioned above is acceptable for anyone, including the *cognoscenti*, we can already reject these versions of propagandism. A conclusion summarizes my main findings (§5.7). The next chapter discusses, and defends, substitutionism, according to which we should substitute our error-riddled moral discourse that expresses untrue beliefs about categorical moral reasons for a discourse that expresses true beliefs about hypothetical "schmoral" reasons (Joyce 2007, p. 51).

Some philosophers fail to recognize one or more of these prescriptive metaethical theories as potential answers to the now what question. For instance, Jussi Suikkanen discusses abolitionism, fictionalism, and conservationism, and writes that these are the "only ... possible answers to this question" (2013, p. 172). I do not claim to have exhausted the logical space of possibilities when it comes to formulating prescriptive metaethical theories. But I do think that I have covered every answer to the now what question that has so far been discussed in the literature.

5.2 Assessment Criteria for Prescriptive Metaethical Theories

In Chap. 4, I argued that the non-existence of moral reasons does not entail the non-existence of epistemic or prudential reasons. So, after moral error theory, there are reasons that constrain what we are permitted to believe (theoretical reasons remain in existence) and there are reasons that constrain what we are permitted to do (practical reasons remain in existence). It is just that the set of practical reasons has shrunk in size, from containing at least moral and prudential reasons to containing at least prudential but no moral reasons ('at least' because I don't want to rule out the possibility that, for instance, aesthetic reasons are practical reasons and that they exist). The task for the moral error theorist is to figure out what she has most reason to do with moral discourse after error theory, given that prudential and epistemic reasons exist and moral reasons do not exist. I think that this is already a formidable task, and I will therefore not consider aesthetic or any other kinds of reasons, such as legal reasons.

Toby Svoboda writes that the relative plausibility of prescriptive metaethical theories should be assessed by

> comparing their respective theoretical advantages and disadvantages. Advantages include possessing the conceptual means to avoid moral error while retaining useful features, such as the ability to allow and to account for moral motivation, moral disagreement, and moral reasoning. These features are useful at least in the sense that they are conducive to desires, goals, and projects many human beings have. Disadvantages include lacking the conceptual means to avoid moral error or to secure one or more of the useful features of morality. (2017, p. 55)

Svoboda defines "moral error" as the mistake of accepting a false moral belief, or uttering a false moral judgement (Svoboda 2017, p. 55). I agree that the ability to avoid moral error is a good-making feature of a prescriptive metaethical theory. After all, if a prescriptive metaethical theory tells us to start using moral discourse in a way that commits us to accepting false beliefs, then we have an epistemic reason to doubt that it is the best answer to the now what question. For as I argued in the previous chapter, we are epistemically required not to accept false beliefs (whether this is sufficient reason to reject conservationism will be discussed in §5.6).

However, I don' think that Svoboda has done enough to justify his claim that a prescriptive metaethical theory's ability to secure moral motivation, moral disagreement, and moral reasoning is a reason to accept this theory as a plausible answer to the now what question. He does say that retaining moral motivation, moral disagreement, and moral reasoning is conducive to desire, goals, and projects that many human beings have. But before we can assess whether these things are indeed useful, we first need to know what we want and what we desire. For once we know in sufficient detail what we want, it may *not* be the case that we need to continue to use a (surrogate) moral discourse that gives us motivation, moral disagreement, or moral reasoning, where this 'or' is an inclusive or. This is because, as Mackie aptly put it, it is not "obvious that what is conventionally accepted as morality is exactly what is required" to be able to see to it that our desires are satisfied and that we can engage in the projects that we find worthwhile and that give meaning to our lives (1977, p. 121). This is why Mackie says that after moral error theory:

> morality is not to be discovered but to be made; we cannot brush this aside by adding 'but it has been made already, long ago'. It may well need to be in part remade. (1977, p. 123)

So what do we desire? I think that most of us have the *non-derivative* desire to live in a world in which we cooperate and benefit from this cooperation; a world in which there is ample room for the enjoyment of the fruits of our labour and in which we acknowledge that this sometimes requires us to make sacrifices (e.g., refraining from stealing from others) for the greater good of a safe world to live in. Mackie writes that we desire to live in a world with "mutually beneficial cooperation" (1977, p. 111). I call this desire *the fundamental desire*. The world that we fundamentally desire to live in is the *opposite* of the world described by Hobbes as the state of nature, a state in which there is no morality:

> In such condition, there is no place for Industry; because the fruit thereof is uncertain; and consequently no Culture of the Earth; no Navigation, nor use of the commodities that may be imported by Sea; no commodious Building; no Instruments of moving, and removing such things as require much force; no Knowledge of the face of the Earth; no account of Time; no Arts; no Letters; no Society. (1651, p. 89)

The fundamental desire provides the best fit with the "desires, goals, and projects many human beings have" (Svoboda 2017, p. 55). Whether we can reach our goals and projects of rearing a family, spending quality leisure time with loved ones, and developing our talents depends on whether we can get ourselves sufficiently often to perform actions that contribute to the satisfaction of this fundamental desire. After all, not cooperating means no society and no commodious living, and that in turn means that it will be harder to reach your goals.

My description of the fundamental desire is, of course, a simplification. To give just one example, I also deeply desire to live in a world in which animals do not suffer as a result of our preference for certain kinds of food, but actions that contribute to the satisfaction of this desire do not necessarily contribute to the satisfaction of the fundamental desire. To see this, imagine a world in which everyone knows that we get fantastic mutually beneficial cooperation on the condition that we torture our animals. I will simply ignore these kinds of complications here. Given the space I have available, I will not be able to figure out exactly what is and what isn't part of my fundamental desire (just mutual cooperation, or also animal welfare, or what-have-you) and I also won't be able to figure out which actions contribute to the satisfaction of this much more complicated and multifaceted fundamental desire. However, I do think that the kinds of considerations that I will discuss here about which prescriptive metaethical theories are, and which are not, conducive to my project of satisfying what I have called the fundamental desire will remain much the same even if we enlarge the content of the fundamental desire.

I have the fundamental desire, and I am confident that you do too. What follows is an assessment of the various prescriptive metaethical theories as answers to the now what question in which I assume that what matters, in a prudential sense of 'matters', is the satisfaction of the fundamental desire. If you don't have this fundamental desire, then my assessment will only be of theoretical but not of practical interest to you. That is, you might continue to read what follows in these pages, and you might be able to object to my arguments on the basis of theoretical considerations such as consistency, but you won't have a prudential reason to adopt my proposal in practice because you lack the fundamental desire.

I have just argued that the fundamental practical assessment criterion by which we should judge the various prescriptive metaethical theories is their ability to enable me to satisfy my fundamental desire. Can we go from here to specific assessment criteria for prescriptive metaethical theories? There are good reasons to think that keeping moral thought and language in some form or other after error theory is beneficial in light of my project of trying to satisfy my fundamental desire (whether there are still better reasons for abolishing moral discourse altogether shall be discussed in §5.6). A number of benefits should be mentioned.

The first benefit of keeping moral thought and language in some form or other is that moral thought provides a *bulwark against practical irrationality*. Consider David Hume's sensible knave. Hume thinks that

> though it is allowed, that, without a regard to property, no society could subsist; yet, according to the imperfect way in which human affairs are conducted, a sensible knave, in particular incidents, may think, that an act of iniquity or infidelity will make a considerable addition to his fortune, without causing any considerable breach in the social union and confederacy. (1751, p. 282)

In other words, we all agree ('allow') that if we want to get ourselves into a position in which we satisfy our fundamental desire, then we should have 'a regard to property' (or perform other morally good actions like giving the poor). But alas, sometimes we become bad reasoners 'due to the imperfect way in which human affairs are conducted'. For example, we may find ourselves incapable of rationality if presented with the lure of immediate and immense gain, so that, even holding fixed the project of trying to satisfy our fundamental desire, we will sometimes think, falsely, that failing to have a regard for property on the occasion is what we should do all things considered.

Similarly, Richard Joyce writes that usually we have good instrumental reasons for acting in a cooperative manner, but he also writes that this would only "be good if we lived in a world populated entirely by humans enjoying perfect rationality", which we don't, and so practical rationality will not prevent all defections from occurring (Joyce 2001, p. 210). Elsewhere he writes:

> since knaves have on their minds the possibility of cheating whenever they are confident of evading detection, they are likely to be tempted to cheat in situations where the chances of evading detection are less than certain, thus ... risking severe punishment. (2005, p. 300)

So, there are at least two mistakes that knaves make and that make them practically irrational: they not only sometimes make the wrong judgement about what is truly in their self-interest, but they also sometimes have unwarranted confidence that their defection will not be noted.

Hume's sensible knave is in relevant respects similar to Hobbes's Foole, who also acknowledges that refraining from stealing and killing is most of the time rationally required but that there are circumstances in which it is rational to steal and kill instead:

> The Foole hath sayd in his heart, there is no such thing as Justice; and sometimes also with this tongue; seriously alleaging, that every mans conservation, and contentment, being committed to his own care, there could be no reason, why every man might not do what he thought conduced thereunto; and therefore also to make, or not make; keep, or not keep Covenants, was not against Reason, when it conduced to ones benefit. He does not therein deny, that there be Covenants; and that they are sometimes broken, sometimes kept; and that such breach of them may be called Injustice, and the observance of them Justice; but he questioneth, whether Injustice, taking away the feare of God (for the same Foole hath said in his heart that there is no God,) may not sometimes stand with Reason, which dictateth to every man his own good; and particularly then, when it conduceth to such a benefit, as shall put a man in a condition, to neglect not onely the dispraise, and revilings, but also the power of other men. (Hobbes 1651, p. 101)

Like Hume's knave, Hobbes's Foole thinks that it is sometimes better for him to perform actions that are not conducive to attaining a world full of mutual cooperation, and though he thinks that it stands to "Reason" to do this, in fact it isn't (Hampton 1986).

Hume's answer to the sensible knave, which Joyce thinks is "roughly correct", is that we should "supplement" practical rationality with something that somehow makes it the case that we won't use practical rationality every time we have to make a decision (2001, p. 210). That is, we need something that we can use as a heuristic in making up our minds about what we should do. He explains this as follows:

Because short-term profit is tangible and present whereas long-term profit is distant and faint, the lure of the immediate may subvert the agent's ability to deliberate properly so as to obtain a valuable delayed benefit, leading him to 'rationalize' a poor choice. Hobbes lamented this 'perverse desire for present profit' (Hobbes 1642: §3.27)—something which Hume blamed for 'all dissoluteness and disorder, repentance and misery' (Hume 1751: §6), adding that a person should embrace 'any expedient, by which he may impose a restraint upon himself, and guard against this weakness' (Hume, 1739/40: §III.ii.7). Let me hypothesize that an important value of moral beliefs is that they function as just such an expedient: supplementing and reinforcing the outputs of prudential reasoning. When a person believes that the valued action is morally required—that it must be performed whether he likes it or not—then the possibilities for rationalization diminish. (Joyce 2005, p. 301)

Earlier, Joyce wrote:

Moral thinking ... is ... an expedient [that] functions to bolster self-control against ... practical irrationality ... in this manner, moral beliefs can help us to act in an instrumentally rational manner. (2001, p. 184)

Why think that using a (surrogate) moral thought can perform the role of the required heuristic? The first thing to note is that, as Jon Tresan argues, the fewer cognitive steps are required in thinking about something, or in making a decision, the lower the likelihood becomes that the wrong decision will be made (2010, p. 230). The second thing to note is that the heuristic does not have to be perfect (Joyce 2005). All we need is that using either moral discourse or a surrogate moral discourse such as fictionalist discourse is better than not using either of these. And given the problem that people are sometimes practically irrational and that there is a reason to think that thinking about whether to steal in (surrogate) moral language helps us to avoid lapsing into practical irrationality, using either morality or a surrogate morality after error theory is in fact better than using none of these. Therefore, given that we want to ensure that we behave in a way that furthers cooperation for mutual advantage, which is what we fundamentally desire, and given that we know that we are more likely to exhibit this behaviour if we use heuristics rather than practical rationality itself every time we need to decide, we have a prudential reason to use some form of moral or surrogate moral thought rather than none at all.

There is also a second benefit of using some kind of moral thought rather than none whatsoever. This reason does not concern practical rationality but motivation. To get our fundamental desire satisfied, it is not sufficient to figure out which action is most conducive to this end. We must also muster the *motivation* to perform the action which we have decided we should perform. Given that evolution has selected for humans who have a strong propensity to act on judgements that they believe have moral properties, it stands to reason to think that continuing to use moral language in some form or other will make it easier for us to muster the motivation to do what we think we ought to do compared to not using any moral or surrogate moral thinking at all (Joyce 2006; Street 2006; Green 2013).

Call these the *reasoning bulwark* and *motivation bulwark* benefits of using a moral or surrogate moral discourse. The two assessment criteria that correspond to these benefits are whether a revolutionary metaethical theory can provide the required bulwark against practical irrationality and whether it can provide the required bulwark against lapses in motivation.

These two benefits are both *intra*-personal benefits because they both concern what the individual agent can do, all by herself, to make it more likely that her fundamental desire will be satisfied. However, there are also *inter*-personal benefits of continuing to use moral judgements in some form or other. Suppose that you have your own psychology fully in order. That is, you have arrived at the correct judgements about what you ought to do in order to satisfy your fundamental desire (no practical irrationality) and you have also managed to muster the motivation to act on those judgements (no impaired motivation). You are ready to act but, lo and behold, other agents aren't there yet. They don't yet have their psychologies in order. So, you want to communicate to them what you think they should do so as to jointly achieve a world in which *you* can satisfy *your* fundamental desire.

The first interpersonal benefit of using a surrogate moral language is that it enables you to communicate with like-minded people, that is, people who accept error theory, who have the fundamental desire, and who accept the same prescriptive metaethical theory as you do. I call this the *like-minded communication benefit*, because it concerns the benefit that using a (surrogate) moral discourse enables like-minded error theorists to communicate with each other in an attempt to take joint measures towards reaching the world they all want to live in. The second interpersonal benefit of using some kind of moral language is that it enables you to communicate with people who are not like you in relevantly similar respects, that is, people who do not accept the error theory, or who are error theorists but do not have the fundamental desire, or who accept the error theory and have the fundamental desire, but do not accept the same prescriptive metaethical theory as you do. I call this the *mismatched communication benefit*, because it concerns the benefit that error theorists can reap from continuing to use a (surrogate) moral discourse in their communication with those who are not error theorists.

In this chapter, I will only ask whether the prescriptive theories are able to paint a picture of moral discourse after error theory that is an effective bulwark against practical irrationality and against lapses in motivation. As it will turn out, none of them can secure these benefits, and so I will only discuss the interpersonal benefits for the prescriptive theory that I favour, which I discuss in the next chapter, and which can guarantee the two intra-personal benefits. The reason that I focus on intra-personal benefits first and treat a prescriptive metaethical theory's inability to secure these two benefits as a sufficient reason to reject that theory is that securing intra-personal benefits has lexical priority over securing interpersonal benefits. After all, if I am unable to get my own reasons for action right, then I won't be able to get them right in joint action with you either.

In addition to the two *practical* assessment criteria I have just mentioned, there are also *theoretical* assessment criteria by which I shall judge the various revolutionary metaethical theories. A complicating factor is that contrary to what Toby Svoboda thinks, it is not the case that these criteria are the same for all metaethical theories (2017, p. 50). Instead, which criteria we should use depends on the theory we discuss. For example, a revolutionary metaethical theory that asks us to continue to use moral language in some form or other because doing this will bolster self-control must explain how this works on the level of moral psychology, but this is not something that abolitionism must be able to explain, since this answer to the now what question does not ask us to use moral language or a surrogate moral language at all. This means that I will only be able to mention the various theoretical tasks for the prescriptive metaethical theories on offer as I go along.

The last thing I need to do before I can start the discussion of which prescriptive metaethical theories can provide the required bulwarks against practical irrationality and lapses in motivation is to explain why two other proposed assessment criteria for judging prescriptive metaethical theories will not be considered in this book. First, you might think that we need to be able to answer the following question: is it physically or psychologically possible to stop using moral language, or to start using moral language in a different way? William Lycan has argued that "to produce a genuine freedom from moral intuitions, one would need a steady diet of hard drugs, or some other very powerful alienating force" (2011, p. 10n29). Peter Singer claims that even if we reject moral language "we will find it impossible to prevent ourselves inwardly classifying actions as right or wrong" (1981, p. ix). And Nolan et al. write that error theorists will "find themselves unwilling or unable to refrain from making positive moral judgements" (2005, p. 314).

In contrast, Richard Garner writes that "cutting back on moral pronouncements will be no more difficult than cutting back on swearing, and not nearly as difficult as getting rid of an accent" (2010, p. 232). I think Garner is right. We currently use moral language unreflectively and we intuitively understand that it is important, which, I think, explains why we are unwilling to relinquish it. But after error theory, we will, if my arguments are convincing, use moral language, or a surrogate moral language, reflectively. And having reflected on its pros and cons, we will understand that my proposed surrogate moral language brings us more (prudential) good than bad compared to either continuing to use moral language as it is or ceasing to use it altogether, which will consequently motivate us to effectuate the required change. So I don't use this criterion because it does not discriminate: every prescriptive metaethical theory can satisfy it as easily as every other prescriptive metaethical theory.

Second, you might think that we should be able to answer the following question as well: is it practically possible to convince the folk, first, of the truth of error theory and, second, that any of these answers to the now what questions should be adopted? Cuneo and Christy doubt this because they think that the folk won't be able to understand error theory, and that, even if this is possible

> how would one go about communicating this message to the world (late night commercials?)? (2011, p. 95)

In contrast, Jussi Suikkanen writes:

> I admit that not many people are aware of the moral error theory and the arguments for it. Even fewer people have accepted those arguments. We can still consider what would happen if people were convinced by them. (2013, p. 172)

I think Suikkanen is right. Perhaps there is only a very slim chance that the folk will be convinced that error theory is true. But if at some point they do believe it, we'd better have an answer to the now what question, as there are (prudentially) better and worse reactions to error theory. Moreover, I don't think that error theory is too difficult for the folk to understand. It might be too difficult for the folk to understand what a plausible solution to the Frege-Geach problem should look like, but an argument to the effect that there is something that their language must be about to be true, but that this does not exist, does not seem to be too difficult to understand. So this criterion, like the previous criterion, does not enable us to discriminate between the various prescriptive metaethical theories because every prescriptive metaethical theory can satisfy it as easily as every other prescriptive metaethical theory.

In the remainder of this chapter, I argue that abolitionism, revolutionary fictionalism, revolutionary expressivism, and conservationism are not plausible. The norms for how to use, modify, or stop using moral language that they prescribe are not useful for us in our attempts to satisfy our fundamental desire.

5.3 Revolutionary Fictionalism

The revolutionary fictionalist argues that we should keep moral discourse in one form or other, but rather than continuing to fully believe moral propositions, as the conservationist recommends, we should *pretend* that there is moral truth. This can be done in two ways (Eklund 2011). Attitude-fictionalists (also sometimes called force-fictionalists) say that we should make-believe rather than believe moral propositions. To make-believe a proposition is to adopt an attitude akin to pretence to this proposition, with the consequence that one's attitude becomes insufficiently demanding of the world to be subjected to the correspondence-truth norm, and so judgements that we make-believe escape the charge of being systematically untrue. Schematically:

Attitude of make-believe to: Moral proposition (e.g., 'giving to the poor is morally obligatory')

Content-fictionalists think that we should continue to fully believe propositions, but only after we have first turned them into fictionalist propositions by prefixing them with fictionalist operators to get propositions like: 'in the moral fiction, stealing is wrong'. This also does not commit users of moral language to the systematic falsity of moral judgements in light of the correspondence-truth norm, as it is correspondence-true in the fiction that stealing is wrong. Schematically:

Attitude of believe to: Fictionalist-moral proposition (e.g., 'in the moral fiction, giving to the poor is morally obligatory')

Given that I discuss fictionalism as a prescriptive metaethical theory, I will not discuss Mark Kalderon's *hermeuntic* moral fictionalism, which says that participants in moral discourse already fictionalize their judgements (2005).

First, consider the attitude-fictionalist, who claims that pretending that there is moral truth gets us the bulwark against practical irrationality that we need in order to overcome the inevitable defections that Hume's sensible knave case and Hobbes's Foole case show, whilst at the same time avoiding moral error. As Joyce puts it:

> The crucial question ... is whether some of the costs [of not having any morality] may be avoided by taking a fictionalist stance towards morality— whether the practical benefits of moral belief may still be gained by an attitude that falls short of belief. (2005, p. 302)

But as he immediately admits:

> On the face of it, it seems unlikely. How can a fiction have the kind of practical impact ... that confers on moral belief its instrumental value? ... It seems implausible that a mere fiction could or should have such practical influence on important real-life decisions. (2005, p. 302)

The problem is that the attitude of make-belief is a highly overridable attitude (Oddie and Demetriou 2010, p. 200). Many things can knock us out of the mode of pretence. A child pretends that a chair in the living room is a boat and that the carpet is the sea, but if dinner is served, she simply leaps into the 'water' and runs to the dining room. We pretend to know that our lover isn't cheating on us even in the face of countervailing evidence, but there comes a point where we can no longer fool ourselves. This suggests that fictionalized moral language is not the bulwark against the irrational thoughts, such as the thought that we should steal, that we need.

Joyce however thinks that if we accept morality as a "precommitment", then the fictionalist attitude will be less overridable, and indeed that it will be sufficiently robust to provide the required bulwarks against practical irrationality and lapses in motivation (2005, p. 305; Elster 1984, p. 36). To be precommitted to morality is to develop a stable disposition to think in moral terms—for instance, in the shops, when one is tempted to steal—and yet to remain disposed to "step out of the fiction" in critical contexts such as the philosophy classroom (Joyce 2005, p. 291). A critical context is a context for moral conversations "that carries a strong presumption of truth-telling, such as the court room or the philosophy seminar room" (Cuneo and Christy 2011, p. 87). Such a context "subjects one's attitudes to careful scrutiny" (Joyce 2001, p. 191). On this model, fictional thinking doesn't feel different from moral thinking. One isn't supposed to actively rehearse the truth of the error theory and the conscious decision one made to enter the fiction when one is tempted to steal some chewing gum from the supermarket when no one is looking. If one is precommitted to the moral fiction, the temptation to steel will automatically feel abhorrent, and you will immediately conclude that morally speaking you mustn't steal, just like you would before you had ever heard of the error theory. And so precommitment ensures that your mind won't wonder to ask whether stealing on this particular occasion is to your benefit (it provides a bulwark against practical irrationality) and it also means that you use your motivational system to act on what you believe to be morally wrong (it ensures moral motivation). As Joyce explains:

> If a knave were to say to [an agent who accepts fictionalism] 'Why not steal?' she would answer without hesitation 'No!—Stealing is wrong.' What goes through her mind may be exactly the same as what goes through the mind of the sincere moral believer—it need not 'feel' like make-believe at all (and thus it may have the same influence on behaviour as a belief). The difference between the two need only be a *disposition* that the fictionalist has (though is not paying attention to): the disposition to deny that anything is really morally wrong, when placed in her most critical context. (2005, p. 306; emphasis in original)

My objection to this solution to the problem that the fictionalist attitude is too easily overridable is that it is either too good or not good enough. I call this the *either too good or not good enough objection*. First, it might be too good. If this solution really is to work, then I shouldn't be able to remember *at all*, when it matters, that error theory is true, because if I can remember this, then we have a problem with practical rationality and with motivation. For then, if no one is looking, I will probably be taken in by the lure of immediate gain, and as a result I will probably steal. The problem here is that, if I really can't remember this in these kinds of practical situations, then it looks as though I won't be able to remember this in the philosophy classroom either, in which case I will no longer be an error theorist. But if, alternatively, we admit that we can remember that error theory is true in such detached contexts, then it seems that we will similarly be able to remember that error theory is true in practical contexts in which we are tempted to steal. And that means that we do not have a bulwark against practical irrationality and absence of motivation on this precommitment interpretation of fictionalism either. Whichever horn of this dilemma we choose, fictionalism does not work.

Joyce recognizes that this is a problem and accepts the second horn of the dilemma:

> But what if the knave carries on: 'But in all seriousness, taking into account philosophical issues, bearing in mind John Mackie's arguments—*why not steal?*' Then, *ex hypothesi*, our fictionalist will 'step out' and admit that there is nothing morally wrong with stealing. So does she stuff her pockets? No! For she still has all those Hobbesian and Humean [prudential] reasons to refrain from stealing. (2005, p. 306; emphases in original)

The problem with this response is that it conflates the normative issue of whether it is rational to defect (which we all agree it isn't when we are "cool, calm, and collected") on the one hand, and the issues of how we can insure that we recognize this when we are *not* cool calm and collected, and how we can insure that we muster the motivation to refrain from defecting on the other hand (Smith 1991, p. 406). We all agree that if the agent steps out of the moral fiction, she still has non-moral reasons to act in accordance with what she ought to do in the moral fiction, but this is not at issue and so this is not a solution to my dilemma.

Perhaps *content*-fictionalists do better. According to content-fictionalism, we should continue to fully believe propositions, but only after we have turned them into fictionalist propositions by prefixing them with fictionalist operators to get propositions like: 'in the moral fiction, stealing is wrong.' Unfortunately for the content-fictionalist, believing that things are wrong in the fiction will make it even easier to become distracted by the thought that it might be in one's interest to steal because stealing is merely wrong 'in the fiction'. Precommitment is not possible for a content-fictionalist, because on her proposal for how we should continue to use moral language, the difference between moralizing and fictionalizing is not merely dispositional. Fictional moral thought feels different from moral thought. This is because the fictionalist claims that we should have the thought 'stealing is wrong, *in the fiction*', and this thought is different form the thought that 'stealing is wrong'.

Content-fictionalists might reply that they can accept a "homophonic translation" for moral judgements: although the content of what is being said is altered, what the resulting utterance *sounds like* is not different from the original moral judgement (Burgess 1998, p. 545). Ingram argues that this is possible for a group of moral language users that switch from truth-apt but untrue talk about moral normativity to truth-apt and *true* talk about prudential normativity whilst continuing to use moral terms:

> In an abolitionist society the claim that one ought to φ rather than ψ will be automatically interpreted as the claim that φ-ing is more in one's interests that ψ-ing. It will be naturally interpreted as a prudential claim, stripped of the irreducible and categorically authoritative moral properties integral to moral ascriptions. (2015, p. 236)

The same should be possible, I think, for a society in which we switch from using moral judgements to express truth-apt beliefs about categorically authoritative moral properties to using the same judgements to express fictionalized thoughts along the lines specified by content-fictionalism. If this works, the content-fictionalist might continue, then there will be a bulwark against practical irrationality and there will also be a bulwark against lack of motivation. After all, the content-fictionalist judgements *sound like* moral judgements, and so they will *work like* moral judgements, rendering the option of stealing a non-option. The difference becomes purely dispositional again.

But if this is what the content-fictionalist wants to say, then she falls prey to the same dilemma as the attitude-fictionalist: this solution is either too good or not good at all. First, the solution might be too good. If this solution really is to work, then I shouldn't be able to remember, when it matters, that error theory is true. For if I can remember this, then we have a problem with practical rationality and with motivation. But if I can't remember this in these kinds of practical situations, then I won't be able to remember this in the philosophy classroom either, which means that this kind of view won't be a form of fictionalism anymore and that error theory is out of the window, given that that agent never remembers its truth.

Alternatively, this solution might be not good enough. For if we ensure that we can remember that error theory is true in detached contexts, then it looks as though we can similarly remember that error theory is true in practical contexts in which we are tempted to steal, and that means that we do not have a bulwark against practical irrationality and absence of motivation on this homophonic translation interpretation of content-fictionalism either. In summary, both force-fictionalism and attitude-fictionalism fail as plausible answers to the now what question. We should try a different answer to this question.

5.4 Revolutionary Expressivism

In this section, I discuss revolutionary expressivists who "recommend that we cease making moral utterances and judgements that express false beliefs and instead make moral utterances and judgements that express attitudes that are neither true nor false" (Svoboda 2017, p. 49). Before we can discuss this view, I should make two remarks about it.

First, Svoboda defines error theory as the view that moral judgements express false beliefs, but this is unduly restrictive, given the availability and indeed superiority of the formulation of error theory in terms of moral judgements expressing truth-apt beliefs that are neither true nor false. I therefore think it is better to define revolutionary expressivism as the view that we should 'cease making moral judgements that express truth-apt beliefs that there neither true nor false and instead make moral utterance that express conative non-truth-apt attitudes that are neither true nor false'. Error theory thus understood and revolutionary expressivism are two different views: the first view says that moral judgements are truth-apt but systematically fail to be true, whereas the second view says that moral judgements were never truth-apt to begin with.

Second, Sebastian Köhler and Michael Ridge have defended revolutionary expressivism as a view about what ought to be done with normative language after global normative error theory rather than as a view about what should be done with moral language after a local moral error theory (Köhler and Ridge 2013). As such, their position is not an answer to the question what we should do after *moral* error theory. I will therefore only discuss Svoboda, who has thus far provided the only serious attempt to defend revolutionary expressivism.

Revolutionary expressivists claim that after error theory, we should stop uttering judgements like (3) and should start uttering judgements like (42) or (43):

(3) Giving to the poor is morally obligatory.
(42) Hooray for giving to the poor.
(43) Give to the poor!

Whether we should choose (42) or (43) depends on what kind of revolutionary expressivist we want to be, with (42) standing in the tradition going back to A.J. Ayer's emotivism and (43) stemming from the tradition that goes back to Richard Hare's prescriptivism and C.L. Stevenson's claim that the primary meaning of moral judgements is imperatival (Ayer 1936; Hare 1952; Stevenson 1937).

In what follows, I will just focus on (42). I do this because moral imperatives may express false or at least untrue moral beliefs (Kalf 2017, pp. 113–114). First consider what Josh Parsons has called *cognitivism about imperatives*, according to which imperatives are truth-apt and have truth-conditions (2012, 2013). For Parsons, these truth-conditions are facts about what speakers say, and these facts are not moral facts:

> If imperatives have truth conditions, what are they? There are varying possible answers to this question, but I think the best is as follows: anything you can say using the imperative mood, you could say instead using a performative. For example, instead of saying 'Attack at dawn!', I could have said 'I command that you to attack at dawn!' The thesis of cognitivism, then, is that imperatives are equivalent to the corresponding performatives, and the performatives in turn are true iff they are so commanded. That is to say: 'Attack at dawn!' means the same as 'I command that you to attack at dawn!' 'I command that you attack at dawn' (spoken by me) is true iff I command that you attack at dawn. (2012, p. 49)

Other recent work on imperatives has been done by Peter Vranas, who writes:

> What exactly is it to "endorse" an imperative sentence? To endorse a declarative sentence is to believe that the sentence is true, but imperative sentences cannot be true. I submit that to endorse an imperative sentence which prescribes that an agent perform an action is to believe that there is a reason for the agent to perform the action. For example, to endorse the imperative sentence "John, do your homework" is to believe that there is a reason for John to do his homework. (2010, pp. 59–71)

Though Vranas does not accept Parsons's cognitivism about imperatives, he does think that imperatives can have close ties to reasons; including moral reasons. Take (43). On Vranas's account, to endorse this sentence is to believe that there is a moral reason for the addressee to give to the poor. If we combine Parsons's and Vranas's accounts, then we get a view on which imperatives express truth-apt beliefs whose truth-makers are moral reasons just like declarative, atomic sentences like (3) express truth-apt beliefs whose truth-makers are moral reasons. I find cognitivism about imperatives plausible for moral imperatives, and I therefore advise error theorists to accept not (43) but (42) as the preferred translation for (3).

Mightn't Svoboda *stipulate* that imperatives express non-truth-apt conative states? He might, but then the folk have to keep in mind *two* assumptions if they use (43), that is, that our moral judgements which currently express beliefs that are truth-apt but systematically fail to be true should now express imperatives *and* that imperatives don't take a cognitivist semantics. And that is more difficult than just keeping in mind that our moral judgements, which currently express false beliefs, should now express statements like (42), which, because less cognitively demanding, is more likely to give the revisionary expressivist the required bulwark against lapses in motivation and irrationality.

An important consideration that speaks in favour of Svoboda's revolutionary expressivism based on the emotivist rather than the prescriptivist tradition is that with it everyone will be able to avoid moral error. Another important consideration to take revolutionary expressivism serious is that it can secure, as Svoboda puts it, "moral motivation, moral disagreement, and a kind of moral reasoning" (2017, p. 49). If revisionary expressivism can secure moral motivation, then it can provide the required bulwark against lapses in moral motivation, and if it can give us the right kind of moral reasoning, then it also goes some way towards providing the required bulwark against practical irrationality, as I will explain below. Since moral disagreement concerns an inter-personal rather than an intra-personal benefit, and since I will argue that none of the two required intra-personal benefits can be secured by becoming a revolutionary expressivist, I will not discuss moral disagreement here. I start with moral reasoning.

Moral Reasoning Can revisionary expressivists account for moral reasoning? I don't think they can, given the Frege-Geach problem. Consider this from Peter Geach:

> If doing a thing is bad, getting your little brother to do it is bad. Tormenting the cat is bad. Ergo, getting your little brother to torment the cat is bad. (1965, p. 463)

This seems to be a valid *modus ponens* argument comprised of moral propositions. The problem is that expressivists, regardless of whether they are descriptive or revisionary expressivists, cannot explain how moral utterances can figure in such cases of genuine moral reasoning. For if the argument is not to equivocate, the meaning of the moral terms that feature in its premises and conclusion must be identical. But if expressivism is right, this can't be the case, for according to it, non-embedded moral sentences get their meaning from the conative attitudes that they express, and embedded moral sentences do not express.

The revolutionary expressivist might respond by insisting that being able to account for valid inferences is not a desideratum for her prescriptive metaethical theory, only for a descriptive metaethical theory. But this is not true, for it is important to be able to reason with (surrogate) moral discourse, given our aim of satisfying our fundamental desire. Here is why. Recall, from the previous section, Jon Tresan's claim that the fewer cognitive steps are required in thinking about something, or in making a decision, the more likely it is that the agent reaches a particular conclusion or acts on a particular intention (2010, p. 230). The quick inference that 'if x is wrong, then y is wrong', if one is contemplating whether to do y, makes it less likely that one makes a mistake in doing what one should do (viz., refraining from doing y), given that one wants to satisfy the fundamental desire, compared to doing the actual cost-benefit analysis between doing y and not doing y. There are countless possible actions that contribute to either the satisfaction of the fundamental desire (e.g., giving to the poor) or the frustration of this desire (e.g., engaging in wanton killing). Which of these actions should you perform? Practical reasoning without (surrogate) moral terms, we agreed with Hume (recall the sensible knave example), makes it more likely that we fail in our attempt to satisfy our fundamental desire. You might ask: what is really good for me? Stealing this jacket or not stealing this jacket? And you might think that stealing this jacket will make you look better, and that since no one is looking and stealing one jacket won't erode trust in society to any significant degree, you should steal the jacket. The revolutionary expressivist claims that just like thinking with moral judgements that express beliefs before we accepted the error theory, thinking with moral judgements that express non-truth-apt desires will provide the required bulwark against such faulty practical reasoning. The whole point of Hume-type sensible knave cases is that we should be able to reason like this: 'if frustrating collaboration is wrong and if stealing frustrates collaboration, then stealing is wrong.' The question is whether the expressivist allows us to reason like this. I claim that given the Frege-Geach problem, the expressivist does not enable us to make this inference, and that we therefore can't use it as a bulwark against faulty practical reasoning.

At this point, the revolutionary expressivist might accept the challenge and argue that according to her, surrogate moral inferences work by some other mechanism than transferring truth, via beliefs, from premises to conclusions. To get the required account, the expressivist might appeal to something like Blackburn's *logic of attitudes* (1984, pp. 189–196). For Blackburn, the non-cognitivist attitude that we must adopt towards moral propositions is one of approval or disapproval, and the translation of Geach's valid argument becomes:

Blackburn's Translation

Premise 1: H! (p)→H! (q)
Premise 2: H! (p)
Conclusion: H! (q)

We read this argument as 'Hurray! P entails Hurray! Q', 'Hurray! P', therefore 'Hurray! Q'. Carl Baker explains that what speaks in favour of this reasoning with the logic of attitudes is that in so doing we avoid

> attitudinal inconsistency: if I deny the inference, I am unable to form a consistently realisable ideal. Since Premise 1 is classically equivalent to '¬H! (p) v H! (q)', accepting the premise ties me to a 'tree' of commitments: that is, endorsing the disjunction commits me to endorsing one disjunct should the other become untenable. Here, Premise 2 makes the first disjunct untenable since they are contradictories. So accepting Premise 1 and Premise 2 forces me to accept the second disjunct—H! (q)—which also forms the conclusion of the argument. To endorse P1 and P2 whilst rejecting C is to hold a set of attitudes which is not satisfiable: that is, there is no ideal in which the goals expressed by those attitudes are all realised. (2011, pp. 446–7)

Although no moral judgement expresses a truth-apt belief if we reason with the logic of attitudes, Premise 3 follows from the other premises in the sense that it would be inconsistent to hold the attitudes expressed by the first two sentences but fail to hold the attitude expressed by the third sentence. Blackburn says that this would betray a "fractured sensibility" (1984, pp. 195–196).

My objection is that reaching practical consistency is not a sufficiently effective bulwark against practical irrationality. This is because *another* way to reach consistency among attitudes is to insist that it is not the case that H! (q), apply *modus tollens* rather than *modus ponens*, and reason as follows:

Alternative Consistent Argument

Alternative Premise 1   H! (p)→H! (q)
Alternative Premise 2   Not-H! (q)
Alternative Conclusion   Not-H! (p)

We read this argument as 'Hurray! P entails Hurray! Q', 'Not-Hurray! Q', therefore 'Not-Hurray! P'. If we only have consistency, then we don't have much of a bulwark against faulty reasoning because consistency alone rationally underdetermines the choice between Blackburn's Translation and Alternative Consistent Argument.

The expressivist might respond that this will not happen if you are already committed to the thought that tormenting the cat is bad (p). This is true, but we are considering what would happen in cases in which we experience a lapse in our ability to engage in good practical reasoning (alas, for some of us torturing cats is tempting). And my objection is precisely that by just using attitudinal consistency, we don't have the means to rationally decide between going for p and q or going for not-p and not-q instead.

Svoboda does not agree, and writes:

> Blackburn's account might be sufficient to ground a kind of moral reasoning among revisionary expressivists. If we grant that expressivist moral judgements do not admit of logical relations among one another, they still provide good pragmatic reasons to those who hold them (e.g., to adopt or relinquish some moral attitude), and this may be enough to establish the possibility of moral reasoning … Consider someone who holds the non-cognitive attitude of disapproving of capital punishment. In a moment of unrestrained fervour, this person might express satisfaction at the execution of some particularly heinous criminal. A friend of this individual might point out that this satisfaction is (pragmatically) inconsistent with the attitude of disapproving of capital punishment, and this might open the way for a rational conversation between the two persons regarding how one's various moral attitudes should be modified in order to be consistent. Since non-cognitive attitudes are susceptible to such pragmatic evaluation, they can figure into cases of such moral reasoning. (2017, pp. 69–70)

But this is not a reply to my objection because we still just have consistency as a tiebreaker between these the various desires, and so we still don't have anything to go by in trying to ensure that the choice between dropping a particular desire is not rationally underdetermined. This suggests that revolutionary expressivism cannot secure moral reasoning.

An additional line of response that revolutionary expressivists might try is to say that we should not be conscious of the fact that surrogate moral judgements take a non-cognitivist semantics when we engage in our moral reasoning. When it matters, we should reason with what appear to be moral judgements that express beliefs and for which we only accept a homophonic translation in terms of desires in critical contexts. This idea is similar to the fictionalist's idea discussed above that the difference between users of moral language as it actually is and fictionalists is merely dispositional: they both do exactly the same in practical contexts, but in critical contexts characterized by heightened epistemic standards, the fictionalist agrees that nothing is morally wrong, whereas the meta-ethical realist or success theorist does not. So, in practical contexts, the expressivist reasons just like the folk do now, and it is only in critical contexts that they 'remember' error theory and realize that their Geach-type arguments were not classically valid in terms of the transfer of truth from premises to conclusions and were only indicative of attitudinal consistency. But if this is the proposal, then the objection is again that this is either too good, or not good enough. That is, the view is either inconsistent with error theory because either we can never remember the truth of this theory, or else we can remember error theory, but then we can also remember it in practical contexts, and we will as a result not be able to reap the benefits of a surrogate moral discourse.

Moral Motivation But perhaps expressivists, given that they make much use of motivationally efficacious desires in their semantics, can give us the required bulwark against lapses in motivation. The argument that revisionary expressivism can account for moral motivation piggybacks on the descriptive expressivist's account of moral motivation. Svoboda formulates it as follows:

> Like expressivists in general, revisionary expressivists can understand moral judgements as desire-like attitudes that have inherent motivational force. For example, if the moral judgement that lying is wrong is understood as a desire-like attitude with respect to lying (e.g., disapproval of it), it is easy to

see why the person making this judgement would be motivated to some degree not to lie. The revisionary expressivist thus can help herself to a straightforward account of intrapersonal motivation, thus preserving a very useful feature of morality while avoiding any epistemic error in the process. (2017, p. 67)

In an earlier paper on expressivism and error theory, Svoboda explains that the motivation argument for descriptive expressivism works as follows: if you participate in an anti-war protest and shout 'Stop war!', then "the utterance is used to express a disapproving attitude toward war rather than a belief" (2011, p. 44). During the protest, Svoboda thinks, you will be in some sort of emotional state and disapprove of war, and this conative state of mind is what your imperative expresses.

The problem with this argument is that if we spell out why it is 'easy to see why the person making this judgement would be motivated to some degree not to lie', we find a suppressed premise in this argument. The suppressed premise is that the expression relation is a *causal relation*, such that, if a judgement expresses a conative mental state, then that is so because the utterance of that judgement is *caused by* that conative state (Schroeder 2008, p. 98). Svoboda's argument needs causal expressivism because without it speakers may utter a moral judgement that expresses a state that they are not in, in which case this judgement won't motivate.

Worse, the causal theory of the expression relation is implausible (Schroeder 2008, p. 101). True, Ayer invites this causal interpretation of the expression relation when he writes that moral claims are "ejaculations" of emotions (Ayer 1936, p. 130). Simon Blackburn also seems to accept causal expressivism when he writes that when we "assert values ... we *voice* our states of mind" (1998, p. 50, italics in original). But this theory of the expression relation is not plausible, and to see why, I first explain why it is implausible for the descriptive expressivists. Take (44):

(44) I am sorry.

In saying that (44) expresses regret, we cannot say that 'expresses' denotes a causal relation, for (44) still expresses regret even if its utterer does not experience any regret at all. This is because it is a linguistic convention that (44) expresses regret even when it is uttered insincerely, just as an insincere assertion is still an assertion and an insincere promise is still a promise (Joyce 2006, p. 53). Something similar holds for moral judgements. Take Svoboda's example:

(45) Lying is wrong.

A judgement like (45) expresses, if the expressivist is right, a con-attitude towards lying, but it will do this even if the person who utters (45) is not in that state at all, again because there are linguistic conventions that dictate that (45) means that there is at least something that speaks against lying. So, given how our moral discourse works, descriptive expressivists cannot accept the causal theory of the expression relation. There has to be a gap between the (surrogate) moral judgement and the desire-like state that a speaker is in for it to be possible that others understand what you are communicating, that is, that there is something that speaks against lying. Merely accidentally being in a motivationally efficacious state is not the kind of thing that can "do the speaking against" (Crisp 2006, p. 44). And so, one's interlocutors will justifiably assume that whatever it is that does the speaking against lying, this does not guarantee that the utterer of (45) is in a motivationally efficacious mental state. In other words, expressivism should not collapse into speaker-subjectivism, according to which what moral judgements express are the conative states that speakers are in at that moment in time. Expressivism can only secure moral motivation if it accepts the causal theory of the expression relation, but it mustn't accept the causal theory of the expression relation.

One response that Svoboda could try is to accept an alternative account of the expression relation and claim that it also secures motivation. Mark Schroeder mentions the possibility of understanding the expression relation as a kind of Gricean conventional implicature (2008, p. 101). He also mentions Gibbard's indicatory expressivism, according to which "the mental state that an utterance expresses is the one that the speaker intends to indicate to his audience that he is in" (Schroeder 2008, p. 102; Gibbard

1990). The problem with these accounts of the expression relation is that they allow "for the possibility that an utterance can express a mental state that the speaker is not in" (Schroeder 2008, p. 103). And that won't get us moral motivation.

5.5 Conservationism

The two remaining views are both cognitivist views. I start with the conservationist or preservatist view that says that we should preserve moral discourse as it is (Olson 2014). We ought to continue to moralize without changing anything about our moral discourse in practical contexts, though again in critical contexts we should be able to become aware of the truth of error theory. Olson usefully likens conservationism to the two-level approach to moral thinking as advocated by R.M. Hare (1981):

> we rely on non-Utilitarian moral thinking and reasoning when we find ourselves in 'morally engaged' and everyday contexts and that we turn to Utilitarian thinking and reasoning only in 'detached and critical' contexts. Similarly, conservationism recommends moral belief in morally engaged and everyday contexts and reserves attendance to the belief that moral error theory is true to detached and critical contexts, such as the philosophy classroom. (2014, p. 192)

To avoid the either too good or not good enough objection, Olson recommends that we compartmentalize our first-order and second-order moral thoughts (2014, p. 194). Compartmentalization only allows one's metaethical beliefs to interfere with one's moral beliefs in critical and never in ordinary contexts. Thus, if I am in a supermarket and tempted to steal some chewing gum, then, even though I have the metaethical belief that moral error theory is true, I will not (be able to) access that belief or (be able to) become conscious of it. Instead, I will simply consider my first-order ethical beliefs, and I will conclude that it would be wrong to steal the gum, and in the wake of this I will also become motivated to refrain from doing so. Does compartmentalization enable us to satisfy our fundamental desire by providing a bulwark against practical irrationality and lapses in motivation?

Bulwark Against Practical Irrationality If we can continue to use moral language as it is in ordinary contexts, then we seem to have an effective bulwark against practical irrationality. But can we do this after error theory? I think we can't, for this solution works either too well or not well enough. It works too well if we can never access the belief that error theory is true, but then we are no longer error theorists; or else it does not work well enough because we can always access the belief that error theory is true, which means that we don't have a bulwark against practical irrationality.

Olson disagrees and discusses some examples of cases in which we seem to be "*taken in* by [a thought] even though we are disposed to believe, upon detached and critical reflection, that it is false" (Olson 2014, p. 193; italics in original). For example:

> someone might say truly the following about a cunning politician: 'I knew she was lying, but hearing her speech ... I really believed what she said.' Or a deceived lover might say about his mistress, 'I knew she was lying, but when she told me that she cared about me I really believed her.' ... Something similar might be going on with moral beliefs. The error theorist might say ... 'I knew all along that there is no such thing as moral requirements, but when I realized that breaking the promise would badly hurt his feelings I came to believe that I was morally required not to break it'. (Olson 2014, p. 193)

Olson concludes that it "appears realistic that in morally engaged ... contexts, affective attitudes ... tend to silence beliefs that moral error theory is true" (2014, p. 93). My worry is that even if this is true, we don't have a response to my objection. My objection was that conservationism is either too good or not good enough, and merely pointing out that there are examples in which compartmentalization and silencing work is not a reply to this objection, which is about how we avoid the cases in which we *do* become aware of error theory.

We may be able to glean an additional response to my objection that conservationism either works too well or not well enough from Olson's text. As I reconstruct his argument, the response would be that we can accept the second horn of my dilemma, which was that the belief that error theory is true can be reached, but that even if we reach the belief that error theory is true in critical contexts, we still get the required bulwark against practical irrationality. Thus, it may happen that "speakers who are convinced that error theory is true do not succeed in their compartmentalizing endeavours, i.e. … largely fail to believe first-order moral claims" (Olson 2014, p. 194). Nevertheless, "thinking the thought … that stealing is morally wrong might function as a reminder that one normally, i.e., on reflection, dislikes stealing [and] such a reminder might bolster self-control since normally we want to avoid acting so as to become the objects of our own dislike" (2014, p. 195). But I don't think this works. The problem is that it may be true that I normally dislike stealing, but in this moment, I *like* stealing, and I might precisely become the object of my own dislike in the moment when it matters if I were to refrain from doing what I like doing now.

Bulwark Against Lack of Moral Motivation Can the continued use of moral language provide a bulwark against lack of motivation? I fear that the either the view is too good or not good enough objection applies here as well. Either this account is too good because we always continue to believe in morality and thus always reap its motivational benefits, but then we also get moral error. Or else, this account is not good enough, because if we allow the belief that error theory is true to interfere in our practical deliberations, then it stands to reason that that this belief will eliminate our desire to be moral. Again, I think we are justified to look elsewhere.

5.6 Abolitionism

The only two remaining options are that we should abolish moral thought and talk completely, as the abolitionist thinks, and that we should substitute thinking and talking about moral facts for thinking and talking about *schmoral* facts, as the substitutionist thinks. The former view will be discussed, and rejected, in this section. The latter view will be discussed, and accepted, in the next chapter.

Abolitionists suggest the following translations for moral judgement (3):

Abolitionist Surrogate Discourse

(3) Giving to the poor is morally obligatory.
(46) I desire to live in a world with mutual cooperation, and given that giving to the poor is a good means to attaining this end, I should desire to give to the poor.
(47) I desire to live in a world with mutual cooperation, and if you do too, then, given that giving to the poor is a good means to attaining this end, you should also give to the poor.

In (46) and (47), the 'should' is a prudential 'should', as it is in all translations of moral judgements, according to the abolitionist. Shorter versions of these abolitionist judgements are also possible:

Shorter Abolitionist Surrogate Discourse

(3) Giving to the poor is morally obligatory.
(48) I should desire to give to the poor.
(49) You should desire to give to the poor.

Translations (48) and (49) will, at least after some time, be understood to stand for (46) and (47).

The abolitionist cannot avail herself of the benefits of continuing to use moral language in some form or other. The abolitionist asks us to think directly in terms of what we desire and to communicate what we think we and others should desire, and that precisely invites thoughts like 'but on this occasion, perhaps it is better to perform an action that is not conducive to getting a world in which we all cooperate because then I can get even more of what I want; I can have that *and* cheat—I can be a free-rider'. The bulwark against practical irrationality is missing, and clearly the bulwark against lapses in motivation cannot be provided either. In what follows, I ask whether there are benefits to not using any form of (surrogate) moral language after error theory that abolitionists can claim, and that are so beneficial for us, given our aim to satisfy our fundamental desire, that they epistemically oblige us to accept abolitionism rather than a view that recommends that we continue to use (surrogate) moral language. I reject these arguments, and I conclude that abolitionism doesn't work.

The first benefit that abolitionists claim for their position that does not use the idea that we must bolster self-control is that without moral discourse we will be able to reach agreement on issues that we used to call morally important (but that after error theory are not morally anything) quicker and that the content of our agreement will be better. The sense in which these agreements are 'better' is that being able to reach agreement on such issues will improve mutual cooperation (which we fundamentally desire) as it easier to cooperate with people who accept roughly the same values as you do. Richard Garner writes:

> Not only does the moral overlay inflame disputes and make compromise difficult, the lack of an actual truth of the matter opens the game to everyone. Every possible moral value and argument can be met by an equal and opposing value or argument. The moral overlay adds an entire level of controversy to any dispute, and it introduces unanswerable questions that usurp the original question, which is always some practical question about what to do or support. This "moral turn" guarantees that the participants will be distracted from the real issue, and that the disagreement will flounder in rhetoric, confusion, or metaethics. (2010, p. 220)

Take the "controversy over abortion", which:

> would not be nearly as intractable as it has become if the fiction of moral rights had not been appropriated by both sides. If the issue is not moralized, Roe v. Wade looks like a sensible compromise between two extreme positions, but when the right to life is set against the right to choose, neither side can yield without violating morality. A human embryo is what it is, but someone who insists on describing it with morally loaded terms like "person"

or "innocent human baby" leaves no room for compromise over issues like abortion or embryonic stem cell research. How can anyone compromise with someone they see as wanting to murder babies? (2010, p. 220)

The problem with this argument is that this benefit is also open to every other prescriptive metaethical theory, except conservationism. After all, every prescriptive metaethical theory except conservationism denies that there is such a thing as a moral overlay, and so every prescriptive metaethical theory except conservationism avoids employing "philosophical double talk which would repudiate an ontology while simultaneously enjoying its benefits" (Quine 1960, p. 242). True, some revisionary metaethical views say that there should be a moral overlay of a kind, such as a moral overlay 'in the moral fiction'. But that is not a *moral* overlay and only an overlay 'in the moral fiction'. This is therefore not support for abolitionism but for any prescriptive view except conservationism. It does not give us a reason to favour specifically abolitionism.

The second benefit that abolitionism may provide is that morality and moral discourse preserve unfair arrangements and facilitate the misuse of power, and that with error theory and abolitionism there will be fewer of these unfair arrangements. Of course, the abolitionist cannot mean 'morally unfair', so I will interpret her as saying that these arrangements result in a world in which cooperation is less frequent and less effective. In defence of this suggestion, Garner writes that the "addition of moral overtones to a practice" will tend to stabilize the differential advantages that various parties initially have, regardless of what these differential advantages start out to be (2010, p. 220). Garner attributes this argument to Mackie, who gives the example of property laws that enjoy a moral defence (1980, p. 154). Reformers of such laws will, because of the moral overtone, be condemned as traitors and criminals. This means that moral language is a barrier to improvement understood as a change to a world in which there is more mutual cooperation. Garner admits that moral laws can also *help* those who are in an initial position of differential disadvantage and that it might be beneficial to have moral laws for the purpose of attaining a world with mutual cooperation, but these moral principles

> protect us only if those with the power to abuse us accept the idea of morality and are moved by it. It is likely that they do accept morality and that they

are moved by it when it tells them what they want to hear; but it is also likely that they will never accept a moral directive as authentic if it threatens to deprive them of any property or privilege they cherish. (2010, p. 220)

And so, thinks Garner, the strong and rich use morality for the purpose they want, which is getting themselves in a better bargaining position, and this is a position that is not conducive to mutual cooperation. If it helps the strong and rich to appeal to morality to secure their position, then they will, but if morality calls for changes that are not in their advantage, then they will simply not take it seriously, in which case there is also no positive effect of appealing to morality. Abandoning morality gets us more mutual cooperation.

However, again this benefit of abandoning morality does not depend on whether we adopt the abolitionist answer to the now what question. With the exception of conservationism, every other prescriptive metaethical theory asks us to abandon morality. Abolitionism is not a plausible response to moral error theory.

5.7 Conclusion

In this chapter, I have argued that none of the existing prescriptive metaethical theories that are currently being discussed in the literature gives us a satisfactory answer to the now what question. In the next chapter, I will argue that the only solution that I haven't yet discussed, and which has not yet been discussed in the literature, is plausible.

References

Ayer, A.J. 1936. *Language, Truth and Logic*. London: Victor Gollancz.
Baker, C. 2011. Expressivism and Moral Dilemmas. *Ethical Theory and Moral Practice* 14: 445–455.
Blackburn, S. 1984. *Spreading the Word*. Oxford: Clarendon Press..
———. 1998. *Ruling Passions*. Oxford: OUP.
Burgess, J.A. 1998. Error Theories and Values. *Australasian Journal of Philosophy* 76: 534–552.

Crisp, R. 2006. *Reasons and the Good.* Oxford: OUP.
Cuneo, T., and S. Christy. 2011. The Myth of Moral Fictionalism. In *New Waves in Metaethics*, ed. M. Brady, 85–102. New York: Palgrave Macmillan.
Eklund, M. 2011. Fictionalism. In *The Stanford Enclyclopedia of Philosophy*, ed. E.N. Zalta. Stanford: Stanford University Press.
Elster, J. 1984. *Ulysses and the Sirens.* Cambridge: CUP.
Garner, R. 2010. Abolishing Morality. In *A World Without Values*, ed. R. Joyce and S. Kirchin, 217–234. Dordrecht: Springer.
Geach, P.T. 1965. Assertion. *Philosophical Review* 74: 449–465.
Gibbard, A. 1990. *Wise Choices, Apt Feelings.* Cambridge, MA: Harvard University Press.
Green, J. 2013. *Moral Tribes.* New York: Penguin Press.
Hampton, J. 1986. *Hobbes and the Social Contract Tradition.* Cambridge: CUP.
Hare, R.M. 1952. *The Language of Morals.* Oxford: Clarendon Press.
———. 1981. *Moral Thinking: Its Levels, Point and Method.* Oxford: OUP.
Hobbes, T. 1642[1983]. *De Cive*, ed. H. Warrender. Oxford: OUP.
———. 1651. *Leviathan*, ed. R. Tuck, 1991. Cambridge: CUP.
Hume, D. 1739/40. *A Treatise of Human Nature*, ed. L.A. Selby-Bigge, 1978. Oxford: Clarendon Press.
———. 1751. *Enquiries Concerning Human Understanding and Concerning the Principles of Morals*, ed. P.H. Nidditch, 1975. Oxford: Clarendon Press
Ingram, S. 2015. After Moral Error Theory, After Moral Realism. *The Southern Journal of Philosophy* 53: 227–248.
Joyce, R. 2001. *The Myth of Morality.* Cambridge: CUP.
———. 2005. Moral Fictionalism. In *Fictionalism in Metaphysics*, ed. M.E. Kalderon, 287–313. Oxford: Oxford University Press.
———. 2006. *The Evolution of Morality.* Cambridge, MA: MIT Press.
———. 2007. Morality, Schmorality. In *Morality and Self-Interest*, ed. P. Bloomfield, 51–75. Oxford: OUP.
Kalderon, M.E. 2005. *Moral Fictionalism.* Oxford: OUP.
Kalf, W.F. 2017. Against Hybrid Expressivist-Error Theory. *Journal of Value Inquiry* 51: 105–122.
Köhler, S., and M. Ridge. 2013. Revolutionary Expressivism. *Ratio* 26: 428–449.
Lutz, M. 2014. The 'Now What' Problem for Error Theory. *Philosophical Studies* 171: 351–371.
Lycan, W. 2011. *Judgement and Justification.* Cambridge: CUP.
Mackie, J.L. 1977. *Ethics: Inventing Right and Wrong.* Harmondsworth: Penguin Publishers.
———. 1980. *Hume's Moral Theory.* London: Routledge.

Nolan, D., G. Restall, and C. West. 2005. Moral Fictionalism Versus the Rest. *Australasian Journal of Philosophy* 83: 307–330.

Oddie, G., and D. Demetriou. 2010. The Fictionalist's Attitude Problem. In *A World Without Values*, ed. R. Joyce and S. Kirchin, 199–216. Dordrecht: Springer.

Olson, J. 2014. *Moral Error Theory: History, Critique, Defence*. Oxford: OUP.

Parsons, J. 2012. Cognitivism About Imperatives. *Analysis* 72: 49–54.

———. 2013. Command and Consequence. *Philosophical Studies* 164: 61–92.

Quine, W.V. 1960. *Word and Object*. Cambridge, MA: MIT Press.

Schroeder, M. 2008. Expression for Expressivists. *Philosophy and Phenomenological Research* 76: 86–116.

Singer, P. 1981. *The Expanding Circle*. Oxford: OUP.

Smith, M. 1991. Realism. In *A Companion to Ethics*, ed. P. Singer, 399–410. London: Blackwell.

Southwood, N. 2010. *Contractualism and the Foundations of Morality*. Oxford: OUP.

Stevenson, C.L. 1937. The Emotive Meaning of Ethical Terms. *Mind* 46: 14–31.

Street, S. 2006. A Darwinian Dilemma for Realist Theories of Value. *Philosophical Studies* 127: 109–166.

Suikkanen, J. 2013. Moral Error Theory and the Belief Problem. In *Oxford Studies in Metaethics*, ed. R. Shafer-Landau, vol. 8, 168–194. Oxford: OUP.

Svoboda, T. 2011. Hybridizing Moral Expressivism and Moral Error Theory. *Journal of Value Inquiry* 45: 37–38.

———. 2017. Why Moral Error Theorists Should Become Revisionary Moral Expressivists. *Journal of Moral Philosophy* 14: 48–72.

Timmons, M. 1999. *Morality Without Foundations*. Oxford: OUP.

Tresan, J. 2010. Question Authority: In Defense of Moral Naturalism Without Clout. *Philosophical Studies* 150: 221–238.

Vranas, P. 2010. In Defense of Imperative Inference. *Journal of Philosophical Logic* 39: 59–71.

6

Substitutionism

6.1 Introduction

In this chapter, I defend my preferred solution to the now what problem. We should substitute our error-riddled moral discourse that pragmatically presupposes moral reasons, which don't exist, with a schmoral discourse that pragmatically presupposes schmoral reasons, which do exist. Schmoral reasons belong to the set of hypothetical prudential reasons, so they are reasons that, when you act on them, contribute to the satisfaction of one of your desires that you are rationally permitted but not required or forbidden to have (which is what makes them hypothetical reasons, see §4.4). But what sets schmoral reasons apart from other prudential reasons is their content: they are reasons that, when you act them, enable you to satisfy not just any desire but your *fundamental* desire to live in world full of mutually beneficial cooperation.

Some philosophers fail to recognize the substitutionist answer to the now what question as an option at all (Suikkanen 2013, pp. 172–76; Ingram 2015, p. 231). In what follows, I argue that neglecting substitutionism is unwarranted. I first explain Mackie's version of substitutionism, according to which we should substitute our moral discourse that *conceptually entails* moral reasons, which don't exist, with a schmoral discourse that *conceptually entails* schmoral reasons, which do exist (§6.2). My argument is exegetical, but it also teaches us a number of important things about substitutionism, and I use these insights in the remainder of this chapter to defend *pragmatic presupposition* substitutionism.

I start my own defence of substitutionism by first explaining how we can achieve the required change from participating in a discourse that pragmatically presupposes moral reasons to a discourse that pragmatically presupposes schmoral reasons (§6.3). I then argue that pragmatic presupposition error theory enjoys four important benefits. It gives us the two intra-personal bulwarks against lapses in rationality and motivation (§6.4). It also secures the two inter-personal benefits of continuing to use moral language, that is, the ability to talk to like-minded pragmatic presupposition substitutionist error theorists who share your fundamental desire, and the ability to talk to everyone else (§6.5). Having discussed these positive arguments for my view, I continue to rebut two objections to pragmatic presupposition error theory. First, I argue against propagandist substitutionism, according to which we should hide the truth about error theory from the folk and according to which only the *cognoscenti* should be pragmatic presupposition substitutionists, and, second, I argue that my view does not collapses into a success theory of moral discourse (§6.6). A final section summarizes my main findings and introduces the topic of the next chapter (§6.7).

6.2 Mackie's Conceptual Entailment Substitutionism

In this section, I defend my claim that Mackie was a conceptual entailment substitutionist (I also sometimes refer to this position as the conceptual reformist position). As we saw in Chap. 5, there are many possible answers to the now what question, and unfortunately, Mackie was not entirely clear about his own position. His work has invited a conservationist interpretation (West 2010, pp. 184–5; Oddie and Demetriou 2010, p. 200; Fisher 2011, p. 46) and a fictionalist interpretation (Joyce

2005, p. 288; Lillehammer 2004, p. 105; Sainsbury 2010, p. 204). Mackie has also been interpreted as a substitutionist, but this interpretation has only been mentioned in passing and has not been defended (Burgess 1998, p. 545; Kahane 2013, p. 152; Lutz 2014, p. 354, 365n23). Other philosophers do defend substitutionism. For instance, Hallvard Lillehammer argues that error theorists about categorical moral reasons should say that such "reasons should be construed as response dependent regardless of the conceptual commitments embodied in common sense ethical discourse" (2000, p. 174). And Mark Balaguer suggests that after error theory we "might decide that we would be better off if we altered our moral practices, i.e., if we started using our moral terms slightly differently, so that they expressed slightly different concepts, concepts that were ... more natural or coherent, or some such thing" (2011, p. 374). But these philosophers don't attribute this view to Mackie.

Mackie believed that moral concepts entail categorical moral reasons and that there are no categorical moral reasons (§2.3). His solution to the now what problem is that after error theory we should reform our error-infected moral concepts. We should change the instantiation conditions for moral properties that moral concepts legislate, from requiring the world to exhibit objective prescriptivity to just requiring the world to exhibit subjective prescriptivity. This 'should' is a prudential and not a moral 'should'. In his Chap. 5, which commences Part II in his *Ethics*, Mackie first summarizes Part I as an argument for the claim that "there are no objective values" (p. 105; page references in this section are to Mackie's 1977 *Ethics*, unless specified otherwise). There are no moral constraints on what we are permitted to do with moral discourse after error theory, because there are no moral constraints at all. For the same reason, there are no moral obligations telling us what we should do with moral discourse after error theory, and so on. But given that there are hypothetical reasons, which consist of our desires and causal relations, and given that we desire to live a world full of "mutually beneficial cooperation", Mackie argues that we should use a surrogate moral discourse as a causal means to the satisfaction of this desire (p. 111).

In this vein, Mackie writes that we are

free to mould or remould our moral system so as better to promote whatever it is that we do value. (p. 146)

A surrogate moral discourse is a causal means to the satisfaction of our desire to live in a world with mutually beneficial cooperation because engaging in it enables us to overcome the problem that "our motives are mainly selfish" (p. 110):

> The function of morality is primarily to counteract this limitation of men's sympathies (p. 108) ... [for] prudence is not enough and the rational calculation of long-term self-interest is not sufficient ... to lead men to make mutually beneficial agreements. (p. 119)

The rational calculation of long-term self-interest is not sufficient to achieve the world with all the cooperation that we want because, as we saw in the previous chapter, sometimes we are practically irrational. We sometimes display unwarranted confidence in the claim that our defection will not be noted, and we sometimes have an impaired ability to reason about what is truly in our self-interest. Mackie thinks that given that we are practically irrational in this way, and given that we want to live in a world with mutually beneficial cooperation, we should supplement practical rationality with something that obviates the need to use practical rationality every time we have to make a practical decision. This should be something that we can use as a heuristic as we make up our minds about what we should do. He thinks that we will be able to make this work if we "trim down moral demands to fit present human capacity" and "look for rules ... that can fit with the relatively permanent tendencies of human motives and thought" (pp. 133–134). What also helps, he thinks, is the knowledge that if you don't desire to perform actions that foster social cooperation, then there is a real penalty that awaits you, that is, a sacrifice of "inward peace of mind" (p. 35).

At this point, you might ask: if we want to reap these benefits of engaging in moral discourse, why not accept conservationism? Here we find part of the evidence for the claim that Mackie was not a conservationist or a fictionalist. For Mackie claims that it is not "obvious that what is conventionally accepted as morality is exactly what is required" to get a world with mutual cooperation (p. 121). So,

> morality is not to be discovered but to be made; we cannot brush this aside by adding 'but it has been made already, long ago'. It may well need to be in part remade. (p. 123)

Conserving morality as it is, as the conservationist proposes, or make-believing that it still exists, as the fictionalist proposes, are not good reactions to error theory because these two stances do not enable us to change the content of morality where it needs to be changed in order to deal with continuing alterations in the circumstances of justice. Given our fundamental desire, we should change the content of morality so that its obligations become maximally conducive to our attempts to satisfy this desire. Conceptual reform enables us to do precisely this.

How does conceptual reform work? Consider the non-moral concept WITCH. Presently, conceptual analysis of WITCH tells us that this concept refers if, and only if, there are women with supernatural powers. As we know that there are no women with supernatural powers, this concept does not refer (Joyce 2001, pp. 156–7). However, we could decide to change this, accepting that from tomorrow onwards WITCH refers just in case there are women who wear black clothes and are marginalized by society even though they don't have supernatural powers. Given that there are such women, from tomorrow onwards WITCH will refer. Similarly, we can say, for moral concepts. We know from conceptual analysis that today they refer just in case there are objectively prescriptive properties, and so today, given error theory, they do not refer. But we could decide that tomorrow they refer just in case there exist subjectively prescriptive properties, which do exist, and so tomorrow, they will refer. The conceptual reformist proposes to keep the correspondence theory of truth but to change moral judgements' truth-makers: from being objectively prescriptive properties to being subjectively prescriptive properties.

A year before he wrote his *Ethics*, Mackie argued, in a different book, that our current concept of personal identity is not instantiated in the world but that a different concept of personal identity, which demands less of the world, is instantiated, and that

> [a] similar conceptual reform, rather than mere analysis of our present concepts, is, I believe, needed in ethics. I hope to discuss this topic in another book. (1976, p. 196n27)

This other book became the *Ethics*. In it, Mackie distinguishes between "morality in the broad sense" and "morality in the narrow sense" (pp. 106–107). Morality in the broad sense is a general, all-inclusive theory of conduct which provides rules for behaviour that reflect objective truth, and which requires objectively prescriptive facts. Call the practice of discovering and communicating rules of morality in the broad sense moralizing. Morality in the narrow sense is limited to constraints on the pursuit of self-interest (pp. 107–111). Its rules do not reflect objective truth:

> the psychopath of the kind that is quite lacking in sympathy and shows no capacity for moral feeling or moral reasoning simply stands outside the system of control which we have identified as morality in the narrow sense. (p. 213)

Morality in the narrow sense is man-made ('invented' rather than 'discovered'—hence the subtitle of Mackie's *Ethics: Inventing Right and Wrong*). Call this practice of inventing and communicating moral rules in the narrow sense schmoralizing. Mackie's proposal is that after error theory we should stop moralizing and start schmoralizing.

There are two steps in the process of moving from moralizing to schmoralizing. The first and easy step occurs at the general metaethical level and a more difficult step happens at the level of the content of morality in the narrow sense. Regarding the first step, Mackie writes:

> There is no point in discussing whether the broad or the narrow sense of 'morality' is the more correct. Both are used, and both have important roots and connections in our thought. But it is essential not to confuse them, not to think that what we recognize as (in the narrow sense) peculiarly moral considerations are (jumping to the broad sense) necessarily finally authoritative with regard to our actions. (p. 107)

The distinction is not Mackie's. About a decade earlier, William K. Frankena similarly wrote: "we ought to employ *both* the wider and the narrower concepts of morality, using 'moral' and 'morality' in both senses, though perhaps in different contexts" (1966, p. 688, emphasis in original). Mackie also writes that such institution-dependent moral requirements are "written into ordinary moral language" (p. 79). This suggests that on the general metaethical level we do not have to make much effort to switch from thinking and talking in terms of morality in the broad sense to thinking and talking in terms of morality in the narrow sense. Morality in the narrow sense is already with us and all we have to do after error theory is to start thinking and talking solely in terms of it and to stop thinking and talking in terms of morality in the broad sense.

Mackie considers the content of morality in the narrow sense in his Chaps. 6, 7, and 8. In Chap. 6, he argues that, in order to get to the content of schmorality, we need to go beyond a purely utilitarian consequentialism (according to which happiness is the only state of affairs that can properly be called morally good) and say that additional states of affairs or properties can be called good. In Chap. 7, he argues that we should combine non-utilitarian consequentialism and deontology. And in Chap. 8, he applies the combined non-utilitarian consequentialist-deontological account to such issues as liberty (pp. 180–182), suicide (p. 196), and abortion (p. 197).

At the start of Chap. 7, Mackie writes:

> Having rejected utilitarianism ... we could *replace* the goal of utility or happiness ... with some other *concept* of the good. (p. 149, both italics mine)

Mackie also says that after utilitarianism we can "retain the consequentialist structure of utilitarian theory" or "reject the consequentialist structure, and develop a moral system built ... round ... some kind of deontological system" (p. 149). And then he says:

> In fact I want to move in both these directions, to *introduce* both some non-utilitarian consequentialism and some deontological elements (p. 149, italics mine)

I think we can draw two lessons from this. First, Mackie's project of inventing rather than discovering morality in the narrow sense is in full swing at this stage of the book. It is not as though Mackie has discovered, given the evidence as it lies before us (facilitated, for instance, by direct perception of objective moral facts), that morality is partly consequentialist, partly deontological. Rather, Mackie wants to introduce both a form of consequentialism and a form of deontology into our schmoral thinking. Mackie starts from the idea that schmorality is about furthering cooperation and "counteracting limited sympathies" (p. 107) and, given the problems we face today, he argues that a system that combines elements of non-utilitarian consequentialism and deontology enables us to get along better than a system that is purely utilitarian. The second lesson is about Mackie's use of the word concept. Mackie proposes that we "replace" our concept of the good understood in purely utilitarian terms with "some other concept of the good" (p. 149). So, Mackie also says in so many words that we should change our moral concepts.

How does this get us the required bulwarks against practical irrationality and lapses in motivation? Regarding the bulwark against practical irrationality, the idea here, and I will provide a full defence of it in §6.4, is that thinking the thought that we mustn't steal because it is morally wrong to steal will, even though its true meaning is that stealing is schmorally wrong, provides a counterweight against countervailing considerations, such as that stealing is exciting. And moral motivation is secured because thinking the thought that we mustn't steal because it is morally wrong to steal will, and even though its true meaning is that stealing is schmorally wrong, allow us to make use of the evolutionarily programmed mental process that secures motivation to perform the action that we think we are morally obligated to perform. I will provide a full defence of this claim in §6.4 as well.

We need a fuller, and better, defence than this because if we leave these claims as they are, then the objections that I used to justify abandoning alternative prescriptive metaethical theories, such as revolutionary expressivism and revolutionary fictionalism, also have purchase against this view. Recall, for instance, the objection that thinking moral thoughts provides a bulwark against practical rationality either works too well (because it will make it impossible for the agent to recall error theory even in critical contexts) or that it isn't capable of doing the work (because, if the agent can remember the truth of error theory in critical contexts, she will also be able to remember its truth in contexts in which she needs to act, in which case the required bulwark cannot be attained).

But most importantly, I cannot accept Mackie's formulation of the substitutionist answer to the now what question because it rests on the assumption that the mode of commitment of moral discourse to categorical reasons uses conceptual entailment, which I deny. Nevertheless, I think that Mackie has formulated a promising answer to the now what question, and in what follows, I will adopt many of Mackie's ideas. Substitutionism is plausible, I will argue, but it must be formulated on the basis of pragmatic presupposition rather than conceptual entailment.

6.3 Pragmatic Presupposition Substitutionism

The remainder of this chapter defends pragmatic presupposition substitutionism, according to which we should replace our current moral discourse, which pragmatically presupposes categorical moral reasons, with a surrogate schmoral discourse that pragmatically presupposes hypothetical schmoral reasons. Mackie argued that we can get a substitution moral discourse by changing the content of moral concepts, but that cannot work for me, since I reject conceptual entailment error theory. My question is: how do we get from moral judgements that carry the false pragmatic presupposition to categorical moral reasons to a situation in which schmoral judgements carry the true pragmatic presupposition to hypothetical schmoral reasons? In this section, I answer this question.

The basic idea is that if which information we communicate with a moral judgement depends on context, such that a moral judgement uttered in a context that is characterized by both seriousness and the absence of applicability restrictions requires a categorical reason—and such that a moral judgement uttered in a different context does not require such a reason—then we should try to put ourselves into a position in which all the participants to the moral conversation know that everyone is being serious but that applicability restrictions apply. If this works, then moral judgements are truth-apt, pragmatically presuppose that hypothetical reasons exist, and are true if, and only if, they correctly describe the relevant hypothetical reason (and are false otherwise). In Chap. 3, I explained that it is the default assumption of the participants in moral conversations that they are in a context in which their interlocutors are being serious and that the applicability restrictions do not apply. I also explained that certain cues in a conversation about morality can change this. For instance, in normal circumstances, the judgement that a particular medical treatment should be discontinued extends to all people who bear a sufficient number of relevantly similar properties to the patient who is being discussed. But recall Benevolent Doctors from §2.8: the mutual agreement amongst the two doctors that they did not want to set a precedent for other patients constituted a contextual defeater for the normal presupposition to categorical moral reasons.

More generally, the kinds of conversational cues that indicate to one's interlocutor that a shift in the context of the conversation has taken place and that takes you from core cases that license error theory to peripheral cases that are inconsistent with error theory fall under one of the following two rubrics:

a. Utterance of a judgement

Example: Two doctors discuss the permissibility or otherwise of discontinuing a particular treatment of a particular patient. They disagree about this and they engage in a serious conversation, thus considering, among other things, the expected harms and benefits of discontinuing the treatment. During their conversation, one of them utters the judgement: 'let us agree that whatever we decide to do, our decision will not set a precedent for other similarly placed patients'; and the other doctor agrees.

The utterance of this judgement changes the context of this conversation, such that the discussion presupposed categorical moral reasons before the utterance of this judgement and now presupposes hypothetical schmoral reasons.

b. Non-linguistic behaviour
   Example: One day later, the same two doctors have spent the entire morning discussing ethical dilemmas, first, in the hospital's ethics committee, and later in a medical ethics lecture they give to first-year medical students. It is clear to them that, perhaps apart from some of their students, the people they have been interacting with think that the results of moral inquiry are objective and universally valid. They must now discuss the obligatoriness or otherwise of informing the police of suspicious wounds on a young patient's body. They first start discussing rights, harms, benefits, promises, and all the rest of it with full attention. But after some time, they look at each other and raise their eyebrows, and they both know that the other also thinks that in the privacy of their discussion, whatever it is that they end up deciding about whether to disclose the patient's bruises to the police, they do not and will not regard their decision as universally valid or as setting a precedent for other similarly placed patients.
   Their mutual raising of their eyebrows changes the context of this conversation, from presupposing categorical moral reasons to presupposing hypothetical schmoral reasons.

Both these kinds of cues are already in use in moral discourse as it currently exists. But if moral error theorists are serious about becoming pragmatic presupposition substitutionists, as I argue they should be, then they are, I think, best advised to use the clearest cue available to them to get what they want, which, recall, is the satisfaction of their fundamental desire. This is clearly the utterance of the judgement 'error theory is true and let us therefore cancel the presupposition to categorical reasons'. After some time, and once the truth of error theory and the desirability of the pragmatic presupposition substitutionist solution to the now what problem have become sufficiently well known, speakers can revert to a simple nod, adopt a sign from sign language, invent a new word for the purpose of altering the conversational context, or what have you.

Like the conceptual entailment substitutionist, the pragmatic presupposition substitutionist offers a "homophonic translation" of moral judgements to get schmoral judgements (Burgess 1998, p. 545). Metaethicists discussing the pros and cons of substitutionism should use the nomenclature of 'morality' and 'schmorality' in order to avoid confusion. However, for the folk the translation from moral to schmoral judgements is homophonic because although the content of what is being said is altered, what the resulting utterance *sounds like* is not different from the original utterance. The folk can continue to say things like 'giving to the poor is morally obligatory' as long as what they mean by that is that there is a hypothetical and not a categorical reason to give to the poor.

When are schmoral judgements true? If Pete talks to Jan and utters a schmoral judgement like (50), then this judgement is false if there is no hypothetical reason for Jan to give to the poor, but if there is such a reason, then this judgement is true:

(50) Giving to the poor is schmorally obligatory.

Whether there is a hypothetical reason for Jan to give to the poor depends on whether she has the fundamental desire. If she does, and given that giving to the poor is a good means to satisfying the fundamental desire, then she has a hypothetical reason that, when she acts on it, contributes to the satisfaction of her fundamental desire. If she does not have this desire, then there is no such reason for her to give to the poor, though recall that this is consistent with the existence of a legal requirement that gives Jan a legal reason to give to the poor regardless of whether or not she also has a moral or a schmoral reason to do so.

This sounds deceptively simple, for we should not underestimate how difficult even this kind of means-end reasoning can be. As Hallvard Lillehammer writes:

> the falsity of [moral] judgements [does not] entail the falsity of judgements which say whether or not different practical options are consistent with each other, given certain constraints or given certain circumstances. There is an indefinite number of truths about how ends can be promoted and related to each other, necessarily or contingently. The [error theorist] can invoke these facts to explain why informative, insightful, deep and useful ethical thinking can be undertaken even if there are no [moral] reasons. If the ends involved are of the requisite kind and the problem situation sufficiently complex, the thinking required to make sense of the situation can

easily amount to highly systematic and illuminating moral theorizing. (1999, p. 211)

Moreover, says Lillehammer, schmoral

theorizing can also provide interesting impossibility and possibility proofs based on either the logical consistency or the practical compatibility of different conceptions of the good or the right. For example, one might try to prove that a system of human rights can be implemented consistently with a utilitarian moral theory ... All the [error theorist] denies is that [a certain] approach [to the question of our ultimate ends] is intrinsically rationally privileged. (1999, p. 213)

In the next chapter, I give an example of how this kind of reasoning works, as I offer a preliminary discussion of how like-minded error theorists can come to an agreement about which course of conduct regarding the distribution of rescourses in society they should accept, given that they both have the fundamental desire.

A final and crucially important feature of schmoralizing is that whilst engaging in this activity we are allowed and indeed encouraged to change the *content* of our schmoral obligations to ensure that what we tell ourselves (and others) we are schmorally obligated to do is more likely to express a reason that, if we act on it, contributes to the satisfaction of the fundamental desire compared to when we adopt another non-abolitionist answer to the now what question. Contrastingly, the revolutionary fictionalist says that we should either make-believe that there are moral obligations or believe that (in the moral fiction) there are moral obligations, but he or she does not say that we should also change the content of these obligations. The same holds for the revolutionary expressivist and the conservationist.

I think this means that there is reason to be optimistic about whether error theorists can enable themselves to continue to engage in something that looks a lot like normative ethics and thus that they can "avoid a gaping hole in their normative lives" (Lutz 2014, p. 352). To further make my case, I will now argue that pragmatic presupposition substitutionism can guarantee the four intra- and inter-personal benefits of schmoralizing.

6.4 Intra-Personal Benefits of Schmoralizing

In the previous chapter, I argued that prescriptive metaethical theories can be judged on the basis of four criteria. These are: their ability to provide a bulwark against practical irrationality, their ability to provide a bulwark against lapses in moral motivation, and their ability to enable communication, both with people who share your outlook on life (i.e., are both error theorists and substitutionists and have the fundamental desire) and with those who do not share your outlook on life (e.g., are not error theorists, or if they are, are not substitutionists, or do not have the fundamental desire). In this section, I argue that the substitutionist can give us both intra-personal benefits. I argue that she can secure the two inter-personal benefits in the next section.

Bulwark Against Practical Irrationality Although we often know what we should do when we are "cool, calm, and collected", we sometimes find it difficult to reach this conclusion when we stand to gain a lot from performing an action, such as stealing, that promises to satisfy a desire that does come up in the heat of the moment, but that we would not keep after checking it for consistency with the rational requirements that exist or with our other desires, including our fundamental desire (Smith 1991, p. 406). Why is adopting the belief-attitude towards schmoral propositions a better policy than make-believing moral propositions or accepting any other non-abolitionist solution to the now what problem?

First, consider the case for thinking that adopting the belief-attitude towards schmoral propositions provides a bulwark against practical irrationality. The reason is that, just as with all the other prescriptive metaethical theories except abolitionism, thinking the thought 'stealing is wrong' provides a short-cut or a heuristic that makes it less likely that you will reconsider your reasoning for not stealing in the heat of the moment. When you were cool, calm, and collected, you realized that adopting the policy of refraining from stealing, and of giving to the poor, was your best means to satisfying your fundamental desire. By thinking the thought 'stealing is morally wrong', you use the fact that thinking moral thoughts makes it less likely that you will reopen practical deliberation about this. This puts you in a better position to satisfy your fundamental desire compared to the situation in which you do not think in moral terms.

So far so good, but recall, from the previous chapter, that there were two main problems with the other, non-abolitionist answers to the now what question when it comes to their account of how this bulwark against practical irrationality can be achieved, that is, the either too good or not good enough objection and the moral reasoning objection. I formulated the latter objection exclusively for the revolutionary expressivist position, and I will now argue that neither of these objections applies to my version of substitutionism.

Start with the objection that a prescriptive metaethical theory might either be too successful in enabling us to reap the benefits of continuing to use moral terms in our practical deliberation (by making it impossible for us to become conscious of the thought that error theory is true, in any context), or else that it is completely unable to help us to reap these benefits (because if we can become conscious of the thought that error theory is true, then we can become conscious of it when it matters in the heat of the moment). As I explained, this objection sinks the revolutionary fictionalist, revolutionary expressivist, and conservationist proposals—that is, every proposal except the abolitionist theory. But what all these prescriptive metaethical theories have in common is that they propose to keep the content of morality exactly as it is, and this is something that the substitutionist denies. Here is how this difference helps.

One consequence of keeping the content of morality as it is, is that there will always be a chance that what morality requires is different from what will satisfy my fundamental desire. For instance, consider the generally recognized moral obligation to refrain from lying, and suppose that this obligation trumps other moral obligations and generates less mutual human cooperation than the policy that lying is always wrong except when lying improves people's happiness, which in turn makes them better cooperators. What all the prescriptive metaethical theories from the previous chapter except abolitionism recommend is that in the heat of the moment we should think the thought that we are morally obliged to refrain from lying after error theory, even though on reflection and when we are cool, calm, and collected, we may decide that following *this* moral thought does not enable us to satisfy our fundamental desire *in the relevant situation*. This means that thinking the thought that error theory is true, in the moment when it matters, might actually cause people to reopen their practical deliberations about the costs and benefits of lying or stealing at that point in time. For after all, the content of the obligation might not be conducive to people's aim to satisfy their fundamental desire.

Compare this to what the substitutionist says we should do. Imagine that you have accepted error theory, pragmatic presupposition substitutionism, and that you have the fundamental desire. Imagine further that you agree that when you are calm and collected that you must not steal, and imagine that in the shops you feel the temptation to steal. You think the thought 'stealing is morally wrong', and this has the result that you are less likely to engage in a cost-benefit analysis of stealing with the potentially prudentially bad consequence that you end up stealing (prudentially bad because this will frustrate your fundamental desire for mutual cooperation). This substitutionist prescriptive metaethic is, thus far, identical with the other non-abolitionist prescriptive metaethics. And if you don't think the that error theory is true, you have your bulwark against practical irrationality, just like you have this bulwark if you accept one of the other prescriptive metaethical theories. Finally, imagine that in the shops you think the thought that error theory is true, which, we should admit, might happen if we want to avoid the first and implausible horn of the either too good or not good enough objection. After all, if we can never remember that error theory is true, then our prescriptive metaethical theory collapses into preservatism. The consideration that supports the claim that substitutionism is more plausible than the other non-abolitionist prescriptive metaethical theories when it comes to providing an effective bulwark against faulty practical reasoning is that, when you remember that error theory is true in the heat of the moment, you can also remember that following every schmoral obligation is likely to bring you closer to the satisfaction of this desire. You can remember that your substitutionism has enabled you to change the content of morality with the aim of satisfying the fundamental desire when you were cool, calm and collected. Therefore, becoming conscious of the thought that error theory is true will be less likely to trigger the thought that *this particular* surrogate moral obligation might not actually enable you to satisfy your fundamental desire. Had the content of your surrogate moral obligation been identical to the content of the old moral obligations, then the thought 'but perhaps following *this* moral obligation doesn't contribute to the satisfaction of my fundamental desire' would be worrisome. But now that you are a substitutionist, this thought, though it may come up, is less likely to cause you to reconsider your cost-benefit analysis, because you know that when you were cool, calm, and collected, you worked hard towards ensuring that the content of your schmoral obligations is in line with the satisfaction of your fundamental desire. This means that substitutionists make it much less likely that you succumb to the temptation to reopen your practical deliberation about whether you should steal in the moment than the other non-abolitionist metaethical theories. And that means that it provides a better bulwark against practical irrationality than the other prescriptive metaethical theories.

True, it might still happen that you nevertheless stubbornly end up going over the pros and cons of stealing anyway and, taken in by the heat of the moment, end up with the wrong conclusion that you ought to steal. But this is not very problematic. Morality itself does not guarantee that we always do what we should do, morally speaking, and neither does schmorality. So it would be an unfair objection against the substitutionist to insist that she has to guarantee that we always do what we are schmorally obligated to do. In summary, it is not the case that substitutionism works too well, for we are allowed to think the thought that error theory is true in all contexts. And it is also not the case that it does not work well enough, for even if we think the thought that error theory is true in the heat of the moment, we have a sufficiently robust bulwark against faulty practical reasoning.

Next, consider the other objection to the claim that a surrogate moral discourse can provide a bulwark against practical irrationality. This objection, I argued, only besets revolutionary expressivism. The objection was that we must be able to explain how surrogate moral reasoning works but that the revolutionary expressivist cannot explain this. It is useful to be able to explain how surrogate moral reasoning works, recall, because being able to reason with moral terms makes it easier to satisfy our fundamental desire. After all, suppose we realize when we are cool, calm, and collected that if killing is wrong then stealing is wrong, that killing is wrong, and, thus, that stealing is wrong. If, when we are in the heat of the moment, we decide that killing is wrong and that if killing is wrong then stealing is wrong, we will be able, if we can engage in what sounds and feels like moral reasoning, to reach the further conclusion that killing is wrong without having to engage in difficult and error-prone cost-benefit prudential reasoning. However, revolutionary expressivists cannot give us this kind of moral reasoning, because that they cannot solve the Frege-Geach problem. They can only point to consistency requirements amongst conative attitudes, which allows agents to turn a *modus ponens* that moves from the fundamental desire to a derivative desire into a *modus tollens* that moves from not accepting the derivative desire to not accepting the fundamental desire. After all, both patterns of reasoning generate attitudinal consistency.

Substitutionism does better because it is a cognitivist view, which means that it can use the standard truth-preserving properties of reasoning, and which in turn makes it less likely that agents will turn a *modus ponens* into a *modus tollens*. True, in the wake of error theory, the substitutionist also cannot ensure that agents do not abandon the fundamental desire because they are not rationally required to accept this desire. But since in everyday life we are, I think it is safe to assume, more impressed with truth-preserving practical reasoning from accepted beliefs to other beliefs compared to thinking in terms of consistency relations between conative attitudes, it is, from the point of view of trying to get yourself into a position in which you make it as likely as possible that you perform actions that satisfy the fundamental desire after error theory, prudentially wiser to accept substitutionism rather than revolutionary expressivism.

Bulwark Against Lapses in Motivation The reason that substitutionism provides a bulwark against lapses in motivation is that thinking moralized thoughts triggers the evolutionarily advantageous propensity to be motivated to act on what you think is your moral obligation. Moral motivation is useful from an evolutionary perspective because acting on my moral judgements lowers my chance to be ostracized by my group or society, as people don't want others in their group that steal and kill, and I need to be part of a group to be able pass on my genes to the next generation. The question in the current dialectic is whether the substitutionist is on better grounds than the other revolutionary metaethical theories that also tried to secure this benefit of continuing to use moral terms in practical deliberation. The answer to this question can be stated briefly: a successful bulwark against lapses in motivation piggybacks on a successful bulwark against practical irrationality. If it happens too often that I abandon my moralized thought as a consequence of the belief in moral error theory surfacing in my consciousness when I must act, then I cannot use this moralized thought to get the moral motivation that I need to act. But given that, as I just argued, the substitutionist position has an argument for the claim that, compared to accepting any of the other prescriptive metaethical theories, we are less likely to abandon a moralized thought even if the belief that error theory is true comes to the fore, this moralized thought will be able to give me the motivation that I need.

In sum, substitutionism can give us an effective bulwark against practical irrationality and, consequently, an effective bulwark against lapses in motivation. The question that I will now answer is whether my position can also give us the two interpersonal benefits of engaging in a surrogate moral discourse after moral error theory.

6.5 Inter-Personal Benefits of Schmoralizing

In this section, I discuss two interpersonal benefits of schmoral communication. They mimic the first intra-personal benefit of schmoralizing, that is, the bulwark against practical irrationality that engaging in schmoral discourse provides. For a similar benefit with schmoralizing materializes on the interpersonal level. In order to get what I want (viz., the satisfaction of my fundamental desire), it will be useful for me if I can provide *for you* the bulwark against practical irrationality that *you* need to be able to skip some cognitive steps and reach the conclusion that you mustn't steal and must give to the poor. After all, this is what I want you to do, given that if you perform these actions, I get closer to the world I want via the satisfaction of my fundamental desire. To give a simple example: you are about to steal chewing gum from the shop and I can see you wondering about what to do. I interfere by yelling at you: 'but stealing is morally wrong!' The fact that I can do this is beneficial in two situations. The first situation is when I talk with like-minded error theorists who share my fundamental desire. The second situation is when I talk to people who aren't like-minded error theorists who share my fundamental desire.

Start with the world in which you and I are both error theorists and both have the fundamental desire. We will be more successful in attaining the world we both want to live in if we can tell each other that stealing is schmorally wrong compared to when we communicate in the following, highly convoluted way: 'stealing is inconsistent with my fundamental desire, I know you also share the fundamental desire, so let us refrain from stealing.' After all, the appeal to morality here when I simply say 'but stealing is morally wrong', just as it does inside my own head, makes it less likely that we together engage in potentially faulty practical reasoning in the heat of the moment ('but no one is looking, as you can also see, so let us steal this chewing gum') and it also engages both of our motivational systems.

By way of comparison, consider Stephen Schiffer's similar argument for substitutionism after having defended his own moral error theory, which, recall from §2.7, derives from an alleged absence of sufficiently determinate referential intentions for moral concepts:

> What would happen to moral language if *everyone* became convinced that there were no determinately true moral propositions? Clearly, no one could sincerely make unqualified moral judgements, because those judgements couldn't express propositions we [believed] to a very high degree. At the same time, I think an invisible-hand mechanism would lead us to introduce concepts that *were in many ways like the moral concepts we actually have*. For we would find that there was considerable agreement between ourselves and certain recognizable others about the kind of world we wished to inhabit, and if these others included people with whom we had to plan joint ventures and otherwise coordinate behaviour, then we would want quick and easy ways to mark the kinds of actions we mutually approved or disapproved. Perhaps we would introduce an indexical word 'shmwrong' such that when A said to B that it would be shmwrong for so-and-so to do such-and-such she was expressing a belief whose cash-value was that A and B would want so-and-so not to do such-and-such if they were agreed about all relevant facts … Come to think of it, what I have just described is my own continuing use of moral terms. My use is instrumental, but it gets across what I need to get across, and which I couldn't begin to get across if I had to express the truth in what I was saying without use of those terms. (2003, p. 261, italics in original)

Schiffer and I agree that error theorists should be substitutionists and that our use of schmoral judgements after error theory is prudentially wise at least in part because it fosters interpersonal communication among like-minded error theorists. But there are also important differences between Schiffer and myself. Apart from the fact that Schiffer defends a conceptual entailment error theory, whereas I defend a presupposition error theory, I first of all don't think that it is true that 'we couldn't begin to get across' these behaviour-cooperation plans without a moral or schmoral language. I think we can, but doing this would simply make it more likely that we make mistakes in our practical reasoning. Second, I don't think we should trust an 'invisible-hand mechanism' to give us the right kind of substitutionist moral discourse, given that means–end, instrumental schmoral reasoning is highly complicated and that, as I will continue to argue below, the stakes are high as the satisfaction of our fundamental desire depends on the availability of a good answer to the now what question.

I have just considered the benefit of using schmoral discourse to influence the behaviour of those who, like me, accept (a) moral error theory, (b) pragmatic presupposition substitutionism, and (c) the fundamental desire. I will now argue that it is also useful, given that I want to satisfy my fundamental desire, to use a schmoral discourse to communicate with those who don't have at least one of the properties (a)–(c). But note: since I have assumed that you also have the fundamental desire (see §5.2) and that since I think that you should also accept error theory and pragmatic substitutionism, what follows is at the same time an argument for you to use substitutionist moral discourse in your dealings with people who do not share one or more of the properties (a)–(c) with you.

Distinguish, with J.L. Austin, between the locutionary and perlocutionary act of uttering words (Austin also recognizes illocutionary speech acts, but these are more complicated and not relevant for my purpose here). I perform a *locutionary act* in uttering a sentence if I am "saying something" in the "full normal sense" (Austin 1975, p. 94). So, when I say 'the building is high', the locutionary act I perform is that of saying that the building is high. But in uttering the same sentence I can also perform the perlocutionary act of scaring someone who is afraid heights. Which *perlocutionary act* I perform in uttering a judgement depends, at least in part, on the hearer's reaction. I can only scare you with the sentence 'the building is high' if you are afraid of heights. As Alexander Bird explains this phenomenon:

> As the title of J.L. Austin's famous book tells us, we do things with words. In speaking we not only utter words, which Austin calls locution, but we also perform other kinds of acts ... Perlocutionary acts are acts whose essence involves some fact caused by the utterance of words. If I amuse you with an anecdote, that act is a perlocutionary one—your being amused is the effect of my locution. (2002, p. 1)

A surrogate moral language like the substitutionist language that I propose can likewise be used for performing actions other than uttering words in the full normal sense of communicating what the speaker believes to be true or false. For instance, I can use the substitutionist schmoral discourse to "bluff" John into believing that he shouldn't steal (Williams 1981, p. 111; see also McDowell 1995, p. 75; Lillehammer 1999, p. 205; Gibbard 1990, p. 171; Gaus 1996, p. 124). Whether this works depends on such things as our relation, his perception of my power, his general propensity to be impressed by what people say, *et cetera*. But *if* John is usually impressed by what I say, then I can bluff him into believing that he should not steal, even if he fails to share one or more of the properties (a)–(c) with me. This is because getting him to accept a desire to refrain from stealing can be a perlocutionary effect of the schmoral judgement that I utter.

I use the word 'bluff' in reference to Williams's critique of external reason claims, which I discussed in §3.4. Williams writes about external reasons claims that:

> there may be no reason to see [them] as more than bluff and brow-beating. (2001, p. 95)

External reason claims are claims about what agents have reason to do for which it is not part of their truth-conditions that the addressee has a desire that will be fulfilled if she acted on that reason (or can reach that desire through procedurally rational modifications of her existing set of desires 'S'). It was precisely Williams's view that external reason claims aren't anything other than attempts to *bluff* agents into doing something because they aren't really reasons. Instead, they are merely attempts by the speaker to make the hearer confirm to the speaker's preferences. But although an external reason claim cannot give the hearer a normative reason to perform an action, it can have the perlocutionary effect of causing the hearer to adopt the speaker's outlook in ethics, that is, to give her a merely motivating reason.

Is this an outrageous proposal? It is not, for, first, we have to remember that it is not morally wrong to bluff others into believing what you believe they should believe. After all, nothing is morally wrong, given error theory. Second, the stakes are high. What's on the line is the realization of your ideal world, and you really think that trying to satisfy your fundamental desire is for the better, and so it is a good thing, in the prudential sense of good, that we can use schmoral language for the purpose of bluffing other agents into believing what we think they should believe. Third, agents who accept the fundamental desire probably believe that the world should contain as little suffering as possible, for actions that procure suffering stand in the way of mutual cooperation. This means that speakers will be careful using the perlocutionary force of their schmoral judgements, taking into account that their hearers' feelings must not be hurt. I therefore don't think that this proposal is outrageous.

In summary, pragmatic presupposition substitutionism provides the required bulwarks against practical irrationality and lapses in motivation (intra-personal) and it is also useful when it comes to communicating with like-minded error theorists as well as with other people (interpersonal). I continue my defence of my formulation of the substitutionist solution to the now what problem by arguing, first, that it shouldn't be reformulated as a propagandist theory and, second, that it doesn't collapse into a moral success theory.

6.6 Propagandism and Moral Success Theory

In the previous chapter, I explained that in addition to the various prescriptive metaethical theories that I discussed, there is also the propagandist option, which can be used to reformulate each of these theories. Propagandism has been mentioned as an option for error theory by

Terrence Cuneo and Sean Christy, and also by Jonas Olson, though none of them accepts propagandism (Cuneo and Christy 2011; Olson 2014, p. 196n48). Propagandism says, first, that error theorists should keep the truth of the error theory to themselves, ensuring that the folk won't find out about it. This is supposed to ensure that we don't get a moral apocalypse after error theory, that is, a situation in which people kill and steal (even) more than they do now. Second, error theorists should themselves accept the most defensible answer to the now what question, which, as I have argued, is the substitutionist answer. Should we reformulate substitutionism as 'propagandist substitutionism'?

Richard Joyce offers the following argument against propagandism:

> I will not give serious consideration to the proposal we might call 'propagandism': that some people may be 'in the know' about the moral error theory while, for the greater good, keeping it quiet and encouraging the *hoi polloi* to continue with their sincere (false) moral beliefs. Such a situation really would amount to the promulgation of manipulative lies, which, I will assume, leads ultimately to no good ... It is not wise to risk having a society of epistemological wrecks in order to achieve some projected good through massive deception. (2005, p. 299, italics in original)

I agree that we each *individually* have a categorical epistemic reason to avoid becoming epistemic wrecks; after all, if I were to become an epistemic wreck, then I would make it impossible for my psychology to perform its function, which is, in part, to amass true beliefs (§4.4). But I argued that this does not extend to a universal requirement to protect others from becoming epistemic wrecks (§4.5). If I can get myself into a better position (better, that is, from the point of view of trying to satisfy my fundamental desire) by refraining from informing the *hoi polloi* about the truth of error theory, then I should do this. So Joyce's objection to propagandism fails. The relevant question is not whether we all have categorical reason to perform actions that ensure that none of us becomes an epistemological wreck. Instead, the relevant question is: is it, or is it not, conducive to my attempt to satisfy my fundamental desire to keep the truth about error theory from the folk?

To answer this question, let us compare the following two worlds, that is, the propagandist world in which I hide the truth about error theory from the folk and the 'open world' in which I do inform them about error theory. In the propagandist world, the folk have no clue about error theory and continue to follow their own morality, which includes obligations to give to the poor, and which the substitutionist recognizes as conducive to the satisfaction of the fundamental desire, but which also includes the obligation not to lie. As I argued in §6.4, the problem is that the obligation not to lie as it derives from the old morality is not sufficiently flexible to be conducive to the end of achieving a world in which mutual cooperation is maximally promoted. On the plus side, many other 'old' moral obligations, such as the obligation to give to the poor, are conducive to this end, and so hiding the truth about error theory from the folk is still a pretty good means to my end of satisfying my fundamental desire.

In the open world, by contrast, we allow the folk to learn about error theory and we actively try to convince them of its truth, for instance by making available books, TED talks, tweets, YouTube videos, et cetera that propagate this view. This means that this world will probably contain more people who are convinced by error theory and substitutionism than the previous world that I described. After all, we are all required to, and often do, believe what we have most evidence to believe, and if I am right, we have most evidence to believe error theory and pragmatic presupposition substitutionism. Further, if, which is likely, these people also have the fundamental desire, then there will be more people in this world who perform actions that further mutual cooperation compared to the propagandist world, as they will also have been able to think about the content of their new schmoral obligations, bringing these obligations closer to what actually satisfies their fundamental desire. So, this world is instrumentally better for me from the point of view of my attempt to satisfy my fundamental desire. And so, propagandism is not plausible.

The second question I discuss here is whether the substitutionist alternative is theoretically stable. You might object that it collapses into a naturalist realist moral success theory. For, as Jon Tresan says, once we have made the change from uttering moral propositions to schmoral propositions, then it is probable that we have thereby created new moral terms. After all, the substitutions would pick out the very properties naturalists say are the moral properties. (2010 p. 236)

According to this objection, error theory coupled with substitutionism collapses into a naturalist realist moral success theory because the properties we pick out with schmoral terms are identical to the properties we pick out with moral terms, albeit bereft of categorical reason-giving force.

There are many problems with this objection. First, the folk would not, at least not on reflection, mistake the naturalist surrogate schmoral discourse for moral discourse (see Chap. 3). After all, this leaves out the absolute to-be-doneness of moral facts. Second, although all the other prescriptive metaethical theories (with the exception of abolitionism) demand that the content of morality stays the same, the substitutionist does not make this demand. She says that the content of schmorality also changes, from consisting of rules and obligations that sometimes do but sometimes don't contribute to the satisfaction of the fundamental desire, as morality currently has it, to a normative system that only contains obligations that, when you act on them, contribute to the satisfaction of the fundamental desire. So, the descriptive properties that a moral discourse with a naturalist semantics picks out are not identical to the properties that a schmoral discourse picks out. And so, even if my first response fails, it will not be the case that the substitution judgements pick out the same properties as naturalist judgements, which means that Tresan's objection cannot get off the ground to begin with.

6.7 Conclusion

David Brink, who defends a version of naturalist moral realism, once wrote:

> If, as I argued, rejection of moral realism would undermine the nature of existing normative practices and beliefs, then [accepting the false proposition that there are categorical moral reasons] may seem a small price to pay to preserve [our moral] practices and beliefs. (1989, p. 173)

The importance of our moral practices (e.g., arguing about moral truth, reminding others of promises, teaching our children how to live) and moral beliefs (e.g., having the belief that killing and stealing is morally wrong) lies in the effect that they have on our mental lives. With these practices and beliefs, we get to live in a nicer world; without them, we don't. Brink presents a dilemma: either accept moral realism, possibly by accepting a claim that one knows is false, namely the claim that that moral success theory is true (which is bad), or reject realism and deprive ourselves of the possibility to live in a nicer world (which is even worse).

In this chapter, I have argued that pragmatic presupposition substitutionism is the best prescriptive metaethical theory currently on offer. If what I have argued is correct, then Brink's dilemma is spurious. After error theory, we can—indeed, we prudentially should—preserve our moral practices, albeit with some changes so that we will be in a better position to get what we want, that is the satisfaction of our fundamental desire.

In the next chapter, I will offer a preliminary discussion of how my pragmatic presupposition error conjoined with the substitutionist answer to the now what question can be applied to a pressing problem in normative ethics.

References

Austin, J.L. 1975. *How to Do Things with Words*. Oxford: OUP.
Balaguer, M. 2011. Bare Bones Moral Realism and the Objections from Relativism. In *A Companion to Relativism*, ed. S.D. Hales, 368–390. Oxford: Wiley-Blackwell.
Bird, A. 2002. Illocutionary Silencing. *Pacific Philosophical Quarterly* 83: 1–15.
Brink, D.O. 1989. *Moral Realism and the Foundations of Ethics*. Cambridge: CUP.
Burgess, J.A. 1998. Error Theories and Values. *Australasian Journal of Philosophy* 76: 534–552.
Cuneo, T., and S. Christy. 2011. The Myth of Moral Fictionalism. In *New Waves in Metaethics*, ed. M. Brady, 85–102. New York: Palgrave Macmillan.
Fisher, A. 2011. *Metaethics*. Durham: Acumen.

Frankena, W.K. 1966. The Concept of Morality. *Journal of Philosophy* 63: 688–696.
Gaus, G.F. 1996. *Justificatory Liberalism*. Oxford: OUP.
Gibbard, A. 1990. *Wise Choices, Apt Feelings*. Cambridge, MA: Harvard University Press.
Ingram, S. 2015. After Moral Error Theory, After Moral Realism. *The Southern Journal of Philosophy* 53: 227–248.
Joyce, R. 2001. *The Myth of Morality*. Cambridge: CUP.
———. 2005. Moral Fictionalism. In *Fictionalism in Metaphysics*, ed. M.E. Kalderon, 287–313. Oxford: OUP.
Kahane, G. 2013. Must Metaethical Realism Make a Semantic Claim? *Journal of Moral Philosophy* 10: 148–178.
Lillehammer, H. 1999. Normative Antirealism. *The Southern Journal of Philosophy* 37: 201–225.
———. 2000. Revisionary Dispositionalism and Practical Reason. *Journal of Ethics* 4: 173–190.
———. 2004. Moral Error Theory. *Proceedings of the Aristotelian Society* 104: 95–111.
Lutz, M. 2014. The 'Now What' Problem for Error Theory. *Philosophical Studies* 171: 351–371.
Mackie, J.L. 1976. *Problems from Locke*. Oxford: Clarendon Press.
———. 1977. *Ethics: Inventing Right and Wrong*. Harmondsworth: Penguin Publishers.
McDowell, J. 1995. Might There Be External Reasons? In *World, Mind, and Ethics*, ed. J.E.J. Altham and R. Harrison, 68–85. Cambridge: CUP.
Oddie, G., and D. Demetriou. 2010. The Fictionalist's Attitude Problem. In *A World Without Values*, ed. R. Joyce and S. Kirchin, 199–216. Dordrecht: Springer.
Olson, J. 2014. *Moral Error Theory: History, Critique, Defence*. Oxford: OUP.
Sainsbury, R.M. 2010. *Fiction and Fictionalism*. London: Routledge.
Schiffer, S. 2003. *The Things We Mean*. Oxford: Oxford University Press.
Smith, M. 1991. Realism. In *A Companion to Ethics*, ed. P. Singer, 399–410. London: Blackwell.
Suikkanen, J. 2013. Moral Error Theory and the Belief Problem. In *Oxford Studies in Metaethics*, ed. R. Shafer-Landau, vol. 8, 168–194. Oxford: OUP.
Tresan, J. 2010. Question Authority: In Defense of Moral Naturalism Without Clout. *Philosophical Studies* 150: 221–238.

West, C. 2010. Business as Usual? The Error Theory, Internalism, and the Function of Morality. In *A World Without Values*, ed. R. Joyce and S. Kirchin, 183–198. Dordrecht: Springer.
Williams, B. 1981. *Moral Luck*. Cambridge: CUP.
———. 2001. Postscript: Some Further Notes on Internal and External Reasons. In *Varieties of Practical Reasoning*, ed. E. Millgram, 91–97. Cambridge, MA: MIT Press.

7

Application

7.1 Introduction

So far, I have argued that moral error theory is plausible and that pragmatic presupposition substitutionism is the best answer to the now what question. This set of claims commits me to a metanormative theory that has consequences for our thinking about prudential oughts (these exist), epistemic oughts (these also exist), and moral oughts (these don't exist). In this chapter, I discuss how we might use this metanormative theory to answer a pressing question in normative ethics. The question is: what are the circumstances under which someone is entitled to own a resource, such as land, if anyone is entitled to private property at all?

In §1.1, I explained why I call this a question in normative ethics. My reasons were, first, that I believe that the topic of distributive justice should be more central to normative ethics because it deals with the issue of how we should treat other human beings. And second, that after moral error theory there is no longer a clear sense in which questions about morality differ from the more general questions discussed in practical philosophy, which include questions in social and political philosophy. Jonas Olson further illustrates this second point when he considers Mackie's error theory and writes:

> After having rejected objective values and moral properties … in the first part of his *Ethics: Inventing Right and Wrong,* Mackie proceeded in the second and third parts to discuss among other things substantive normative theories, the human good, and political morality. The normative theory Mackie ends up advocating is largely contractualist and right-based. It involves rights to liberty and self-determination, property rights, and equal opportunity rights. These rights are of course not self-evident normative truths. They are to be determined partly in terms of the extent to which they turn out conducive to the human good, and partly via political processes. (2014, p. 196)

Doing normative ethics after error theory requires an investigation into the nature of political processes and the topic of property rights itself, which teaches us something about how we can achieve a world that promotes mutually beneficial cooperation. Given what I have just argued, the issue of how we should distribute resources in society is an appropriate test case for pragmatic presupposition substitutionist schmoral discourse.

In what follows, I compare John Rawls's liberal egalitarian account of distributive justice with Robert Nozick's libertarian theory of property rights (Rawls 1971, 1985, 1993, 1999; Nozick 1974, 1997). I first explain the essentials of their debate, and I conclude that both theories of distributive justice assume the truth of moral success theory and that for this reason, neither of them can be adopted by the error theorist (§7.2 and 7.3). After this, I explain how substitutionism provides an account of distributive justice that should be accepted by every error theorist who has the fundamental desire to live in a world with mutually beneficial cooperation (§7.4). A final section summarizes my argument (§7.5).

7.2 Rawls on Distributive Justice

In his landmark 1971 book *A Theory of Justice*, John Rawls revived normative political philosophy. This was needed, first, because, in the decades before this book, "non-cognitivism bested the competition and dominated the scene … Stasis—the less charitable would say *rigor mortis*—set in" (Darwall et al. 1992, pp. 120–1). 'Stasis' because ethicists, and political philosophers in their wake, saw non-cognitivism as a reason to reject the idea that they could give arguments for first-order normative ethical claims about what people should do. Instead, they thought that they were only able to say something about *how we talk about* what we should do, morally speaking. With A.J. Ayer, they analysed the nature of moral language as consisting in "ejaculations" of emotions that do not admit of rational assessment (1936, p. 130). Ayer wrote:

> When someone disagrees with us about the moral value of a certain action or type of action, we do admittedly resort to argument in order to win him over to our way of thinking. But we do not attempt to show by our arguments that he has the 'wrong' ethical feeling towards a situation whose nature he has correctly apprehended. What we attempt to show is that he is mistaken about the facts of the case. We argue that he has misconceived the agent's motive: or that he has misjudged the effects of the action [etc.] … if our opponent happens to have undergone a different process of moral 'conditioning' from ourselves, so that, even when he acknowledges all the facts, he still disagrees with us about the moral value of the actions under discussion, then we abandon the attempt to convince him by argument … We feel that our own system of values is superior, and therefore speak in such derogatory terms of his. But we cannot bring forward any arguments to show that our system is superior. (1936, pp. 146–7)

When we discuss ethical issues, we do argue about what we should believe. Yet these arguments are confined to the assessment of non-ethical, empirical matters of fact that might sway your interlocutor to come to believe what you believe is right or wrong *if you both share the same ethical feeling*. But we cannot engage in a meaningful discussion about which ethical feeling one should have.

The second reason that political philosophy needed to be revitalized was that those who did not accept the non-cognitivist creed were either Utilitarians or intuitionists (Rawls 1971, p. xvii). Utilitarians believe that an action is right if, and only if, it maximizes utility impartially conceived, where classical Utilitarians believe that utility is to be understood as the balance of pleasure over pain. Intuitionists believe that a whole array of different actions can be right or wrong, irrespective of whether or not they maximize utility impartially conceived, depending just on what we intuitively conceive of as being right or wrong. The problem with this was that neither option seemed to work. Utilitarianism were unable to "provide a satisfactory account of the basic rights and liberties of citizens as free and equal persons, a requirement of absolutely first importance for an account of democratic institutions" (Rawls 1971, pp. xi–xii). After all, if by taking away your right to something I can maximize utility, then I should do this, morally speaking. Unfortunately, their Intuitionist critics, said Rawls, have

> failed … to construct a workable and systematic moral conception to oppose it. The outcome is that we often seem forced to choose between utilitarianism and intuitionism. Most likely we finally settle upon a variant of the utility principle circumscribed and restricted in certain ad hoc ways by intuitionistic constraints. Such a view is not irrational; and there is no assurance that we can do better. But this is no reason not to try. (1971, pp. xvii–xviii)

The solution that Rawls offers is a version of a social contract theory (1971, p. 10). We get the basic rights and liberties that free and equal persons should get in a democratic society because we (or rather, our rational selves) agree that each person gets these rights and liberties.

In presenting this argument, Rawls placed himself in a tradition of thinkers that, with Immanuel Kant, believed that investigating the principles of practical reason could vindicate objectivity in ethics (Darwall et al. 1992, pp. 122–3). But although Rawls placed himself in this tradition, he did not accept the strong claim that practical reason vindicates objective ethics. There may be strands in his early writings that suggest otherwise, but the later Rawls abandoned the project of appealing to metaphysical claims in favour of a political conception of justice (1985). He also did not believe that his arguments prescribed all-things-considered oughts for every society to adopt his liberal egalitarian political theory (1999). His argument was that, at least for some peoples, the principles of practical reason generate an intersubjective agreement about how we should treat each other, though it remains rationally permissible for some other, non-liberal peoples to remain non-liberal.

How do we reach this agreement or 'social contract', and what kind of agreement regarding the distribution of resources in particular do we get? Rawls argues that people are both *reasonable* (they have a sense of justice, they care about others, they want to live by fair terms of cooperation even at some expense of their own interests, etc.) and *rational* (they have a conception of the good, they care about themselves, they employ instrumental reasoning to get what they want, etc.) (1971, p. xi, 5, 11; 1999, p. 25, 28, 31). Reasonable and rational people will agree on a method for dividing the primary goods in life (such as basic rights and liberties, income and wealth, and social status) that is fair to everyone and that, within these limits, puts them in the best position to pursue their own private objectives in life. Rawls thought that given that people want to be reasonable and rational, they will want to have a procedure for deciding "who gets what, when, and how" that gives expression to these two ideals (Lasswell 1936). Rawls argues that we can achieve such "justice as fairness" if the decision about how the primary goods are to be distributed will be made by people who have managed to temporarily abstract from their individual properties, such as being male or female, being physically fit or challenged, et cetera (1971, p. 11).

The principles that will be chosen behind this 'veil of ignorance' are the following.

> First: each person is to have an equal right to the most extensive scheme of equal basic liberties compatible with a similar scheme of liberties for others.
> Second: social and economic inequalities are to be arranged so that they are both (a) reasonably expected to be to everyone's advantage, and (b) attached to positions and offices open to all. (1971, p. 53)

The first principle has lexical priority over the second: giving up a right to freedom in order to guarantee greater equality or more overall welfare is never justified (Rawls 1993, p. 6). Thus, we should give everyone the same basic liberties, and as many of these as possible; moreover, we should divide our resources equally unless an unequal distribution benefits the least well off. You might have thought that you are morally permitted to hoard resources if, say, you have given someone else at least a fair chance of getting what they want to get (as I will explain in the next section, Nozick attempts to spruce up this thought into a theory of justice). And you might also have thought that even if the inequality that ensues is not to the advantage of everyone, as long as you did not harm anyone in the process, you are allowed to acquire even more resources. However, in fact, if Rawls is right, then you are not allowed to do this because it entails violating principle of justice no. 2a.

Rawls's theory is attractive for error theorists who, like me, think that what you should do, all things considered, depends on what rational deliberation says you should do, all things considered, but who think that rationality does not supply categorical or universally applicable moral imperatives. For one of the elements of Rawls's theory is that behind the veil of ignorance, one is supposed to try to maximize one's chance that one gets what one wants. But error theorists cannot accept this theory because Rawls also assumes that people, both in society and behind the veil of ignorance, are reasonable, that is, that they have a sense of justice. In other words, according to Rawls, there exists a rational requirement with moral content that takes the following form:

Sense of Justice
RR (you develop a sense of justice that enables you to care about others).

This means that Rawls's theory is a moral success theory that will be debunked by the argument developed in Part I of this book.

7.3 Nozick on Distributive Justice

An alternative approach to the issue of distributive justice has been offered by Robert Nozick in his 1974 *Anarchy, State and Utopia*. Nozick's argument does not require us to postulate a rational requirement with moral content, such as Sense of Justice. Instead, Nozick presents a thoroughgoing individualist theory of moral and political life that seems to make just those commitments that can be accepted by moral error theorists.

Nozick's philosophy is naturalistic in the sense that he does not postulate properties that aren't postulated or discovered by scientists (Nozick 1981, p. 294). Consider his theory of free will, which is incompatibilist because it takes free will and determinism to be incompatible. Incompatibilists face the problem of control: it may be true that human behaviour that was completely determined to happen in exactly one particular way ever since the big bang is not consistent with freedom of the will. But likewise, if we perform action A because we were caused to perform this action by a random occurrence of activity A' in our brain, then, even though we could have performed action B because we could have been caused to perform this action by a random occurrence of activity B' in our brain, we are not free either, unless we somehow control the indeterminacy to make the resulting action *our* action. Agent-causal incompatibilists postulate a Cartesian soul or Kantian noumenal self to control these indeterminacies in an attempt to get free will, but Nozick rejects this idea because such properties are too queer to exist. Instead, he thinks that we, as agents, can be identified with certain complex brain processes, such that the occurrence of one process where another process could have occurred results in free action so long as the first process was the result of a reflexively, self-subsuming, weight-bestowing decision, where each of these elements is itself wholly explicable in terms of natural events that do not require the postulation of an agent or Cartesian soul that controls these events (Nozick 1981, pp. 294–301).

This theory of free will is in the background of Nozick's claim that being a certain person and choosing your own life is what it means to have a meaningful life (1974, p. 43, p. 50). Nozick is a voluntarist: what is good for you is the life you choose for yourself. This is a thoroughgoing individualism without appeal to a sense of justice. It is so extremely individualistic that Katrin Flikschuh describes it as follows:

> Nozick's metaphysics of free will – his account of individuals as reflexively self-determining sources of original value – contains no interpersonal dimension at all. In choosing and building a conception of life for themselves, individuals appear to be intensely and exclusively preoccupied with themselves. They appear to be unaware of others and of how others' existence may shape or affect their conception of their own life: Nozick's individual self-choosers appear to live the lives of monads. (2007, pp. 78–9)

Monads are self-sufficient metaphysical entities in Leibniz's metaphysical philosophy that were entirely inward-looking and the universe was entirely comprised of these monads (Leibniz 1714). All of this means that Nozick's picture of human life appears to match the picture of human life that I have presented in this book: although individuals are rationally required to perform many actions (to take the means to their ends or drop their ends, to believe what they have conclusive evidence to believe, etc.), they are not required to protect other human beings, or to perform actions that further other people's interests, unless they themselves happen to have the desire to protect or further other people's interests. And so Nozick's overall philosophical outlook seems to have the right kind of shape to provide the error theorist with input about distributive justice.

What does Nozick say about distributive justice? The first sentence of Nozick's book about the topic reads as follows:

> Individuals have rights, and there are things no person or group may do to them (without violating their rights). (1974, p. xix)

Nozick uses this claim to argue that a theory of justice in distribution—or as he prefers, "justice in holdings" (1974, p. 150)—is correct if, and only if, agents have acquired their resources by a process that did not involve the violation of anyone else's rights, regardless of whether the distribution that results is egalitarian, such as in the Rawlsian sense that everyone gets exactly the same unless an unequal distribution is to the benefit of the least well off. Nozick writes:

> the following inductive definition would exhaustively cover the subject of justice in holdings.
>
> 1. A person who acquires a holding in accordance with the principle of justice in acquisition is entitled to that holding.
> 2. A person who acquires a holding in accordance with the principle of justice in transfer, from someone else entitled to that holding, is entitled to the holding.
> 3. No one is entitled to a holding expect by (repeated) applications of 1 and 2. (1974, p. 151)

In other words, according to Nozick:

> A distribution is just if it arises from another just distribution by legitimate means. (1974, p. 151)

This also explains why Nozick prefers to talk about justice in holdings, for talking about justice in distribution suggests that there has to be a distributor that gives people resources according to some principle, such as, for instance, "the principle of distribution according to moral merit"

(1974, p. 156). Nozick argues that his own principles of justice in holdings are entailed by the principle of self-ownership, which gives expression to the idea that individuals have rights. Property right in things in the world is transferred from my right to own myself (the principle of self-ownership) to a thing in the world, at least so long as I leave enough behind for you or compensate you appropriately for not being able to appropriate things (Nozick 1974, pp. 171–182).

The most important question for the error theorist is this: although Nozick's theory is appropriately individualistic and although it does not ask us to accept a rational requirement with moral content, where do these individual rights in the first sentence of his *Anarchy, State and Utopia* come from? We can ask: whence the principle of self-ownership? Katrin Flikschuh has argued that there are two interpretations of this claim. First, there is "the majority view" on which "Nozick's appeal to rights is philosophically unfounded" (2007, p. 64). Nozick just postulates it because he has to start somewhere to be able to get down to business. Second, there is the view on which "society must respect these rights" because of the Kantian principle that people are "separate existences" and "ends and not merely means" (Nozick 1974, p. 30, 33; Kymlicka 2002, p. 108; Flikschuh 2007, p. 65). But if these are the only options, then error theorists cannot accept Nozick's programme, no matter how much it otherwise appeals to them. For if the decision to grant other people rights is (philosophically) unfounded, then there is also no rational foundation to accept it, and error theorists cannot wield their epistemic rational requirement to believe what they have good or most evidence believe to stay on board with Nozick's project. Alternatively, if the reason that we should accept Nozick's claim that we have important rights is that this gives expression to the Kantian thought that people are ends in themselves, then we also have a problem, because error theorists are not required to accept this kind of rational requirement with moral content.

7.4 Distributive Justice after Error Theory

This debate between right libertarians like Nozick and liberal egalitarians like Rawls continues until today, and in the meantime, other theories have been formulated, including left libertarian theories (Otsuka 2003), luck egalitarian theories (Dworkin 1981, 2002), and many other theories. Moral error theorists have an explanation for why this debate continues, which is that those who participate in the debate accept different fundamental moral principles, which these people cannot make sufficiently plausible in the absence of objective moral truth, and which therefore does not enable them to win over their opponents (§5.6). All those who participate in the debate claim to have found the moral high ground. With this kind of "moral overlay", as Richard Garner has argued, we are going to find it very difficult to reach agreement on how we should distribute our resources (2010, p. 218; see also Lillehammer 1999). Those on the political right think that they have morality on their side and that accepting a theory of justice that requires taxation for the purpose of redistribution of resources amounts to "forced labour" and is a violation of their moral right to self-determination (Nozick 1974, p. 169). But those on the political left think that not accepting a patterned theory of justice in distribution is, precisely, immoral.

At this point in the dialectic, the question is: how, if at all, can the substitutionist error theorist intervene in this debate? Is a particular distribution of resources schmorally right? In other words, adopting which theory of justice in distribution or holdings best enables us to satisfy our fundamental desire? The answer to this question is extremely complex, and requires, at least, investigation into the relevant empirical facts. Most importantly, it requires information about how people will respond to unpredicted and *unpredictable* changes in their circumstances of justice, for instance what will happen if we have been able to increase, as Hume put it, "to a sufficient degree the benevolence of men or the bounty of nature" (Hume 1739, III.2.ii; Lukes 1985, p. 108). As Karl Popper argued, and this is the mainstream position in contemporary philosophy of the social sciences, it is not possible to predict the future because it is not possible to predict human actions, interactions, responses, and so on. Popper writes:

> physics can arrive at universally valid uniformities, and explain particular events as instances of such uniformities, whereas sociology must be content with the intuitive understanding of unique events, and of the role they play in particular situations, occurring within particular struggles of interests, tendencies, and destinies. (1957, p. 20)

And so, although the essence of a substitutionist moral discourse is that the schmoral obligations that it recommends must express reasons that contribute to the satisfaction of the fundamental desire, sometimes we will find it impossible to specify exactly which actions do and which actions don't contribute to this desire.

And yet we must act, so we must find a way to approximate as well as we can the ideal set of schmoral codes the abiding by which puts us in the best position to perform actions that contribute to the satisfaction of the fundamental desire. Given the fundamental uncertainty about the human predicament and aptly described by Popper, error theorists are best advised to use the various theories of justice on offer as a heuristic in deciding which policy to support. The argument for this claim is, in part, an argument from elimination. One option is to just focus on the facts without seeking the help of a moral or surrogate moral overlay, and to ask the question: adopting which theory of distributive justice, exactly, is the best means to the satisfaction of our fundamental desire? This will result in a stalemate as a proper answer to this question requires us to be able to predict human behaviour, which is, according to the mainstream position in contemporary philosophy of the social sciences, not possible. Deferring to scientists and experts is certainly sometimes called for, but given the fundamental uncertainty about how people will react to changes, this will only work up to a point. A second option is to continue to use morality as conservationists say we should do, but as I have argued throughout Part II, that is not our best bet either, given that we know that the content of morality does not always jibe with what will contribute to the satisfaction of our fundamental desire. But there is a third option.

Imagine a conversation with a fellow error theorist who shares your fundamental desire, and imagine further that neither of you knows what the best causal means to the satisfaction of your fundamental desire is. Should you support a Nozickean or a Rawlsian policy regarding the distribution of resources? You and your interlocutor disagree about which policy to support. The most expedient way to resolve this issue is to adopt a plausible middle position between an egalitarian theory of justice such as Rawls's that suggests an equal distribution unless an unequal distribution is to the advantage of the least well off, and an inegalitarian theory of justice as formulated by Nozick. For in the absence of knowledge about which policy works best, the best we can do is pick a policy that holds the middle between the various theories that been defended and that therefore can also be accepted.

Here J.L. Mackie got matters right, it seems to me, by defending a system of morality in the narrow sense that combines deontological elements and rights on the one hand with consequentialist considerations about maximizing utility on the other hand (1977). Similarly, when it comes to justice in the distribution of resources, we should, with Rawls, accept that the resources in society should be distributed by a government rather than leaving the question of who gets what completely up to individuals, and yet we should accept, with Nozick, that the government should be less invasiveness in people's affairs than it would be if we implemented Rawls's theory. We should accept this because we cannot base our decision on predictions about the future (we cannot know what will be most conducive to satisfying our fundamental desire) and because this position is nevertheless probably acceptable as it holds the middle between two positions that have already been accepted. In this way, we use schmoral discourse as a heuristic for the decision we have to make, since we need to act.

This argument must be qualified in four ways. First, the actual content of this negotiated agreement will have to be specified in collaboration with policymakers, political scientists, economists, and lawyers. I envisage working out what this position that holds the middle between Rawls and Nozick entails on the level of policymaking as an ongoing project. We can go back and forth between our agreement on the abstract level of substitutionist normative ethics after error theory on the one hand, and policy on the other hand, so as to determine what does and what doesn't work. The agreement to hold the middle between Rawls and Nozick stands proxy for a more specific agreement that is forthcoming in collaboration with others. Second, and in line with what I just said, if more and better information becomes available about what does and what doesn't contribute to the satisfaction of the fundamental desire, and if this information turns out to be inconsistent with the agreement to hold the middle between Rawls and Nozick, then we should change the content of this agreement, that is, then we should change the content of our schmoral obligations. The third qualification is that the conversation such as I just imagined it between two participants in moral discourse should continue on the abstract, theoretical level as well, by taking on board further theories of justice, including the alternative theories that I mentioned, such as Otsuka's left libertarianism and Dworkin's luck-egalitarianism (Otsuka 2003; Dworkin 2002).

Fourth, note that what I say here is not inconsistent with my argument from the previous chapter that since on the substitutionist account the content of schmorality can be changed, it is more likely to give us the intra-personal bulwarks against lapses in rationality and motivation. In the previous chapter, I argued that a change in the content of our schmoral obligations gets us closer to the satisfaction of our fundamental desire, yet here I argue that it will be difficult to figure out what that content is. But there is no inconsistency here, for it can both be true that we know what does not contribute to the satisfaction of our fundamental desire (e.g., always refraining from lying) and that we don't know what, exactly, does contribute to the satisfaction of our fundamental desire in a particular situation (e.g., should I use a white lie now?). Since I know that morality certainly contains obligations that are not conducive to my attempt to satisfy my fundamental desire and that my substitutionist normative ethics at least enables me to abandon those obligations, it still seems that the bulwark against practical irrationality (and the bulwark against lapses in motivation on the back of this other bulwark) can be obtained consistently, allowing for the fact that the agent becomes conscious of the belief that error theory is true, especially since the agent also knows that the content of her substitutionist schmoral obligations has been researched thoroughly. This enables the pragmatic presupposition error theorist to avoid the either too good or not good enough objection that sunk all the other prescriptive metaethical theories that we discussed in Chap. 5, and it also enables her to make some headway in solving some issues in traditional normative ethics and political philosophy.

7.5 Conclusion

After moral error theory, we should accept as our preferred theory of justice a theory that holds the middle between (Rawlsian) egalitarianism and (Nozickean) inegalitarianism. This is because this position is, given the unpredictability of human behaviour, most likely to put us in the best situation to satisfy our fundamental desire, though this position, as the pragmatic presupposition error theorist recommends, should be revised in light of comparison with other theories of justice and further empirical research.

References

Ayer, A.J. 1936. *Language, Truth and Logic*. London: Victor Gollancz.
Darwall, S., A. Gibbard, and P. Railton. 1992. Toward Fin de siècle Ethics: Some Trends. *Philosophical Review* 101: 115–189.
Dworkin, R. 1981. What Is Equality I: Equality of Resources. *Philosophy and Public Affairs* 10: 283–345.
———. 2002. *Sovereign Virtue*. Cambridge, MA: Harvard University Press.
Flikschuh, K. 2007. *Freedom*. Cambridge: Polity Press.
Garner, R. 2010. Abolishing Morality. In *A World Without Values*, ed. R. Joyce and S. Kirchin, 217–234. Dordrecht: Springer.
Hume, D. 1739/40. *A Treatise of Human Nature*, ed. L.A. Selby-Bigge, 1978. Oxford, Clarendon Press
Kymlicka, W. 2002. *Contemporary Political Philosophy*. Oxford: OUP.
Lasswell, H.D. 1936. *Politics: Who Gets What, When, and How*. New York: McGraw-Hill Book Co..
Leibniz, G. 1714. *Monadology and Other Philosophical Essays*. Trans. Paul Schrecker and Anne Martin Schrecker. Indianapolis: Bobbs-Merrill.
Lillehammer, H. 1999. Normative Antirealism. *The Southern Journal of Philosophy* 37: 201–225.
Lukes, S. 1985. Taking Morality Seriously. In *Morality and Objectivity*, ed. T. Honderich, 98–109. London: Routledge.
Mackie, J.L. 1977. *Ethics: Inventing Right and Wrong*. Harmondsworth: Penguin Publishers.
Nozick, R. 1974. *Anarchy, State, and Utopia*. New York: Basic Books.
———. 1981. *Philosophical Explanations*. Cambridge, MA: Belknap Press.
———. 1997. *Socratic Puzzles*. Cambridge, MA: Harvard University Press.
Olson, J. 2014. *Moral Error Theory: History, Critique, Defence*. Oxford: OUP.
Otsuka, M. 2003. *Libertarianism Without Inequality*. Oxford: OUP.
Popper, K.R. 1957. *The Poverty of Historicism*. London: Routledge.
Rawls, J. 1971. *A Theory of Justice*. Cambridge, MA: Harvard University Press.
———. 1985. Justice as Fairness: Political Not Metaphysical. *Philosophy and Public Affairs* 14: 223–251.
———. 1993. *Political Liberalism*. New York: Columbia University Press.
———. 1999. *The Law of Peoples*. Harvard: Harvard University Press.

8

Conclusion

In this book, I have argued that pragmatic presupposition moral error theory based on rationality rather than queerness is plausible. I have also argued that pragmatic presupposition substitutionism is the most plausible answer to the now what question. And third, I have explored the connection between what I have said in this book about metanormativity and a topic in normative ethics.

I cannot claim that what I have argued is beyond dispute. For instance, in my defence of error theory, I assumed metaethical cognitivism, a minimally inflationary theory of truth, and the possibility of armchair access to folk intuitions about morality and moral language (see §1.3). But I do think that I have made some progress. For instance, I think that my reply to the companions-in-guilt objection, which focuses on the content rather than the structure of moral and epistemic reasons, has potential. Likewise, I think that my argument for the non-negotiable commitment claim, which uses the pragmatics of moral discourse, offers a new and plausible perspective on this topic. All in all, I believe that my formulation of error theory comes with fewer obstacles and problems than earlier formulations of this theory (§4.9).

If my arguments are convincing, then error theorists face some new challenges. In addition to thinking about the cogency of their arguments and responding to objections, error theorists now face the practical question of how they should go about thinking about the content of their substitutionist, schmoral discourse (Chap. 7). We should continue to think about the tenability of moral error theory, but I think that we should also start taking seriously the question what we should do after error theory, in the prudential sense of should, given that, as Socrates so aptly put it, "we are discussing no small matter, but how we ought to live" (Plato, *Republic*, 352-d). It is just that if I'm right, there are no moral considerations that bear upon this issue. But that hardly makes the issue less important.

Reference

Plato, *Republic*.

Index

A
Abolitionism, 162, 171, 172, 192, 193, 210, 211, 222
Abortion, 5, 192, 193, 203
Alienation objection, 137
Applicability restrictions, 94, 99, 100, 111–113, 205
Atomic Judgements, 36, 38, 94, 106, 110
Authority, 41, 51–55, 57, 58, 102, 104, 151

B
Benevolent Doctors, 74, 96–98
Bluff, 218
Browbeating, 104
Bulwark
  against lapses in motivation, 169, 180, 185, 192, 214, 215
  against practical irrationality, 166, 169, 170, 173, 175–178, 181, 183, 189, 190, 192, 204, 210, 211, 213, 215

C
Categorical epistemic reason, 220
Categorical imperative, 30, 52
Categorical moral reason, 4, 6, 16, 33, 34, 36, 47, 68, 71, 87, 106, 135, 136
Causal interpretation of the expression relation, 186
Cognitivism, 22, 23, 108, 179, 180, 228, 241
Companions-in-guilt objection, 8, 120, 146, 241

Conceptual entailment error theory, 31–33, 36, 39, 41, 59, 64, 66–69, 71, 73–75, 86, 87, 108, 112, 217
Consequentialism, 203, 204
Conservationism, 28, 161–163, 172, 177, 188–190, 193, 194, 200, 219
Content-internalism, 40, 44, 45, 59, 60, 64, 67, 107
Conversational implicatures, 38, 71

D
Deontology, 203, 204
Distributive justice, 228, 232, 234, 237

E
Egalitarian theory of justice, 237
Either too good or not good enough objection, 175, 211, 212
Emotivism, 21, 179
Entailment-cancelling operator, 84
Ethically inflected, 111, 113
Existence theory of reasons, 105, 124, 148

F
Frege-Geach problem, 172, 181, 182, 214
Function theory of normativity, 133, 136, 138, 141, 142, 145, 146, 152
Fundamental desire, 164–166, 169, 172, 181, 189, 192, 197, 198, 201, 207–217, 219–223, 228, 236–239

G
Generic argument for error theory, 4
Global error theory, 4

H
Humean instrumentalism, 126
Hybrid cognitivist-non-cognitivist semantics, 22
Hypothetical imperative, 135

I
Inconsistency objection, 12, 38
Incredulous stare, 20, 123
Indicatory expressivism, 187
Inegalitarian theory of justice, 237
Inescapability, 51, 52, 55, 104
Instrumental Principle, 130, 132, 133, 138, 143
Internal reason, 128

J
Justice
  as fairness, 231
  in holdings, 234

M
Maxim of honesty, 151
Metanormative theory, viii, 8, 9, 227
Metaphysical entailment, 19, 27
Modal operator, 111
Moral apocalypse, 15, 220, 223
Moral disagreement, 22, 65, 163, 180
Moral discourse, 5
Moral overlay, 192, 193, 236, 237

Moral realism, 12, 47, 48, 50, 59, 222, 223
Moral truth, 22, 173, 223

N
Negation operator, 35, 36, 84, 88
No moral considerations are relevant argument, 11, 12, 20, 107
Non-cognitivism, 22, 108
Non-Humean instrumentalism, 125–127
Non-hypothetical imperative, 52
Non-negotiable commitment, 4–6, 15, 18, 27, 30, 31, 40, 59, 63, 81, 82, 88, 104, 109, 114, 119
Normative ethics, viii, 9, 10, 21, 154, 209, 223, 228
Now what question, vii, viii, 8–10, 15, 28, 154, 159–163, 165, 171, 172, 178, 194, 197, 198, 205, 209, 211, 220, 223, 227, 241

O
Objective prescriptivity, 31, 41, 59, 199
Obviously implausible objection, 13
Open world, 221

P
Peripheral moral discussions, 113
Pervasiveness objection, 20, 69–72, 75, 82
Platitude, 46, 47
Practical oomph, 51, 54

Pragmatic presupposition error theory, 19, 82, 86, 91, 93, 94, 96, 98, 101, 112, 113, 198
Pragmatic presupposition substitutionism, 21, 198, 205, 209, 212, 217, 219, 223, 227
Preparatory moral action, 131
Prescriptive metaethical theories, 161
Principle of charity, 63, 64, 68, 69
Principle of epistemic conservatism, 150, 151
Principle of self-ownership, 235
Principle of the excluded middle, 110, 111
Propagandism, 162, 220
Propagandist world, 221

Q
Quasi-realism, 22
Queer, vii, 19, 20, 33, 37, 50, 121–123, 146, 147, 233

R
Rational requirement with moral content, 130, 138–140, 232, 235
Restricted error theory, 35
Revolutionary expressivism, viii, 161, 172, 178, 180, 184, 204, 213
Revolutionary fictionalism, viii, 161, 172, 204

S
Schmorality, 203, 204, 207, 213, 222
Schmoralizing, 209

Semantic presupposition error
 theory, 87, 90, 91, 98
Silencing function argument, 55–57
Social contract theory, 230
Sound deliberative route, 127
Speaker-subjectivism, 187
Specific Argument
 for Error Theory, 153
Supervenience, 98, 122
Synthetic property identity, 50

T
Translation test argument, 46, 47, 50, 54

U
Untrue, 5–7, 9–13, 82, 109, 112

V
Vindicatory reduction, 49, 63

W
Well-formed sceptical
 position, 53, 103, 124, 125
Witch, 3, 5, 6, 54, 90, 201

CPSIA information can be obtained
at www.ICGtesting.com
Printed in the USA
LVOW13*0821030618
579364LV00001B/1/P